Essays on the Patriarchal Narratives

*To the memory of William James Martin (1904-1980),
the Christian scholar whose vision led
to the establishment of Tyndale House, Cambridge.*

ESSAYS ON
THE
PATRIARCHAL
NARRATIVES

Edited by
A. R. Millard & D. J. Wiseman

WINONA LAKE, INDIANA

EISENBRAUNS

This American edition published 1983 through special arrangement with Inter-Varsity Press by Eisenbrauns.

First published 1980

Library of Congress Cataloging in Publication Data

Main entry under title:

Essays on the patriarchal narratives.

    Bibliography: p. 217.
    Includes indexes.
    1. Patriarchs (Bible)—Addresses, essays, lectures. 2. Bible. O. T. Genesis—Criticism, interpretation, etc.—Addresses, essays, lectures. I. Wiseman, D. J. (Donald John) II. Millard, A. R. (Alan Ralph)
BS573.E87 1983   222'.1106   82-21070
ISBN 0-931464-13-7
ISBN 0-931464-12-9 (pbk.)

Contents

Preface

Today there is renewed interest in the history and traditions of the patriarchal period. Recent publications have sought, among other things, to show that the biblical patriarchs were a literary, even fictional, creation of the first millennium B.C., produced to provide the nation of Israel, which came into prominence only then, with 'founding fathers.' Much of this new writing is helpful in distinguishing what are traditional or speculative interpretations from the basic text of Genesis. Sometimes archaeological evidence has been adduced in support of the historicity of the patriarchs and their cultural background in the second millennium B.C. which can no longer be sustained. Sometimes, however, the value of such evidence is ignored or belittled.

In the light of the importance of this subject for the proper understanding of the historical reliability and the theological teaching of the Bible (which cannot be separated), the Council of Tyndale House set up an Old Testament project group to look afresh at aspects of the problems raised. These essays are the first fruits of its work. We are grateful to all who have supported the research and to those scholars who have given time to it.

Since such studies depend largely on the validity of the methods of study, this matter has initial place. Attention is given also to matters of tradition-history and structural analysis of the text. The essays review past work and attempt, in their various ways, to break new ground and stimulate further study. They aim to make a positive contribution, not merely to criticize the works of other writers. Each, necessarily, reflects the views of its own author, rather than of the contributors as a whole.

These essays are offered in the context of a continuing debate, yet with the hope that they will prove of interest and help to many concerned with a subject of absorbing historical and theological importance.

D.J.W
A.R.W

Abbreviations

AASOR	*Annual of the American Schools of Oriental Research*
ANET	*Ancient Near Eastern Texts*, ed. J. B. Pritchard (^{3}1979)
AJA	*American Journal of Archaeology*
Alt, KS	A. Alt, *Kleine Schriften* (1953-54)
AOAT	*Alter Orient and Altes Testament*
AOTS	*Archaeology and Old Testament Study*, ed. D. Winton Thomas (1967)
ASTI	*Annual of the Swedish Theological Institute*
BA	*The Biblical Archaeologist*
BAR	*Biblical Archaeology Review*
BASOR	*Bulletin of the American Schools of Oriental Research*
BJRL	*Bulletin of the John Rylands Library*
Bright	J. Bright, *A History of Israel* (^{2}1972)
CAH^3	*Cambridge Ancient History*, 3rd edn.
CBQ	*Catholic Biblical Quarterly*
Coats, *Canaan*	G. W. Coats, *From Canaan to Egypt (CBQ* Monograph Series 4, 1976)
Cross, *CMHE*	F. M. Cross, *Canaanite Myth and Hebrew Epic* (1973)
CT	Cuneiform Texts, British Museum, London
EAEHL	*Encyclopedia of Archaeological Excavations in the Holy Land*, ed. M. Avi-Yonah, E. Stern (1975-78)
Eissfeldt, KS	O. Eissfeldt, *Kleine Schriften* (1962-68)
ExpT	*The Expository Times*
GK	Gesenius-Kautzsch, *Hebrew Grammar*
Grayson, *ABC*	A. K. Grayson, *Assyrian and Babylonian Chronicles* (1975)
HSS	*Harvard Semitic Studies*
HTR	*Harvard Theological Review*
HUCA	*Hebrew Union College Annual*
IDB	*Interpreter's Dictionary of the Bible* (1962, 1976)

IEJ	*Israel Exploration Journal*
Int	*Interpretation*
JANESCU	*Journal of the Ancient Near Eastern Society of Columbia University*
JAOS	*Journal of the American Oriental Society*
JBL	*Journal of Biblical Literature*
JCS	*Journal of Cuneiform Studies*
JNES	*Journal of Near Eastern Studies*
JSOT	*Journal for the Study of the Old Testament*
King, *Annals*	L. W. King, *Annals of the Kings of Assyria* (1902)
Kitchen, *AOOT*	K. A. Kitchen, *Ancient Orient and Old Testament* (1966)
Kitchen, *BW*	J. A. Kitchen, *The Bible in its World* (1977)
NBD	*The New Bible Dictionary*, ed. J. D. Douglas (1962)
Or	*Orientalia*
OTS	*Oudtestamentische Studien*
PEQ	*Palestine Exploration Quarterly*
POTT	*Peoples of Old Testament Times*, ed. D. J. Wiseman (1973)
RA	*Revue d'Assyriologie*
RB	*Revue Biblique*
RLA	*Reallexicon der Assyriologie*
Saunders, *NEATC*	*Near Eastern Archaeology in the Twentieth Century*, ed. J. A. Saunders (1970)
SBL	Society of Biblical Literature
TB	*Tyndale Bulletin*
Thompson, *Historicity*	T. L. Thompson, *The Historicity of the Patriarchal Narratives*, BZAW, 133 (1974)
TZ	*Theologische Zeitschrift*
UF	*Ugarit-Forschungen*
de Vaux, *History*	R. de Vaux, *The Early History of Israel* (1978)
van Seters, *Abraham*	J. van Seters, *Abraham in History and Tradition* (1975)
VT	*Vetus Testamentum*
VTS	*Vetus Testamentum* Supplement Series

Williamson, *Israel*	H.G.M. Williamson, *Israel in the Books of Chronicles* (1977)
Wilson, *Genealogy*	R. R. Wilson, *Genealogy and History in the Biblical World* (1977)
WTJ	*Westminster Theological Journal*
ZA	*Zeitschrift für Assyriologie*
ZAW	*Zeitschrift, für die alttestamentlische Wissenschaft*
ZDMG	*Zeitschrift der deutschen morgenländischen Gesellschaft*

1
The Patriarchs
in Scripture and History
John Goldingay

The focus of this paper is an attempt to interpret the patriarchal narrative itself. This was, of course, a concern of study of the patriarchs in the pre-critical period, but after that it was long an unfashionable enterprise. It is now becoming once again an object of scholarly interest, as is evidenced by works such as J.P. Fokkelman's *Narrative Art in Genesis*.[1] Such study can now build on insights that have emerged from other critical approaches, and I hope, for instance, in the way I approach the patriarchal narrative, so also to consider some aspects of the ongoing significance of the patriarchal traditions as this was developed in different ways in the period up to the exile.

But I have also another aim. The essays in this volume are concerned with clarifying the historical background of the patriarchs in the second millennium B.C. This was an important feature of Old Testament study in the 1950s but is now itself an unfashionable enterprise; thus in the last section of the paper I shall draw attention to the rationale for this interest which arises from my attempt to interpret the narrative itself.

1. THE THEME OF THE PATRIARCHAL NARRATIVE

What is the patriarchal narrative about? What is it saying? The answer at one level, of course, is that it is saying what it says, and to discover what that is you must read it. But a narrative may express some overall vision of the meaning of the events it relates, and we may be able to verbalize this vision. We must not let our purported grasp of this vision become more important than the narrative itself, yet putting it into words may help us to appreciate the actual narrative as we read it. It is possible, of course, to impose 'visions' or structures on a work. As it happens, however,

[1]Assen: Van Gorcum, 1975

1

certain concrete verbal themes and patterns recur in the fabric of
the patriarchal narrative, and these seem to be the narrative's own
pointers to the meaning it sees in the story it tells. The individual
scenes in the narrative all relate to the theme expressed in the
verbal pointers.

1.1 The story of Abraham

The story of Abraham is prefaced in 11:10-26 by a summary
history in genealogical form from the family of Noah (the second
major figure in Genesis, after Adam) to the family of Terah,
which included Abram (Genesis's third major figure). It is then
introduced in 11:27-32 by Terah's family history. The information
this family history offers (the birth of Lot, the death of his father
Haran, Abram's marriage to Sarai, her inability to have children,
the name of his brother Nahor's wife, the family's departure from
Ur to Haran and Terah's death there) provides the background to
various incidents in the chapters that follow, and seems to be
included for this purpose rather than for its intrinsic interest. In
the Hebrew Bible a new lection begins with Yahweh's summons
to Abram (12:1), and the real opening of the Abram story lies
here.

Grammatically, chapter 12 begins less emphatically than RSV
may imply (there is no 'Now' in the Hebrew). But in terms of
contents, there is an air of moment about 12:1 in that at this point
Yahweh himself speaks, for the first time since the Tower of
Babel story, and thus for the first time in the Abram narrative,
since 11:10-32 has not referred to his involvement. Now he intervenes with a command (12:1) and an undertaking (12:2-3). Abram
expresses his commitment by doing as Yahweh told him (12:4-5a),
a note which recurs later in the story (with 12:4a cf. 17:23b,
21:4b—though the verb is different each time). And when Abram
has travelled to the country he was directed to, Yahweh then
reasserts his commitment by renewing his promise (12:5b-9). He
will give this land to Abram's descendants. Abram himself com-
pletes a preliminary tour of the land, building an altar to worship
Yahweh in the (relative) north at Shechem, another in the centre
of the land between Bethel and Ai, and moving on to the south to
the area of Hebron which will be his home.

But it is not until 13:18 that we are told of the building of a
third altar there. In the meantime some odd notes are struck, such

as to introduce discord into the theme which opened up somewhat idyllically in 12:1-9. Actually, obstacles to the fulfilment of Yahweh's undertaking have been referred to already. 'To your descendants I will give this land' (12:7a). But the land is occupied by someone else (12:6b), so how can Abram have it, and his wife cannot have children (11:30), so how can he have descendants?

12:10-13:4 relate a further threat to the promise. Yahweh intends to make Abram a great nation, to make him a blessing to the nations, and to give the land of Canaan to his descendants. But as a result of an entirely human response to a real crisis, each element in this promise receives a kind of anti-fulfilment. Abram leaves the land of Canaan, watches the potential mother of his descendants join the Pharaoh's harem, and causes Yahweh to bring affliction on the Pharaoh and his house. All ends well (very well, indeed: see 12:16; 13:2), yet the story is a sombre one.

13:5-13 provides another surprise. There is strife within the (wider) family of Abram itself, arising out of the presence of other peoples in the land promised to them. And Abram's generosity in proposing a solution to the problem deprives him of the part of the land that most resembles not only the Egypt from whose prosperity Abram has recently profited but also the Eden from which Genesis's first major figure was expelled. Sombrely, the land which is like the one Adam lost is inhabited by people like those among whom Noah lived (with 13:13 cf. 6:5), and this fact is to be picked up later (Gn. 18-19). Meanwhile Yahweh reaffirms the promise of land and descendants (13:14-17) and Abram begins to enter into his inheritance as he makes the home and offers the worship at Hebron that brings the narrative, interrupted after 12:9, to the end of a section (13:18).

The key theme which emerges from these opening two chapters of the Abraham story is that Yahweh made certain commitments to Abram, commitments which met some measure of fulfilment but were ever threatened by circumstantial and human factors. And every major element in the rest of the Abraham narrative relates to this theme stated in these opening chapters. Yahweh has undertaken to bless Abram with descendants and land and to make him a blessing for other peoples. But the path to the fulfilment of this undertaking is littered with obstacles.

The theme of Yahweh's blessing appears clearly in Genesis 14. In other respects the chapter portrays Abram in a very different way from the other patriarchal stories, and this highlights the theme's appearance when the chapter comes to its narrative climax in its final scene (14:17-24). Here the kings who occupy the stage for the first scene (14:1-12) and Abram and his allies who occupy it for the second (14:13-16) at last appear together. But the centre of the stage is taken by Melchizedek the king of Salem, who appears suddenly in the denouement, though he had been absent from the earlier scenes. And his words bring the chapter directly into the theme announced and first developed in chapters 12-13, because they are words of blessing on Abram (see 14:18-20). They draw our attention to what amounts to a fulfilment of the original promise of blessing in 12:2-3, and coming from the king of Salem constitute a further fulfilment of the words there about Abram's name becoming great among the nations.

The end of the story, however, relates Abram's refusal to be made rich by the king of Sodom (14:21-24). How then is he to become prosperous? 'After these things' Yahweh tells him not to be afraid. The one who delivered Abram's enemies into his hand (14:20) is Abram's deliverer (15:1).[2] Abram has refused possession gained through his involvement with the king of Sodom (14:21-24), so Yahweh promises that his descendants will be given great possessions (15:14).[3] Abram has been in covenant with human allies (14:13),[4] but now Yahweh commits himself to a covenant relationship with him. Thus Genesis 15 takes up several features of Genesis 14.

Genesis 15 itself focuses on the questions of offspring (15:2-6) and of land (15:7-21). The problem with the first is that Abram 'continues childless', but he accepts Yahweh's renewed promise. Then, as Abram finds it difficult to believe in the second under-taking, Yahweh renews this in a more emphatic way in the form of a covenant, though also solemnly revealing how long it will be before the chief obstacle to its fulfilment (the presence of other peoples in the land) can justly be removed.

Chapter 16 returns to the promise of children. Abram begets a son by his wife's maid. The action has been seen as a sinful human attempt to anticipate the fulfilment of Yahweh's words,

---

[2] *magen* (RSV 'shield'), from the same root as the verb *miggen* in 14:20. These are the only occurrences of either word in Genesis to Numbers, so that the link is hardly coincidental.

[3] The word *rekuš* comes five times in 14:11-21 and then in 15:14; cf. 12:5, 13:6, 31:18, 36:7, 46:6.

[4] *bᵉrît* appears in the Hebrew expression for allies.

though the story contains no hint of this judgement. Indeed, Yahweh reasserts his undertaking to Abram with regard to Hagar and her son (16:11; cf. 13:14-17, 15:4-5). The birth of Ishmael is a step towards one aspect of the fulfilment of that undertaking.

Genesis 17 opens with a very full statement of the theme. It begins with God's revelation (17:1a; cf. 12:1a; but especially 15:1a), his self-announcement (17:1b, cf. 15:1b), and his challenge (17:1b; cf. 12:1b; 15:1b). It speaks of descendants and land (17:2-8), but the key-word 'blessing' is replaced by the key-word 'covenant'— which in effect means 'a commitment to bless'. Descendants are explicitly promised as 'blessing' both for Sarai/Sarah through the birth of a son (17:16) and for Hagar's son Ishmael (17:20).

The story of the destruction of Sodom and Gomorrah also keeps relating to the theme of blessing and descendants. The three visitors declare specifically that Sarah will have a son next spring (18:1-15). Abraham's dialogue with Yahweh (18:16-33) arises out of the promise (18:17-19). Although he fails to rescue Sodom (19:1-28), it is not because he is not seeking to be a blessing there, and at least he succeeds in rescuing Lot (19:29). Even the narrative about Lot and his daughters, with which the story closes (19:30-38), relates to the theme of descendants.

Chapter 20, however, reveals that Abraham's capacity for imperilling the promise is not yet exhausted. Although the chapter may not imply that Abraham is outside the promised land (as he was in 12:10-20; cf. 26:1-3) and shows that he can still be a means of blessing as a man of prayer (20:7, 17; cf. 18:22-33), at first he brings trouble to Abimelek instead (20:9, 18).

Then at last the promise of a son is fulfilled (21:1-7). This raises the question of the relationship between Abraham's two sons. 21:8-21 reaffirms that both will become nations, though Isaac will have a special significance (21:12-13, cf. 17:20-21); the pattern is repeated in the story of Esau and Jacob (cf. 27:28-29, 39-40). 21:22-34 returns to Abraham and Abimelek, with a narrative which tacitly illustrates the fulfilment of another aspect of God's undertaking. Abraham is significant enough to be in a special relationship with the king of Gerar, who acknowledges, 'God is with you in all that you do' (21:22). Abraham's name has become great.

Chapter 22 again comes to its climax with a restatement of God's words of blessing (22:15-18). The narrator does not see the command to sacrifice Isaac as a puzzling imperilling of God's purpose to give Abraham descendants through this son, but as God's testing of Abraham (22:1-12). It is when Abraham passes the test that the words of blessing are again reaffirmed.

After a flashback to Haran (22:20-24) which provides the background to chapter 24, Genesis 23 tells of the death of Sarah and of Abraham's purchase of a burial place for her in Hebron. Like the begetting of a child by Hagar, Abraham's purchase of this plot of land might seem a sinful, human act. Why should the one to whom God said he would give the land pay money for it? Is Abraham looking for a false kind of security in the actual legal possession of a foothold (rather, a skeleton-hold!) on the land itself? But the narrative passes no negative judgment. Sarah dies 'in the land of Canaan' (23:2) and the 'possession' of the land of Canaan (17:8; cf. 48:4) begins in the 'posession' of a burial place for her there (23:4, 9, 20; cf. 49:30; 50:13).

Chapter 24 (introduced by 22:20-24) is the last narrative proper in the Abraham story, and, indeed, the longest and most finely worked one of them all. It begins by telling us that the undertaking with which the Abraham story opened has actually been fulfilled: 'Yahweh had blessed Abraham in every way' (24:1; cf. 24:35). But blessings can be lost and inheritances sacrificed. So measures need to be taken to ensure that the descendants are born 'within the family' (24:2-4) and without leaving the land (24:5-8). The chapter is then the account of how the right mother for Abraham's grandchildren is found within these conditions. All that remains is to close off the story of the blessed man Abraham (25:1-11).

The theme of the Abraham narrative, then, is that Yahweh undertook to bless him with descendants and land and to make him a blessing for other peoples, that obstacles to the fulfilment of this commitment presented themselves from many quarters, but that Yahweh kept reaffirming his undertaking and saw it to its partial fulfilment in Abraham's own lifetime.

1.2 *The story of Isaac*

The question now arises whether the Isaac story continues the same theme. That it does is hinted by the closing verse of the Abraham narrative: 'after the death of Abraham God blessed Isaac his son' (25:11). But before the story of Isaac is developed, that of his elder brother is summarized (25:12-18). In his descendants God's words find part, if not the central part, of their fulfilment.

The first real Isaac narrative follows in 25:19-26. In contents, of course, chapters 22 and 24 (and others) have already centred on Isaac. Yet in the structure of Genesis those chapters belong to the Abraham story. Strictly, indeed, it was the Terah story, since 25:12 and 19 are the first formal section headings since 11:27. But the report of Terah's death in 11:32 and Abraham's prominence henceforth suggest that *de facto* 12:1-25:11 is the Abraham story. As the Abraham story has a central concern with his sons, so the Isaac story, which extends from 25:19 to 35:29, includes—indeed, is dominated by—stories about Esau and Jacob. The nature of God's promises no doubt explains the Genesis narrative's pre-occupation with the question of descendants and the consequent prominence of stories about children in the narratives about their parents.

25:19-26 thus constitutes an unexpected but understandable beginning to the Isaac narrative. The event it relates took place in connection with the birth of his twin sons when he was sixty (25:26), and first the author has to summarize for us the first sixty years of his life and the background to this birth, in two or three verses (25:19-21). We are then told of an event from(?) twenty years later (25:27-34), before coming in the next chapter to incidents that seem to have happened before the twins' birth.

So the Isaac narrative unfolds in a rather jerky way. But this gives added emphasis to 25:22-26 and 27-34, and on examination these paragraphs turn out to state the way the blessing theme is to be developed in the Isaac story. As in the Abraham narrative, a word from Yahweh is set at the beginning of the Isaac story. But whereas the word to Abram includes the promise that he will be made a great nation, the word to Isaac's wife speaks of her mothering two nations. In the event, the word to Abram (though often imperilled) also received a double fulfilment, through Ishmael and Isaac; it was the younger of the half-brothers who was to be preferred (17:21; 21:12), but there is no suggestion of rivalry between them—though there was tension between their mothers (16:4-6; 21:9-10). The word to Rebekah, however, already speaks of the preferment of the younger of the two sons she is to bear, and hints at the trouble there will be between them (25:23). Their actual birth sees the beginning of the fulfilment of Yahweh's word (25:26), the differences between them as they grow up relates to it (25:27-28), and the actual supplanting of the elder by the younger begins through the latter's throwing away the right of primogeniture (25:29-34).

The original blessing theme is explicitly resumed in chapter 26. Here Yahweh appears, commands, and promises, as he had to Abraham (26:2-5; cf. 12:1-3). Although Isaac made mistakes very like his father's (26:6-11; cf. 12:10-20; 20:1-18), he also received blessings very like his father's (26:12-14; cf. 13:1-4). He was involved in strife like his father (26:15-22 cf. 13:5-13; 21:25-32), but he was reassured by Yahweh and he worshipped like his father (26:23-25; cf. 13:14-18; 21:33) and was acknowledged by the nations like his father (26:26-33; cf. 14:19-20; 21:22-24). Indeed, it is explicitly because Yahweh committed himself to Abraham, because Abraham obeyed him, and as the God of Abraham, that Yahweh appears to Isaac (26:3, 5, 24). Nevertheless, there is one distinctive motif characteristic of the Isaac narrative, the promise 'I will be with you' (26:3) or 'I am with you' (26:24). It reappears in the form of Abimelek's acknowledgment of Isaac, 'Yahweh is with you' (26:28), as it had featured in Abimelek's acknowledgment of Abraham (21:22). It reappears in the Jacob material in the chapters that follow (28:15, 20, 31:3, 5, 42, 35:3),[5] and constitutes the distinctive aspect to the promise and experience of Yahweh's blessing as this is portrayed in the Isaac narrative.

After chapter 26 the relationship between the two sons dominates the story of Isaac, as 25:19-34 has advertised it would. In chapter 27 at least, however, the theme of who is to receive the blessing is central (27:4, 7, 10, 12, 19, 23, 25, 27, 29, 30, 31, 33, 34, 35, 36, 38, 41), and the specific terms of Isaac's actual blessing recall Yahweh's words to Abraham (26:29, cf. 12:2-3). The modern reader is appalled at Jacob's deceit, and the narrative hints at the poetic justice of his subsequent deceit by Laban, yet it is not so concerned to draw moral lessons as it is to invite us to read the story in the context of 25:23 and to marvel at how Yahweh's word is fulfilled in extraordinary ways.

27:46 takes up another theme of the Abraham story, the provision of a wife for his son. 26:34-35 form the background to this section. Formally set in the context of his diplomatic self-exile from home, Jacob's quest for a wife becomes a central concern for the rest of the Isaac narrative. Yet, although Jacob looks once again to the family of Nahor for a bride, and finds her in the household of the Laban who had so graciously received Abraham's servant seeking a bride for Isaac, the finding of Rachel is so

[5]The prepositions translated 'with' etc. vary.

different from the finding of Rebekah. Isaac's father implies that it is simply inappropriate for his son to marry a Canaanite woman (24:3), Jacob's father acts under wifely pressure that itself arises from a mere concern for domestic harmony (27:46, 28:1). Isaac was on no account to leave the promised land, but Jacob does so to distance himself from Esau (chapter 28). Abraham's servant undertakes his journey by the step-by-step direction of Yahweh and his angel (24:7, 12-21, 27, 50-52), but Yahweh is unmentioned in Jacob's journey once he leaves Canaan (29:1-30). No hitch deprives Isaac of Rebekah, but Jacob is for a while cheated by a trick worthy of his own cunning—and one which reasserts the rights of the first-born (29:26).

Nevertheless, Jacob's journey is set in the context of Yahweh's commitment to him. Before he leaves home Isaac prays for him that he may indeed be fruitful and inherit the land (28:3-4). Before he leaves the land itself Yahweh appears to Jacob in a dream and declares, as he had to Abraham and to Isaac, that he will give Jacob the land, that Jacob's descendants will be very numerous, that other nations will bless themselves by Jacob, and that he will be with Jacob wherever he goes (28:12-15), and Jacob commits himself to Yahweh on the basis of this promise (28:20-22). And indeed the sojourn with Laban sees the fulfilment of Yahweh's undertakings to Jacob. He becomes the father of many sons (29:31-30:24). He is a means of blessing to Laban (30:27, 30). He gains wealth and possessions despite Laban's attempted fraud and despite or through the superstitions that he and Laban seem to have shared (30:25-43). If there is a moral ambiguity about some of Abraham's acts (12:10-13; 16:2-4; 23:1-18), there is no ambiguity about the deceit and theft of the Jacob stories. Yet once more the narrative is more concerned with the conviction that these human acts were the means of Yahweh fulfilling his purpose than it is with moral judgements. Jacob's cocky assertions (31:9-13, 42) are true. God has indeed dealt graciously with him, and he has enough (33:11). Yahweh protects him from the deserved wrath of his father-in-law and turns Laban into his covenant-brother (31:17-55).

But to succeed in escaping from Laban is only to have to face Esau. The fear of Laban (31:31) is replaced by the fear of Esau (32:7, 11), despite the encouragement not to be afraid under whose protection Jacob stands (26:24, cf. 15:1). It is to the blessing that Yahweh gave Jacob as he left the land, and to the command that

Yahweh gave him to return to it, that Jacob himself actually appeals at this point (32:9-12). Land and descendants are once again the focus. And when God (?) appears, Jacob insists on a blessing, and receives one (32:26, 29). Then he finds Esau gracious and welcoming rather than still harbouring revenge. But if Esau is a changed man to make sure that Yahweh's commitment to Jacob is fulfilled, Jacob (for all his changed name) is clearly still the same trickster—and this, too, is the means by which Yahweh prospers him, for Jacob not only buys his piece of land, at Shechem (33:18-20), but also finds reason and means to beat the Shechemites at their own game and to dispossess them of all they own (34:23, 27-29). Then, as the story of Isaac draws to a close, God calls Jacob back to Bethel, where he goes to build an altar to the one who had appeared to him there in his moment of need and had kept his promise to be with him wherever he went (35:1-3), and we are again told of the renaming of Jacob as Israel and of the blessing of descendants and land (35:9-12). Like Abraham, Isaac dies with his two sons together to bury him (35:29; cf. 25:9).

The Isaac narrative, then, is by no means identical with the Abraham narrative. It is more tightly structured and less episodic, there is more irony, and it introduces fewer heroes and more villains. Yet the major themes we perceived in the Abraham narrative appear here too. It relates that Yahweh reaffirmed to Abraham's son and grandson his undertaking to bless Abraham with descendants and land and to make him a means of blessing to others, and that he kept this undertaking despite and frequently through the vagaries of those he committed himself to. This theme holds the narrative together by constituting both a thread running through it and the key motif to which the individual scenes relate.

1.3 *The story of Jacob*

The awareness that the Isaac story, like the Abraham story, centres on the theme of God's blessing, naturally predisposes us to look for the same theme in the Jacob story. We are not disappointed, though the latter, like the two earlier narratives, has at the same time its own distinctiveness.

As was the case with 'the Isaac narrative', to entitle the sequence 'the Jacob narrative' feels somewhat whimsical, since most of the chapters refer explicitly to the life of one of his sons rather than to Jacob himself. Yet it is clearly marked as 'the Jacob story' at its beginning and on its return to Jacob for the closing chapters (47-50), and, indeed, the point about the Joseph material in its context is to explain how Jacob's family came to be in Egypt. Only in 50:22b-26 is Jacob realy left behind and Joseph the focus.

Like the Isaac story, the Jacob narrative is preceded by a brief account of the supplanted elder brother, which ties off that aspect of the preceding narrative (36, cf. 25:12-18). It includes the note that Esau surrenders the land to his brother (36:6-7). The further note that in contrast Jacob himself 'dwelt in the land of his father's sojournings, in the land of Canaan' gains its significance from what has come before (his exile in Haran) and what will follow (his exile in Egypt).

After that, the story proper gets under way in a surprising fashion—though in this respect it again resembles the Isaac story. Like the opening summary verses of the latter, the opening summary verses here (37:2b-4, cf. 25:19b-21) lead in to an event which sets the keynote for the bulk of the story as a whole. Isaac's wife receives a word from God which defines the overall parameters for the chapters that follow; Jacob's son has a dream which reveals the parameters for the chapters that follow it (37:5-11; cf. 25:22-23 and 24-34). Although Jacob and his family respond to the dream in a way that the modern reader is tempted to see as entirely appropriate (37:8, 10-11a), at the same time Jacob, the narrative implies, knows the word of God when he hears it (37:11b, cf. Rebekah's response to the word about Jacob, 25:28b). The Jacob now deceived over Joseph (37:31-35) is a softer character than the one we have met before, but the narrative's interest is not in character development from one set of stories to the next but in the function of Jacob's personality in connection with the theme announced by the dream.

Yet immediately the scene which follows the dream (37:12-36) sets up a contrast with its promise. The main theme of the story from Genesis 37-47 is then how Joseph's dream comes true despite and even through the affliction and humiliation brought about by the brothers who resented him, by the woman who loved him, by the master who misjudged him, and by the steward who forgot him. The theme is expressed in the patterned sequence of the story, which forms an extended narrative unparalleled in Genesis and with few equals elsewhere in the Old Testament.

But it is still the Jacob story, and this is reflected in the transition of attention to Judah in chapter 38. Since Reuben, and Simeon and Levi, have disgraced themselves (34, 35:22), Judah is in a sense Jacob's senior son. Now Joseph, supposedly destined to be leader, seems to be out of the way. So Judah becomes the focus for a while.[6] Marriage and children dominate his story, as we would now expect, and the chapter ends with the birth of twin sons, of whom once again the elder is displaced by the younger (38:27-30). But this pattern affects Judah himself. The chapter's function is once again to tie off the story of a supplanted older brother by telling us of the fulfilment of the promise in the birth of his sons. It seems that Judah is disqualified from leadership by his marrying out and his recourse to an apparent prostitute: in the realm of marriage and sex he behaves more like Reuben (and Shechem, who provoked Simeon and Levi's sin) than Joseph, as chapter 39 will now portray him.

The first verbal markers to the narrative's burden also come in chapter 39, which three times reiterates that Yahweh was with Joseph and thus he met with success (39:2, 3, 23; cf. 21).[7] Then lo and behold, it further reiterates that Joseph was the means of bringing Yahweh's 'blessing' to his owner, Potiphar (39:5). Once a further reverse is behind him, Joseph becomes a blessing to the Pharaoh himself too (40-41), though the term itself does not appear.

But success for the Pharaoh of course also means success for Joseph himself. This is highlighted when his brothers appear in Egypt to bow before him, and Joseph recalls the dreams with which the narrative opened (42:9). Yet the triumph which fulfills the dream has not yet been fully understood. Why has Yahweh elevated the (?arrogant) Joseph in this way? Joseph himself is allowed to tell us, when the story comes to a climax as he reveals himself to his brothers. This was Yahweh's way of providing for the needs of Jacob's whole family (45:5-8).

So Jacob himself is to follow Joseph to Egypt. And immediately the familiar (yet again updated) divine undertakings made to each of the patriarchs reappear. Once more God speaks to Jacob in a

[6]See F. Goldin, 'The youngest son or Where does Genesis 38 belong?', *JBL* 96 (1977), pp. 27-44.

[7]RSV obscures the reiteration; 'successful' and 'prosper' represent forms of the one Hebrew root ṣ-l-ḥ.

vision, identifies himself, and bids Jacob not to fear to go to Egypt, because there he will make Jacob into a great nation and from there he will bring Jacob back to the promised land again (46:2-4). Whether or not Abram's journey to Egypt and Jacob's to Mesopotamia were sinful human initiatives, Jacob's journey to Egypt takes place entirely within the purpose of God. And there in Egypt Jacob blesses Pharaoh (47:7, 10) and the promise of fruitfulness is kept (47:27). As Jacob's death draws near, recalling God's blessing of him, he gives a father's blessing to Joseph's sons, and as he had himself received the elder's blessing from his father so he gives it to Ephraim rather than to Manasseh (48:1-20). He passes on to Joseph (treated as his own senior son, in accordance with Joseph's dream) both the promise that God will be with him and will bring him back to the land of his fathers, and his own personal possession in the land of Shechem (?) (48:21-22). The 'deathbed scene' is prolonged by Jacob's blessing on all his sons in chapter 49 (see 49:28), with a specific reference to blessings for Joseph (see 49:25-26), before Jacob actually dies and returns to the land himself (50:12-13). Genesis closes with Joseph's own final affirmation that the whole story we have been reading (Genesis 37-50) belongs within the purpose of God to keep many people alive, despite the sins of his brothers in their part in the story (50:20), with Joseph's own final passing on of the promise of the land to 'the sons of Israel', and with his dying in living hope of sharing in the fulfilment of that promise himself (50:24-26).

It is possible, then to read through the patriarchal narratives as a whole and perceive one clear theme linking them. The theme is explicit in the actual words of God which promise blessing, land, increase, and influence. These explicit words then form the key which explains the function in their context of the stories which make up the bulk of the narratives as a whole. These stories illustrate the theme, often by showing how God overcomes the obstacles to the fulfilment of his commitment of himself which arise from circumstances that surround those who received God's commitment or from the people that they had to deal with or from the recipients of God's promises themselves.

2. THE PATRIARCHAL NARRATIVE IN ITS CONTEXT

In asking about the theme of the patriarchal narrative, we have presupposed that understandings of the whole and of the parts interact. Now it may be the case that individual patriarchal stories have their own themes as well as relating to the theme of the whole. Genesis 22, for instance, may be setting up Abraham as a model of faith and obedience, may be giving one of the reasons why the temple was eventually built where it was, and may be explaining why Israelites do not offer human sacrifices. In the absence of explicit indications in the narrative itself it is difficult to be sure whether such concerns are intrinsic to the narrative, but they are not alien to it. It was the oath to Abraham (22:15-18) set in the context of parallel words running through the wider patriarchal narrative which suggested that the concern with the blessing of the patriarchs was the starting-point for understanding it.

But the patriarchal narrative as a whole is itself set in a context; it is not a complete literary unit, but part of a longer work. To appreciate its meaning more fully, then, we need to examine it in this internal literary context. This may also help us to see how the particular theme of Genesis 12-50 relates to other themes of Old Testament faith which are dealt with in the work to which it belongs.

A fuller insight into a narrative (or into any other kind of statement) can also be achieved through the parallel study of its external historical context. By its historical context I mean that set of circumstances of a political, social, economic, and religious kind which form the background to the statement we are concerned with and which thus reflect the needs it had to address, the mistakes it had to correct, and the sins it had to confront. The meaning of Amos's declaration, 'You only have I known of all the families of the earth; therefore I will punish you for all your iniquities' (3:2) becomes clearer in the light of the social and economic circumstances of the time (for which the book of Amos is itself our chief source). Again, there are radically different attitudes in different prophets regarding the nature of Yahweh's attitude to his people and regarding the importance he attaches to their corporate worship. It would be possible to misunderstand these differences as conflicts between the prophets, were it not for the differences in the historical and religious circumstances they are addressing which in part account for the consequent differences in emphasis that they manifest. Establishing a work's historical context enables us to see more precisely the point it is making by the words it uses.

This may be even more the case with narrative than it is with (for instance) prophecy. The date of the prophecy of Joel is quite uncertain and we are thus quite unclear as to its historical background, yet the message of the work and the response it seeks from its hearers are nevertheless clear because it is of the nature of prophecy to make them explicit ('Return to me'—Joel 2:12). But it is not of the nature of narrative to make explicit the response it seeks. The story informs us that God called Abram from Haran to Canaan, but it does not reveal how it wishes this statement to engage us except, presumably, by our being interested. Seeing a biblical narrative in its historical context may at least enable us to see what response the narrative actually received or what response was encouraged in circles that seem sympathetic to the thrust of the narrative.

Many of the postulated connections between Genesis and later historical contexts are a matter of inference. It is often suggested, for instance, that the stress on the sabbath, on abstaining from blood, and on circumcision, in the creation, Noah, and Abraham stories, is to be connected with the importance in the exile of these distinctive outward marks of being a Jew. But this is a matter of inference, with little backing outside the Pentateuch in the actual exilic literature.

As some form of control on postulated links between the patriarchal material and later historical contexts, then, I propose to use the actual references to the patriarchs later in its own internal narrative context, the incidences of similar themes or language there, and also specific references outside this from the period to which this narrative as a whole refers or belongs. The first two tell us what points of connection with later contexts are urged by the work as a whole itself, the last tell us what lessons were seen in the patriarchal material by at least some Israelites of this same period.

But what is this narrative context, and to what period does it belong? What is the literary work to which the patriarchal stories belong, and what is its historical background?

There is no controversy over locating the beginning of this literary work, in Genesis 1-11. But where does it end? Even if the material in Genesis once existed on its own, in its present form Genesis looks forward to events that follow, and Exodus presents itself as a continuation of Genesis. Even more clearly the story of Exodus is continued in Leviticus and Numbers (the instructions in Ex. 25-31 are partly fulfilled in Ex. 35-40, partly in Lv. 8-9). Again, Numbers is not the end of a narrative, and Deuteronomy equally leaves us still in the middle of the story of Israel's beginnings, even though it brings the end of the story of Moses.

With the book of Joshua the story comes to some kind of end. Dramatically, the promises made in the patriarchal stories receive a substantial measure of fulfilment (see Gn. 12:1-3; Jos. 23:14), and at the end of Joshua the story as a whole is reviewed (Jos. 24:2-13). But is Joshua 24 the end of the work which Genesis begins? Several considerations make one hesitate to assume this. Although Deuteronomy and Joshua look backward to the story of the patriarchs and exodus, they also look forward to the life to be lived in the promised land. They note that the fulfilment of promises may be succeeded by trouble (e.g. Jos. 23:15-16), and the end of the story of Israel's origins issues its challenge to the next generation (24:14-27). Now the book of Judges takes up precisely these issues, beginning with the other side of the story as regards Israel's occupation of the land (Jdg. 1), and the style and theological concerns of Judges are broadly similar to those of Deuteronomy and Joshua 1 and 23-24. So Judges represents a continuation of Joshua. Similarly the books of Samuel and Kings each take the same story further until the awful warnings of Deuteronomy are finally fulfilled.

The literary context of the patriarchal stories, then, is the narrative from Genesis to Kings as a whole. Against the background of world history it takes Israel from Ur of the Chaldaeans to the peaks of the occupation of Palestine and the story of David and Solomon, and then down to the trough of exile at the hand of the Chaldaeans from whose midst Abram had once been called. It is this total story that is the internal literary context against which we may most fully appreciate the meaning of the particular stories about the patriarchs.

So what is the external historical background of the patriarchal stories? If they form part of the narrative which runs from Genesis to Kings, then in this final form they cannot date from before the exile. John van Seters has recently reasserted the view that they were in fact composed then.[8] The more usual view for the last century has been that the first connected patriarchal

[8]*Abraham in History and Tradition* (New Haven and London: Yale U.P., 1975).

narratives belong to quite early in the period of the monarchy,[9] perhaps even to the Judges period.[10] The traditional view, however, attributes the origin of Genesis, with Exodus to Deuteronomy, to the time of Moses.[11]

There seems no prospect of an early consensus on the dating of the patriarchal material, a question of considerable importance in connection with tracing the pre-history of Israel and of Israelite religion. But I do not think that we necessarily need to know which approach to dating is right in order to be able to interpret the stories against their historical background. For if the patriarchal narratives are to be read in the literary context of Genesis to Kings as a whole, this suggests that the whole historical period covered by this narrative is the right historical context against which the stories are to be understood, no matter what period they first came into being. Since they ultimately came to belong to a work that culminates in the exile, then it is appropriate to interpret them against this historical context. But since this work pays considerable attention to the exodus-conquest period and to the monarchy, it is also appropriate to ask what the stories mean against those historical contexts, even though we cannot be precise as to the degree of fixed form they had reached in the time of (say) Moses or Solomon.

I want, then, to consider the patriarchal narrative in the literary or historical contexts of pre-history as this is described in Genesis 1-11, of the exodus-conquest period as this is described in Exodus to Joshua, of the monarchy as this is described in Judges to Kings, and of the exile with which the work as a whole ends. And to amplify our understanding of the points that the narratives were then taken to make we will note allusions to the patriarchal material in other contemporary literature, which means mainly the prophets.[12]

[9]E.g. J. Wellhausen, *Prolegomena to the History of Ancient Israel* (ET reprinted Gloucester, MA: Peter Smith, 1973; German original 1878, ²1883), O. Eissfeldt, *The Old Testament: An Introduction* (ET New York: Harper and Oxford: Blackwell, 1965, German original, 1934, ³1964).

[10]So M. Noth, *A History of Pentateuchal Traditions* (Englewood Cliffs and London: Prentice-Hall, 1972; German original 1948).

[11]E.g. R. K. Harrison, *Introduction to the Old Testament* (Grand Rapids: Eerdmans, 1969; London: Tyndale, 1970).

[12]It would be appropriate to include a section of the patriarchal stories in the context of the patriarchal period itself, which would involve consideration of

2.1 *The context of universal pre-history*

So how is the meaning of the patriarchal stories made more specific by their being set in the context of universal pre-history in Genesis 1-11? The theme of God's blessing, which is of central importance in Genesis 12-50, is in fact resumed from Genesis 1-11, where it already plays a key role.

Here indeed is where Genesis opens. Genesis 1:1-2:3[13] relates a series of divine commands through which the world's creation comes about, leading to a double climax (or a climax and a coda) in 1:26-31 and 2:1-3. Here God blesses man and speaks of his being fruitful and filling the land (1:28),[14] thus itemizing the blessing in a way which anticipates the patriarchal narrative (cf. especially 17:20; 28:3-4; 35:11-12; 48:3-4). He also blesses the seventh day (2:3). The life of man was to be one lived under God's blessing.

2:4-25 might be seen as further detailing the command and the blessing, but it also leads into the reversal of blessing into curse through man's resistance to the command. As a result of this the serpent is cursed (3:14),the ground is cursed (3:17; 5:29), and man is cursed (4:11). The picture of gloom is lightened by various notes of God's mercy (e.g. 3:21; 4:1, 15, 25-26), and then by the recollection of God's blessing (5:2) with its outworking in the fruitfulness of the race (5:3-32). But man's life is one under a curse which comes to fruition in the destruction of the time of Noah.

But after that act of judgment the curse is lifted (8:21) and the blessing of fruitfulness in the land is restored (9:1-7; cf. 8:17). As will be the case in the experience of Abraham, the divine commitment with regard to descendants and land is then sealed by covenant (9:8-17). Yet immediately the blessing on Noah and his family is partly undone and Noah declares Canaan cursed, though Shem is blessed (9:25-26) and Noah's descendants multiply to fill the earth again (chapter 10).

---

the assertions they make (e.g. about the relationship between Abraham's religion and that of the people he meets) in response to aspects of the situation in the period to which the patriarchs belonged, but this is more directly the focus of other essays in this volume.

[13]Or perhaps 1:1-2:4a: for the view that such formulae in Genesis are conclusions, not introductions, see P. J. Wiseman, *New Discoveries in Babylonia about Genesis* (London: Marshall, 1963), reprinted in *Clues to Creation in Genesis* (London: Marshall, 1977).

[14]The Hebrew word ʾereṣ means both 'earth' and 'land'.

Genesis 1-11, then, describes the blessing and the curse on Adam, and the blessing and the curse on Noah. Now in the promise in Genesis 12:1-3 there is an ambiguity about the reference to the nations (12:3). Are they the recipients of blessing themselves, or only the admirers of Israel's blessing? When we perceive that Genesis 1-11 is centrally concerned with the theme of the blessing of the whole world, this leads us to conclude that this context resolves the ambiguity of 12:3. As far as Abraham (and later Israel) was concerned, the focus of concern lay in his own blessing. But in the purpose of God, the narrative affirms, Abraham received God's call and the promise of God's blessing as a means of God's restoring the blessing of creation to a lost world. The curse does not have the last word; blessing is reasserted in Genesis 12:1-3, though the patriarchal narrative goes on to make it clear that the curse continues ever to threaten the blessing. And the blessing on Abraham is a re-statement of the blessing of creation.

2.2 *The patriarchs in the context of the exodus and conquest*

The nature of the theme of Genesis 12-50 makes one form of link with Exodus to Joshua inevitable. God's undertaking to bless Abraham with many descendants and to give them the land of Canaan (albeit after a time away from it) is here fulfilled (see e.g. Ex. 1:7; 12:40; 13:19; 33:1; Num. 23:10; Dt. 1:8; 9:5). The exodus happens because God remembers his covenant with the patriarchs (Ex. 2:24; 6:2-8), and Moses's appeal to Yahweh not to cast Israel off bases itself on Yahweh's undertakings to the patriarchs (32:13; Dt. 9:27). It is for this faithfulness to his commitments that Israel is to worship Yahweh in the land (Dt. 26:3).

As the fulfilment of God's undertakings, the exodus and the conquest form the conclusion of a story begun in the life of Abraham. This point is made by some of the narratives' geographical references. Abram first arrives in the land at Shechem (Gn. 12:6), Jacob buys land at Shechem (33:18-19) and passes this on to Joseph (48:22), and the story of the patriarchs, exodus, and conquest ends in the land where it began in an assembly of Israel at Shechem (Jos. 24), where Joseph's bones are re-interred as he had planned (24:32). The completing of the series of acts stretching from the call of Abraham to the giving of the land is then the reason why Israel serves Yahweh in the present (24:2-14; cf. Dt. 26:5-11).

But a second form of link between the patriarchal and the exodus-conquest narratives involves the latter picturing Israel in a position before God parallel to that portrayed in the former. God's undertakings and blessings are repeated, as well as being fulfilled and completed. This theme appears particularly clearly in the account of Israel in the plains of Moab, after her wilderness wanderings (Nu. 22-24). There the Moabite king sends for an Aramaean seer, Balaam, to curse Israel. But Balaam cannot do this, because Yahweh himself has declared Israel blessed. All Balaam can therefore do is bless Israel, reasserting the patriarchal promises of descendants (23:9-10), of God's active presence with them (23:21-24), of possessing a land (24:5-7), and of having kings and defeating enemies (24:17-19). There are particular verbal parallels in 24:9 with Genesis 27:29 and 49:9. The immediately following account of Israel's worship of Moabite gods (Nu. 25:1-5), however, illustrates the obstacles to the fulfilment of this blessing, as the patriarchal stories often do.

The theme of blessing is further reaffirmed in Moses's address to Israel in Moab in the book of Deuteronomy, and the blessing is often specified here as involving increase in numbers and enjoyment of the land. Moses urges Israel to obey Yahweh's commands because then she will experience these blessings (e.g. 7:13; 30:16), he prays for further fulfilment of God's promises (26:15), he looks forward to the worship Israel will offer when she does experience them (e.g. 16:15), and he makes Yahweh's blessing the standard for Israel's generosity to others (15:14). The theme of blessing (and curse, if she disobeys) is particularly prominent in Moses's closing exhortation (chapters 27-28). Other specific parallels with patriarchal promises appear in the closing chapters of Deuteronomy. Moses promises that Yahweh will be with Israel as he was with Jacob (31:6-8; cf. Gn. 28:15). He blesses the twelve tribes as Jacob had (33:1-29, cf. Gn. 49:1-28), acknowledging Joseph's dominion foreshadowed in his dream (33:13-17; cf. Gn. 37:8; 49:22-26; there is another particular verbal parallel in 33:13 with Gn. 27:28). On the other hand, we are now the other side of the fulfilment of many of the patriarchal promises, while the remaining fulfilment is imminent. Israel is thus in a new situation before God, enjoying a covenant relationship that was promised to the patriarchs and may be regarded as foreshadowed by the patriarchal covenant, yet one which was not actually fully experienced by the fathers (Dt. 4:31; 5:2-3; 29:10-15). Deuteronomy thus emphasizes the obligations that follow from actually experiencing the covenant relationship, the blessings of Yahweh, the fulfilled promises. The patriarchal promises, addressed to people for whom the blessings are future, make little reference to such obligations. Deuteronomy stresses the commitment to Yahweh which must be the people's response to their experience of the commitment of Yahweh if the blessing is to abide.

The parallel between Israel's relationship with God during the patriarchal period and at the time of the exodus is expressed theologically in both narratives. On the one hand, the God of the patriarchs is referred to as Yahweh, although this actual name may not have been known until the exodus period.[15] On the other hand, the God of the exodus is identified as 'the God of your fathers, the God of Abraham, of Isaac, and of Jacob' (Ex. 3:16). The parallel is also expressed typologically in Genesis 12:10-13:2. Abram 'goes down' into Egypt as Jacob's family later would and 'goes up' from Egypt as the Israelites would, 'plundering the Egyptians' in the process.

In the context of the exodus-conquest narrative, then, the patriarchal narrative appears both as an instructive parallel to what living before God means for Israel in that later period, and also as the beginning of a story which will be completed then and the giving of an undertaking which will be fulfilled then. The people's place in Canaan is explained by Yahweh's promise of blessing to their fathers and by the sin of those who lived in the land before them. They were promised and given the land by God himself.

2.3. *The patriarchs in the context of the monarchy*

In the structure of Genesis to Kings the period of the monarchy in turn links sequentially with the patriarchal period. It takes the same story a stage further. This linking is expressed at the micro-level in Samuel's address to Israel at the anointing of Saul (1 Sa. 12:7-15). What God has done from Abraham to the monarchy challenges Israel to obedience now, as earlier in the narrative what God has done from Abraham to the conquest challenged Israel to obedience at an earlier point (Jos. 24).

The motif of the fulfilment of Yahweh's undertakings to the patriarchs is less prominent and less explicit in Judges-Samuel-

---

[15]See Gordon Wenham's paper in this volume.

Kings than it is in Exodus to Joshua, but it is present. Abram was promised an empire that would extend from Egypt to the Euphrates and would include the territory of ten peoples (Gn. 15:18-21), and the time of David is the one in which this vision comes nearest to realization. Then 'the princes of the peoples gather as the people of the God of Abraham. For the shields[16] of the land belong to God; he is highly exalted' (Ps. 47:9). The peoples contemporary with Davidic Israel (see especially 2 Sa. 8) are broadly those whose origins and activities are spoken of in Genesis, though the parallel is not exact.

Again, Abraham is told that kings will be among his descendants (Gn. 17:6). Although this comes about in Edom before it does in Israel (36:31-39), the narrative itself probably sees the Davidic monarchy as the most important fulfilment of this promise, which is meanwhile repeated to Jacob (35:11). After the institution of the Israelite monarchy Edom is at first subordinate to but then in rebellion against Israel (1 Ki. 11:14-22; 2 Ki. 8:20-22), and this, too, takes up a patriarchal blessing (Gn. 27:40).

At this point the experience and destiny of the man foreshadows that of the people. The same is true of the sons of Jacob. Many of the details of Jacob's blessing (Gn. 49) are of uncertain significance, but some central points are clear. As in the actual story Joseph—one of the youngest sons—comes to be the leader, so here Joseph receives the fullest blessing, and later among the tribes Joseph, divided into Ephraim and Manasseh (n.b. Gn. 48) gains a dominant position after the division of the kingdom, so that 'Ephraim' becomes a natural title for the dominant northern kingdom which already inherits the very title 'Israel' (e.g. Is. 7; Ho. 5).

Yet this dominance of Ephraim is something of an anomaly. After all, God 'rejected the tent of Joseph, he did not choose the tribe of Ephraim; but he chose the tribe of Judah, Mount Zion, which he loves . . . He chose David his servant' (Ps. 78:67, 68, 70). This conviction has its foreshadowing in the patriarchal story. Judah becomes Jacob's senior son, and even after being displaced by Joseph acts as leader and spokesman among his brothers (see Gn. 43; 44; 46:28). Then Jacob's blessing declares that the brothers will actually bow down before Judah; he is the one to whom

---

[16]On 'shields' see note 2 above on Gn. 14:20, 15:1.

sceptre and staff belong and whom peoples will obey (Gn. 49:8, 10; 10c is difficult, but the verses as a whole are clear enough).

This vision is fulfilled in David, a descendant of Judah's son Perez (Ru. 4:18-22) who himself supplanted his elder brother (Gn. 38:27-30). David's own original centre was Hebron (2 Sa. 2-5), and a connection with Hebron is one of many points at which David parallels Abraham as well as experiencing the fulfilment of his promises. It was at Mamre/Hebron that Abram really settled in the land (Gn. 13:18) and here he entered into his token legal possession of it (Gn. 23).

When Abraham received the promise of an empire, this was sealed by a covenant (15:18-21), and when he was promised that kings would be among his descendants, God made an everlasting covenant with him (17:1-8). Both narratives probably imply Mamre/Hebron as their location (and cf. Gn. 18). With David, too, God sealed his promises by making an everlasting covenant (2 Sa. 23:5; Ps. 89; cf. 2 Sa. 7:16; Ps. 132:12). To Abraham God promises that he will make his name great, to David he promises a great name (Gn. 12:2; 2 Sa. 7:9). To Abraham he promises that nations will pray to be blessed as his descendants are blessed (Gn. 22:18; repeated for Isaac 26:4; cf. 12:3; 18:18; 28:14), for the Davidic king the psalmist prays that his name may endure and men pray to be blessed as his is (Ps. 72:17).[17] (Otherwise, however, the explicit blessing theme is not prominent in Samuel-Kings— though note David's prayer for blessing, 2 Sa. 7:29, and Solomon's prayer of blessing, 1 Kings 8). Psalm 72 also emphasizes the king's responsibility for justice and righteousness, which Abraham shares, too (Gn. 18:19).

In the story of the monarchy, David and the temple are closely linked (cf. Ps. 78:68, 70 quoted above; Ps. 132). In Genesis, Abraham passes his supreme test on a mount in the land of Moriah (Gn. 22:2), and the temple site is called Mount Moriah in 2 Chronicles 3:1. The place comes to have attached to it the phrase, 'On the mountain of Yahweh he will appear' (Gn. 22:14),[18] which to a later generation can only imply the temple mount.

Earlier Genesis 14:17-20 raises the question of the relationship of Abram and the royal-priesthood of Salem—identified at least

---

[17] The hitpael of the verb *barak* is used in Gn. 22:18, 26:4, Ps. 72:17.
[18] The translation of the verb is uncertain, but the noun phrase is enough.

by Psalm 76:2 with Jerusalem. The supplementary identification of the valley of Shaveh as the King's Valley (Gn. 14:17) also presupposes that the scene here is Jerusalem (cf. 2 Sa. 18:18). But here the implicit relationship with David is a different one. As king of Jerusalem David inherits the position of Melchizedek (Ps. 110). But in Genesis 14 Abram acknowledges Melchizedek, paying tithes to him, as, later, Jacob pomised to pay tithes at Bethel (28:22). In applying Genesis 14 and Psalm 110 to Jesus, Hebrews makes explicit the argument that is implicit here. David's authority in Jerusalem is buttressed by the fact that Abram acknowledged his predecessor in Jerusalem.

But the typological relationship between patriarchal figures and those of the monarchy can work both ways. If there are encouraging (though implicit) parallels between the monarchy and Abraham, there are also uncomfortable (and explicit) parallels between the monarchy and Sodom. Sodom is a paradigm of sin and judgment not only in respect of the nations (Is. 3:9, 13:19) but also in respect of Israel (Is. 1:9, 10); Genesis 18-19 sets us its challenge (and its invitation to prayer) regarding the Israel of the monarchy. And there is an explicit and uncomfortable parallel between Jacob and later Israel (see Ho. 12:2-5, 12; also Is. 43:27). As in the patriarchal narrative itself, the reason for Yahweh's continuing forbearance towards Israel is not their deserve but his own covenant commitment (2 Ki. 13:23).

Finally the Joseph story resonates with the account of the monarchy, in the latter's picture of the archetypal wise man Solomon. Joseph is the man who proves that success comes from having Yahweh with one and acting honourably (notably, resisting the seductions of another man's wife), and these are emphases of the wisdom tradition which finds its link with Israel's history in the person of Solomon.

So the story of the monarchy and the story of the patriarchs are told in similar terms, as are the story of the exodus and conquest and the story of the patriarchs. The Abrahamic and Davidic covenants mirror and interpret each other. Israel prays for the Davidic king to continue to experience what God promised to Abraham (Ps. 72:17). The parallel suggests that the Abrahamic covenant foreshadows the Davidic as it foreshadows the Sinai covenant—hence, perhaps, the fact that the prophets usually refer back to one of the latter two (Sinai or Davidic covenant) rather than to the one that foreshadows them. And further, the achievements of the monarchy are explained by the divine undertakings of the patriarchal period, as the exodus and conquest were. Yahweh himself had promised to make Abraham's descendants famous and destined them to rule over Canaan, and this is the explanation and basis of the fact that they now do.

2.4 *The patriarchs in the context of the exile*

The narrative that begins in Genesis by creating order from formlessness and then by taking Abram out of Ur of the Chaldeans into the promised land ends in 2 Kings with chaos triumphant and Israel back in the power of the Chaldeans.[19] What does this literary and historical context add to an appreciation of the patriarchal narrative?

Yahweh's words to the patriarchs had spoken of blessing, but the possibiltiy of the curse had remained in the background. In Deuteronomy 27-28 the two possibilities are straight alternatives, and by the time of 2 Kings 25 the curse seems to be triumphant. In this context, what is the narrative inviting us to make of those words about blessing? The question is sharpened by the fact that some of the promises speak of the blessings being given for ever. The covenant was eternal (Gn. 17:7, 13, 19) and the land was to be enjoyed as a permanent possession (13:15; 17:8; 48:4). These assertions are particularly striking in a context when the covenant seems to be broken and the land lost. Do the promises stand? How permanent is permanent?

In warning of the possibility of exile, both Leviticus and Deuteronomy declare that this need not be the end. Deuteronomy promises that if Israel returns to Yahweh, he will bless them again as he did their fathers (30:9). They can appeal to his covenant with their fathers (4:30-31). A reference to the patriarchs is also explicit in Leviticus 26:40-45. If Israel repents, Yahweh says, he will remember his covenant with Jacob, Isaac, and Abraham, and will remember the land (26:42). The permanencies can be permanent. The defection that led to exile is perhaps

---

[19]'Chaldaeans' is a term that strictly belongs only to the first millennium (cf. its prominence in Isaiah, Jeremiah, etc.), and in Genesis 11 it may deliberately make the point that Israel has returned to the land that Abram was called from.

foreshadowed in the defection even at Sinai, and there one basis for appeal to God's mercy was that he should remember Abraham, Isaac, and Jacob (Dt. 9:27).

The promise that by the grace of God the permanencies can be permanent is explicit in the prophecies which either look forward to exile or arise from it. The God who redeemed Abraham cares for sinful Israel now (Is. 29:22). The commitment Yahweh swore to Abraham and Jacob still applies to their sinful descendants (Mi. 7:20). Jacob's shame will be put to an end when Yahweh restores his children (Is. 29:22-24) and Rachel's grief can be assuaged because Yahweh is going to bring her children back to the land (Je. 31:15-17).

The re-application of the patriarchal traditions is most systematic in Isaiah 40-55. These chapters begin and close with the proclamation that Yahweh's word stands 'for ever' and will achieve its purpose (40:8; 55:10-11). Yahweh has stirred up a new Abraham from the east (or north) to win victories over the Mesopotamian kings like Abraham's own (41:2-4, 25; cf. Gn. 14).[20] Because Jacob/Israel is the offspring of Yahweh's friend Abraham, and in him is taken from the ends of the earth, she need not fear, for he is with her and is her God; Yahweh reiterates his undertaking to Jacob (41:8-10; 43:5; cf. Gn. 28:15, 21; 46:3-4, etc.).

Various specific features of Yahweh's relationship with the patriarchs appear in Isaiah 40-55: the blessing itself (44:3, 51:1-3), the covenant commitment (42:6; 49:8; 54:10; 55:3), the acknowledgment of the nations (45:14; 49:7, 23; cf. especially Gn. 27:29), the return to the land (43:5-6; cf. especially Gn. 28:15). But it is striking that the theme of descendants, and not that of the land, is the one which is most developed. At the beginning of the exile Ezekiel warned Israel not to appeal too easily to Yahweh's promise to Abraham when he was but one man (Ezk. 33:24). But in the context of the exiles' now having suffered enough (Is. 40:2) Yahweh encourages them by the precedent of Abraham: 'For when he was but one I called him, and I blessed him and made him many'. This he will do for Israel now (Is. 51:1-3; cf. 44:1-5; Je. 3:16; 23:3).

---

[20]I take it that Isaiah 41:2-4, 25 refers neither to Abraham as opposed to Cyrus, nor vice versa, but to Cyrus (as 44:28, 45:1 will make explicit) pictured in Abrahamic terms.

The apparently barren, forsaken wife will bear miraculously, as Sarah did (Is. 49:14-21; 54).

In the context of the end of Genesis to Kings in exile, then, the patriarchal narratives carry a simple, clear message. The commitments Yahweh made to the patriarchs and their descendants were permanent and thus they apply to the exile generation, too. The promise of blessing, of land, of increase, of God's own presence, of the acknowledgment of the nations, sealed by the covenant relationship, were not based on the patriarchs' achievements but on the gracious initiative of Yahweh, and they are not brought to an end by Israel's sins, because the divine commitment still stands. This is the basis for hope when the covenant is broken and the blessing gone, the people is decimated and the land lost, and when Yahweh has left them and they are the laughing-stock of the nations.

3. THE PATRIARCHS IN SCRIPTURE AND HISTORY

One of the aims of the attempt to interpret the patriarchal narratives above has been to see what kind of implied vested interest they may have in the historicity of the events they narrate. Are they the kind of stories that could be completely fictional but still be coherent and carry conviction? A parable is fictional, but nevertheless carries conviction on the basis of who it is that tells it and of the validity of his world-view as it expresses it. A gospel, however, invites commitment to the person portrayed in it, and in my view this implies that it cannot be both fictional and true. The kind of response it invites demands that the events it narrates bear a reasonably close relationship to events that took place at the time. Without this it cannot be coherent and carry conviction. In the absence of reference, it cannot even really have sense.

The patriarchal stories seem meaningful. Do they have to be fundamentally historical in order actually to be true? Are they more like a parable or a gospel?

Thomas L. Thompson closes his book *The Historicity of the Patriarchal Narratives*[21] by suggesting that they do not have to have any historical value in order to be true. He contrasts his own

[21]*BZAW* 133; Berlin and New York: De Gruyter, 1974; pp. 326-330.

view with that expressed by scholars such as G. E. Wright,[22] who believe that the true locus of God's revelation to Israel is the events of her history, not the Bible itself. Logically, Wright then assumes, the factuality of Israel's account of these events is of key importance to the believer, and to establish it is a prime task of the historian. In opposition to this understanding, Thompson suggests that Israel's faith is rather a response of hope in God in some present situation, which expresses itself by drawing an imaginative picture of the past to embody its present hope. It is in this sense that salvation history is not something which actually happened but is a literary form arising out of a particular historical context (p. 328). The present is affirmed by creating a past of which it is the fulfilment. The believer therefore has no interest in the historical factuality of an Old Testament narrative. The Bible is a revelation of Israel's faith (embodied in an imaginative portrayal of the past) which makes it possible for us to share the experience of God that she had in the present and to respond with our faith.

As Thompson's historical views represent an extreme form of the current reaction against the Wright-Bright-Albright approach to biblical history, so his theological views represent an extreme form of the current reaction against the Wright-Cullmann approach to salvation history. This latter reaction is expressed in F. Hesse's desire to say goodbye to salvation history,[23] in the trenchant critique of the idea of salvation history in A. H. J. Gunneweg's *Understanding the Old Testament*,[24] and in R. E. Clements' scant attention to it in his *Old Testament Theology: A Fresh Approach*.[25] In various respects this reaction is quite justified, and in particular Thompson is correct that Wright's approach to history ignores the revelation in word or in language embodied in the Bible itself. Event and word are both part of revelation.

But Thompson's own position is as open to criticism on one flank as Wright's is on the other. The way in which the biblical testimonies to faith refer us to past historical events for their

[22]E.g. *God Who Acts* (Chicago: Regnery and London: SCM, 1952), pp. 126-127.
[23]See his *Abschied von der Heilsgeschichte* (Zurich: TVZ, 1971); also J. L. McKenzie, *CBQ* 34 (1972), pp. 504-505.
[24]ET Philadelphia: Westminster and London: SCM, 1978.
[25]London: Marshall and Atlanta: John Knox, 1978.

explanation and justification makes it difficult to believe that they imply no claim for their story's factuality.

Let us consider again some aspects of how the patriarchal traditions are set in a subsequent literary and historical context. First, Yahweh's words to the patriarchs constitute the divine undertaking fulfilled in exodus and conquest. They constitute Israel's charter for her possession of the land of Canaan. They explain how this was Yahweh's gift rather than the Israelites' desert. They set Israel's position in the land in the context of the sweep of a divine purpose concerned with the destiny of the nations. If the patriarchal narrative is pure fiction (which Thompson suggests it may as well be), is anything lost? Surely much is, because the exodus-conquest narrative grounds its statements of faith in these events. If the events did not take place, the grounds of faith are removed.

We should note that Thompson is right that the mere factuality of certain patriarchal events would not in itself prove the validity of the faith perspective set up by the patriarchal narrative. We have seen that the narrative involves a perspective or an interpretation (the theme of blessing) as well as an account of events, and the historicity of the events does not prove the truth of the narrative. But while the historicity of the events is not a sufficient evidence of the truth of the narrative's interpretation, it is a necessary evidence of its truth. The narrative builds its interpretation on the factuality of the patriarchal events, so that without this factuality, faith in Yahweh as the giver of blessing, the one who keeps his promises, the God of grace, and so on, may be true but is nevertheless groundless. If they are not fundamentally factual, the patriarchal narratives have sense but not reference.

Similar considerations apply to the patriarchal narrative in the context of the monarchy and—with more tragic force—in the context of the exile.

> Hearken to me, you who pursue deliverance,
> you who seek Yahweh,
> Look to the rock from which you were hewn,
> and to the quarry from which you were digged.
> Look to Abraham your father
> and to Sarah who bore you,
> for when he was but one I called him,
> and I blessed him and made him many. (Is. 51:1-2)

But on Thompson's thesis it does not matter that the call, the blessing, and the increase of Abraham are imaginative creations of faith! The prophet's position seems to be the opposite—not that faith creates Abraham, but that Abraham creates faith.

The debate in Old Testament scholarship in which Thompson sets his own position over against Wright's is by no means one confined to the United States. Indeed, much of the past two or three decades' discussion of the relationship between faith and history has taken place on the continent and refers back to Gerhard von Rad's exposition in his *Old Testament Theology*[26] of the problem of the 'two histories'—one related by faith, in the Bible itself, the other related by the use of critical historical method. This exposition is anticipated in the Introduction to his commentary on *Genesis*[27] where von Rad describes the patriarchal stories as 'saga'. By the use of this term, he seeks to hold two convictions together. One is that a story in Genesis 'narrates an actual event that occurred once for all in the realm of history.' It is not 'a product of poetic fantasy' (p. 31/[3]p. 32). But the other conviction is that saga is not concerned with history as mere this-worldly events of the past which are now dead and gone. It represents an intuitive response of faith that sees the activity of God in events, and portrays them accordingly. And it assumes that these events are thus relevant to and mirrored in the experience of later believers. 'These narratives express everything that Israel had learnt from her association with Yahweh right down to the narrator's own time' ([3]p. 40). This does not mean 'that these figures and the traditions about them are nothing more than subsequent projections of popular faith back into the primeval period. It means, rather, that this material did not lie in the archives untouched but was moulded and substantially enlarged by being handed down for centuries' (p. 34/[3]p. 35). 'At the beginning, the saga in most cases certainly contained a 'historical' fact as its actual crystallizing point. But in addition it reflects an historical experience of the relevant community which extends into the present time of the narrator' (p. 33/[3]p. 34). Thus, for instance, the story of Jacob at the Jabbok (Gn. 32:22-32) is 'the

[26]Volume 1 (ET Edinburgh: Oliver and Boyd and New York: Harper, 1962), pp. 106-108.

[27]London: SCM and Philadelphia: Westminster, 1961, [2]1963, [3]1972 (German original 1949).

witness of a past, and at the same time completely contemporary, act of God' (p. 34/³p. 35).

Von Rad's use of the word 'saga' parallels Karl Barth's. For Barth, saga is 'an intuitive and poetic picture of a pre-historical reality of history which is enacted once and for all within the confines of time and space'.[28] Both von Rad and Barth can give the impression that they have abandoned the historical nature of biblical events. Yet Barth emphasizes their objective factuality, and in discussing the factuality of Christ's resurrection contrasts his own position with Rudolf Bultmann's.[29] Von Rad, similarly, responds to his critics on this point by affirming that the nature of Israel's faith is such that 'there is little reason to fear . . . that in these descriptions of her early period Israel may have lost contact with actual history. They are rather utterances . . . of a people obsessed with its actual history'.[30]

Barth and von Rad can give the impression that the events they discuss did not happen, because they recognize the limitations that, for good or ill, are imposed by modern assumptions regarding what can be described as 'historical'. Such 'history' cannot include events or statements that the historian cannot control, such as God calling Abraham from Mesopotamia or raising Jesus from the dead. So to say that these events are not historical is not to imply that they did not happen; it is only to imply that they cannot be investigated by the historical method. We can in principle investigate whether Abraham moved from Ur via Haran to Canaan or whether a body disappeared from a tomb belonging to Joseph of Arimathea; we cannot in the same way check the transcendent interpretation which the Bible gives to these events. Part of the difficulty of investigating the factuality of the Bible's history lies in the this-worldly assumptions of the historical method.

Yet this insight does not deal with all aspects of the question of the historicity of the patriarchs. Let us consider statements that are in fact capable of being checked by the historical method.

---

[28]*Church Dogmatics* III, 1 (ET Edinburgh: Clark and New York: Scribner's, 1958), p. 81.

[29]*Church Dogmatics* III, 2 (ET Edinburgh: Clark and New York: Scribner's, 1960), pp. 440-445.

[30]*Old Testament Theology* 2 (ET Edinburgh: Oliver and Boyd and New York: Harper, 1965), p. 424.

Does the ancestry of the Israelites go back to certain pre-Israelite figures who believed that God promised them many descendants and the possession of the land of Canaan, so that the Israelites' own possession of the land could be explained by a promise believed to have been given then? In principle this question can be investigated 'historically' and indeed it has been so investigated, and the conclusion of many scholars is that the answer is 'no'. Does the faith that has based itself on these historical statements then collapse? To describe these stories as saga testifies to their background in some historical event, but if in the stories there is really more of the faith of the tellers than there is of actual events, we still seem to have faith creating Abraham rather than vice versa.

Von Rad himself hints at one resolution of this dilemma. Where did the material in the Genesis sagas that is not strictly 'historical' come from? 'It reflects an historical experience of the relevant community which extends into the present time of the narrator' (p. 33/³p. 34). One could say that the narrative of the jeopardizing of Sarah 'is not 'historical', but the experience that God miraculously preserves the promise beyond human failure was eminently historical (*geschichtlich*) for the community' (p. 39/³p. 41).

In contributions to the 1961 von Rad *Festschrift, Studien zur Theologie der alttestamentlichen Überlieferung*,[31] and in subsequent writings,[32] R. Rendtorff and W. Pannenberg have developed this point. The growth of Israel's traditions (in which Israel's faith is expressed) was itself part of her history. So the faith did arise out of the historical activity of Yahweh—his activity in the development of her understanding of him. Indeed, Israel's national experience included Yahweh proving himself as her protector and provider, an historical experience that could then be seen as retrojected into the patriarchal narrative. Again, there is real historical experience here. From another perspective, Paul Ricoeur has pointed out that 'fact' and 'fiction' should not be distinguished

[31]Neukirchen: Neukirchener Verlag der Buchhandlung der Erziehungsvereins, 1961. ET of Pannenberg's essay in his *Basic Questions in Theology* 1 (London: SCM and Philadelphia: Fortress, 1970), pp. 81-95.

[32]E.g. Rendtorff's *Gesammelte Studien zum Alten Testament* (Munich: Kaiser, 1975).

by suggesting that only the former is historical. 'History's reference and fiction's reference *intersect* upon the plane of the basic historicity of human experience'.[33]

All these points are valid, but they actually reinforce rather than dissolve the significance of the fact that large tracts of the Old Testament such as Genesis are put in the form of narrative about the factual past. Israel was capable of producing fictional parable and present testimony, but in the patriarchal stories she did not: she makes a point of telling a story about the factual past, and refers to it (in a passage such as Is. 51) in such a way as to make it rather clear that she understands the story to be fundamentally factual.

The fashion of current Old Testament scholarship is to replace 'history' by 'story' as the best category for Old Testament narrative, and my own approach will have made clear that I accept the validity of this insight. It is the story told in Genesis to which we are invited to listen and respond in faith, not whatever bare events of ancient near-eastern history lie behind it. And when (as is currently the case) it is difficult to be sure on historical grounds what actual events lie behind the Genesis narrative, this realization enables us still to interpret and profit from this story even when we have to be agnostic about at least some aspects of the history.

On the other hand, while (as R. J. Coggins puts it[34]) 'we should laugh out of court anyone who approached *Hamlet* primarily with a view to improving his knowledge of Danish history, or *Henry V* as a source of knowledge of fifteenth-century England' and ought to query a parallel approach to Genesis, this does not mean that the investigation of the historical facts to which Genesis refers is irrelevant to the value of Genesis, as may be the case with Shakespeare's plays. In Genesis (and in cross-references to Genesis) the Bible appeals to factual history as the overt grounds of its faith statements, and it does therefore invite investigation by the historical method.[35]

[33]*The narrative function, Semeia 13 (The Poetics of Faith: Essays Offered to Amos Niven Wilder* Part 2, ed. W. A. Beardslee; Missoula: SBL, 1978), p. 195.

[34]History and story in Old Testament Study, *Journal for the Study of the OT* 11 (1979), p. 43.

[35]Cf. A. Jepsen, 'The Scientific study of the Old Testament', *Essays on Old Testament Interpretation* (ed. C. Westermann; ET London: SCM; = *Essays on Old Testament Hermeneutics*, Richmond: John Knox, 1963), pp. 267-271.

In his closing paragraphs, Thompson (pp. 329-330) notes that Wright's approach, which bases faith on history, thereby places a severe strain on faith when it is difficult (intellectually) to accept the factuality of the events that faith is supposed to be based on. The same observation applies to the position being defended here, that historical factuality is a necessary though not a sufficient basis for faith. It is not possible to have the advantages of history without its risks. But the pentateuchal narrative, like the preaching preserved in the book of Isaiah, invites us to take this risk.[36]

[36]See further my paper ' "That you may know that Yahweh is God": a study in the relationship between theology and historical truth in the Old Testament', *Tyndale Bulletin* 23 (1972), pp. 58-93. I hope shortly to publish a study of recent critical approaches to salvation history in a volume on 'Interpreting the Old Testament'.

2
Methods of Studying the Patriarchal Narratives as Ancient Texts
A. R. Millard

The stories of the patriarchs of Israel have been handed down in their present form since the third century B.C. at least. The witness of the LXX and the texts from Qumran assures us of that, for their variations are only small. We are dealing, therefore, with literature that is more than 2,300 years old. Unless earlier manuscripts are found, we cannot establish the earlier history of the stories with any certainty; every account we may give will be hypothetical and speculative. It is important to recognize and accept this fact, and so to avoid claiming as certain conclusions what are only deductions built upon theories and assumptions.

As they stand, the stories of Genesis 12-50 are part of a large work that traces the history of Israel from its beginnings to its climax in the possession of the promised land. It is natural to assume that these chapters reached their final form after that event (without, at present, discussing how long after it). The stories share the promise theme as their most obvious link, and that also relates them to the rest of the Old Testament. The promise theme, however, immediately involves a strong theological element. The promise was made by God to Abraham and repeated to his descendants, being fulfilled only after many generations. It is not difficult to argue that stories about the patriarchs could have been quite unrelated, originating among various peoples or tribes at different times and places. At a certain time some of these stories were selected, consciously or unconsciously, and moulded around the promise idea. So formed, they served to legitimize Israel's occupation of Canaan and to unify her religious faith, centring it upon the one promise-keeping God. Anyone concentrating on this approach may find himself arguing not only for the diverse roots of the stories but also for invention or insertion of elements in them, or even distortion, to suit the theological end. This approach is obviously an important one, for it deals with, and accounts for, basic themes. It has the attraction that it can be neither proved or disproved! How satisfactory it is we may consider later.

Approaches to the patriarchal narratives as theological constructions usually stand upon the classical Old Testament literary criticism. This method, as is well known, starts with a detailed analysis of the text to distinguish sources or units within it by means of various internal criteria, principally lexical stock. Once isolated, the sources become the objects of further investigations that aim to discover the circumstances in which they arose. By comparing the actual or supposed histories of ancient stories from other parts of the world, their roots are traced back, by many, to individual shrines or places of pilgrimage. There they may have begun as explanations for the existence of the sacred sites, their founders, and the deities who presided in them. Once the birth-place of a story has been located in this way, the career of the story is followed until it is grouped with others and ultimately interlaced to form part of Genesis. The fusion of the strands into their final form is seen as an achievement of the exilic or post-exilic era. The literary sources themselves are given dates variously from Solomon downwards, although some features within them are nowadays allowed to be of greater age than classic formulations of the documentary hypothesis conceived. The dating, it should be remembered, does not arise from literary considerations primarily, but from a combination of historical and religious views. Since the work of Wellhausen, who commenced with the dictum 'the Law came after the Prophets', and erected a scheme of religious development growing from what he saw as an idyllic family affair to a restrictive priest-ruled liturgy, the basic concept has remained unchanged. Just as it underlies most theological approaches to the patriarchal narratives, so it underlies the work of most form critics, and of most students of the history of traditions.

These attitudes arose in the nineteenth century when knowledge of the ancient Near East was beginning to be widely available. Main-line Old Testament scholarship took relatively little note of it, however; Wellhausen, indeed, practically ignored it, or minimized its value (see, for example, his estimate of Shishak's list of towns captured in Palestine, or his treatment of Manasseh's

Babylonian captivity[1]). Sadly, current work reflects the same stance. Of course, some discoveries have been absorbed into standard works, the Babylonian Flood Story and the Egyptian Teaching of Amenemope being the most widely cited, along with the historical notices for the Divided Monarchy. But the patriarchal narratives, and the Pentateuch as a whole, are still studied along the lines established by Wellhausen's *Prolegomena*. Even the fresh paths taken in recent years by a few operate, with much the same basic criteria while disputing the common distinction of sources.[2]

Now the literary analysis of Genesis is an important and proper exercise; from it we may hope to learn about the construction of the book and the presentation of its contents. We may learn something about its history. All the work described so far has been carried out within the Old Testament alone. Little or no attention has been paid to the world in which the stories came into being, nor have the methods of study applied to them been tested and proved with other literary products of that world.[3] Again, it is perfectly proper to discuss the form and construction of a piece of literature in vacuo, as one might, for example, examine the structure of *Hamlet* or *King Lear*. Hermann Gunkel did draw upon other sources for his study of the literary history of Genesis, but those sources were the legends and traditions of the Greeks, the early Germans, and the Norsemen. They encouraged him to see in Genesis the product of long eras of oral tradition or

[1]See the note on Wellhausen's attitude to Shishak's list in K. A. Kitchen, *The Third Intermediate Period in Egypt* (Aris and Phillips, Warminster, 1973), p. 432, n. 49, and the very different attitudes taken by later scholars whose work is discussed by Kitchen. On Manasseh see Wellhausen's *Prolegomena*, p. 207. While it was wrong to assume that the mention of Manasseh as a tributary in an Assyrian text made the whole Hebrew account credible, as Wellhausen scornfully showed, it was equally wrong to assume that the Hebrew text was without foundation because theological motives could be traced to explain its presentation, as Wellhausen did.

[2]Recent publications make this abundantly clear: R. E. Clements, *A Century of Old Testsament Study* (Lutterworth, London, 1976); H. Donner, *Die Literarische Gestalt der alttestamentlichen Josephgeschichte* (Winter, Heidelberg, 1976), are two. R. Rendtorff's somewhat reoriented approach is conveniently summarized in *JSOT* 3, 1977, pp. 2-56.

[3]W. J. Martin, *Stylistic Criteria and the Analysis of the Pentateuch* (Tyndale Press, London, 1955).

'saga', and of individual stories attached to separate cult-sites. None of these sources belongs to the ancient near-eastern world, and none provides a straightforward analogy to Genesis.[4] (In contrast, Gunkel's form-critical study of the Psalms is based upon compositions from Babylonia which are likely to have much more in common with ancient Hebrew modes of thought). Yet the discussion of Genesis cannot stay in the literary sphere; it reaches out into history and religion, and cannot expect to reach anything approaching a full appreciation of the book without doing so, just as a full appreciation of Shakespeare's plays includes understanding of the Elizabethan theatre and audience. (Where those trained in modern linguistics have applied their techniques to the Pentateuch, the old criteria can be said to be irrelevant.[5])

There seems, therefore, to be good reaon to scrutinize the patriarchal narratives in the context of the ancient Near East. With the works of Shakespeare there is a major advantage for the literary critic in that the period of composition is known, and there is no real dispute about authorship, facts which are lacking for Genesis. At the outset this major problem has to be studied: what is the ancient context of the patriarchal narratives?

This is a question on several levels. At some time the narratives were integrated to become part of Genesis and of the Pentateuch. The reasons for that have long been thought worthy of study. Other parts of the Old Testament and the New Testament reflect attitudes towards the patriarchs at various dates within the biblical period. Then there is the long history of tradition and interpretation within Judaism and Christianity. Each of these is separate, to some extent, and the way in which the patriarchs are treated in the last context is not necessarily helpful to modern appreciation of them. Our present concern is with their place in ancient history. We are asking what age the stories reflect, a question which may have no simple answer, for they may be stories about one age composed in another, and containing traits

[4]Note here the recent critique by S. M. Warner, 'Primitive Saga Men', *VT* 29, 1979, pp. 325-335.

[5]For example, F. I. Andersen, *The Hebrew Verbless Clause in the Pentateuch* (Abingdon Press, Nashville, 1970); R. E. Longacre, 'The Discourse Structure of the Flood Narrative' in G. Macrae (ed.), *SBL Seminar Papers* (Scholars Press, Missoula, Montana, 1976), pp. 235-262.

from both of them. As those who investigate the history of traditions emphasize, a change of context may cause changes in the traditions themselves, but there is no controllable means for determining the presence or absence of such changes, or even a shift of context.

For Wellhausen the answer to our question was straightforward: the patriarchal narratives were retrojections from the time of the monarchy, mirroring ideals of that time, void of any 'historical' content that could inform about the age in which the stories were supposed to be set. That is the view zealously espoused by T. L. Thompson. For a great many readers of the same text that the answer is unsatisfactory, if for no other reason than that the text appears to contradict it.

1. THE USE OF PARALLELS

As information from the ancient Near East accumulated, similarities were noted between ancient customs and events in the patriarchal narratives. When C. J. Gadd made the first major edition of cuneiform tablets from Kirkuk, tablets now called 'Nuzi tablets', in 1926, Sidney Smith called attention to the similarity between a contract of adoption and the position of Jacob and Rachel and the teraphim.[6] With the recovery of many more texts from the site of Nuzi, the discovery of 'parallels' became almost an end in itself. The work of C. H. Gordon and E. A. Speiser in this matter had great influence, but, we now realize, has to be viewed critically and, partly, jettisoned.[7] In reaction to the stress laid upon these 'parallels' as both explanatory of patriarchal practices and as corroborative evidence for their second-millennium B.C. setting, J. van Seters has sought another 'parallel' in a neo-Assyrian contract of the seventh century B.C.[8] Whether the Nuzi contracts or the later one offer a closer 'parallel' to Genesis' accounts of steps taken by barren wives to acquire sons is not pertinent here.[9]

What we should consider is the way in which these 'parallels' are found and applied. The impression left by many of the essays noting or commenting on them is of their haphazard occurrence.

---

[6]*RA* 23, 1926, p. 127.

[7]See the study by M. J. Selman in this volume, and his paper in *TB* 27, 1976, pp. 114-136.

[8]*JBL* 87, 1969, pp. 401-408.

[9]For discussion see Selman, *TB* 27, p. 129.

More than one writer has noted this.[10] The 'parallels' have not
resulted from comprehensive studies of ancient adoption procedures (to continue the example), but from the finding of a tablet
here and another there, each in some way reminiscent of the
biblical incidents. Sometimes a single text has been the basis for
comparison; sometimes a group from one locality; sometimes, as
we have said already, scattered documents. Concentration upon
the archives of a single site can bring imbalance. C. H. Gordon's
date for the patriarchs in the fifteenth century B.C. arose from the
comparisons made with Nuzi texts of that date in the first place.[11]
On the other hand, personal names current especially in documents written two or three centuries earlier were being set beside
the patriarchal names by other scholars to indicate their age and
linguistic horizon. Countering the use of those names, T. L.
Thompson has adduced names from the first millennium B.C.[12]
Once more, we should observe how study has been undertaken for
either period. Yet the names, too, are held to point to one date or
another for the setting of the stories.

Such a selective employment of ancient documents seems to be
unsatisfactory. It has the air, still, of a search for proof, of an
attempt to support a view or a hypothesis by choosing the most
suitable evidence—and this applies to those who invoke texts for
a first-millenium date as much as to those who invoke others for
a higher date. Further, this approach can be shown quite easily to
be unbalanced or distorted by the random nature of the records
extant. When all is said, 'parallels' prove nothing. At worst, they
can be misleading, as additional evidence shows a custom to be
local or to be commonplace. At best they show the possibility that
the patriarchal narratives exhibit the same practices, so permiting
us to conclude that they may tell of the same times. They are not
to be neglected, however, when they are thoroughly understood in
their context.

2. THE ANCIENT CONTEXT OF THE PATRIARCHAL NARRATIVES

To set a text in its context we need to establish our attitude to the
text first. The witness of the text itself should take pride of place

---

[10]Selman, loc. cit.

[11]*Introduction to Old Testament Times* (Ventnor Publishers, New Jersey,
1953).

[12]*Historicity*, ch. 2.

until unassailable cases are made against it. Here, in my opinion, modern scholarship has shown too critical and too sceptical a mind. If some refuse to accord to Genesis, or to any other ancient work, the common privelege of the accused in British law, 'innocent until proved guilty', the converse of that maxim should be vigorously opposed. Repeatedly ridicule and charges of misrepresentation brought by modern scholars against statements made by ancient writers have been utterly refuted through archaeological and linguistic research, and branded as false.[13] This is not a plea for a blind acceptance of the biblical accounts; it is good to investigate them, their composition, motifs, relationships, and purposes, so long as we are aware of the presuppositions on which we act. Scholars too readily ignore alternatives, avoiding attempts to harmonize apparent discrepancies, and treat the text as raw material for them to model; whereas it is the text that is primary, and our modern opinions and theories that need to be ready to accommodate it.

The contents of the patriarchal stories set some limits to their possible context. The geographical horizon is clear: from Mesopotamia through Canaan to Egypt. Unfortunately, the narratives are devoid of any plain reference to events known from other sources. Consequently, any proposal will rest on indirect evidence. Some point to the lack of any extrabiblical documentation for the patriarchs as evidence against their existence. No case can stand on this ground. It would be extraordinary to find their names in the archives of the cities with whose rulers the stories connect them, even if those archives were found. As it is, documents of the second millennium B.C. have been found at only a few sites in Canaan, and in small numbers, while documents of the first millennium, though slightly more numerous, are limited in scope and distribution. Even from Egypt there are hardly any government records. Let us remind ourselves again how fragmentary and incomplete is the information that does survive from the ancient world, even though we have access to tens of thousands of its documents.[14] That only the Hebrew records name Abraham and his family and relate their affairs is neither unusual nor

[13]I gave three examples in *The Bible BC* (Inter-Varsity Press, Leicester, 1977), pp. 5-7; many more could be offered.

[14]This is vividly explained by E. Yamauchi, *The Stones and the Scriptures* (Inter-Varsity Press, London, 1973), ch. 4.

remarkable, and is certainly no reason against treating them as historical accounts.

Let us consider how we might treat the Pentateuch if it were freshly disinterred from some ancient deposit like the Dead Sea Scrolls, giving us a terminal date of 300 B.C. for its composition.

The books of the Pentateuch are undoubtedly works that have been current in a religious tradition, perhaps produced and affected by it, just like many Babylonian and Egyptian texts known to us. Without earlier copies it is impossible to tell how old the composition may be, a situation also obtaining in the other societies. For the purpose of the exercise, we shall suppose that, like the Babylonian and Egyptian works, the Pentateuch has no religious relevance to us.

Within the Pentateuch are records concerning a people, Israel, known to us from inscriptions of the Assyrian kings who campaigned in the Levant from the ninth to the seventh centuries B.C., and from monuments of the pharaoh Merenptah at the end of the thirteenth century B.C. Our Pentateuch relates the arrival of Israel at the border of Canaan after a period of homelessness. It traces her history back to a single figure, Abraham, who, with his immediate descendants, is the subject of the extensive patriarchal narratives. Here we have a phenomenon unique in the ancient Near East; no other people has left us a family history that explains their occupation of their land. This fact alone demands a critical appraisal of the stories. Do they give hints that they were composed long after the times they describe by men living in a different culture, in order to justify their position? Here we approach the stance of the theological attitude outlined earlier. Proof is as hard to produce as disproof.

The one valuable type of evidence that can be sought to support a positive reply to the question is the evidence of anachronism. A single example would be insufficient; a series of indisputable anachronisms alone could carry weight in assessing the age of a composition. We have to ask, too, whether or not an ancient writer would have been alert to the possibility of anachronisms. Blatant examples might be avoided (e.g. Moses speaking in Persian), but the incidental ones that betray the writer's era might not.

The presence of camels and of the Philistines in the patriarchal narratives are regularly asserted to be such unconscious anachronisms, revealing the time of the stories' production. The stories evidently claim to tell of a time several generations before the Israelites entered Canaan (before 1200 B.C.), and therefore prior to the time when both camels and Philistines appear in the Near East, according to extrabiblical sources. Neither case is satisfactory, contrary to the dogmatic statements of many writers. There are evidences for the presence and use of the camel earlier in the second millennium B.C., both written and pictorial.[15] The nature of the camel is relevant, also, for, 'the camel is not an urban creature; it is kept outside settlements and used primarily in the steppe, and there it would die. The likelihood of camel bones being found is small, as is the likelihood of city scribes frequently naming it.'[16] In this case we see too facile a conclusion drawn: absence of camels apart from the patriarchal narratives meant that those narratives came from a period after other texts prove the arrival of the animal. The possibility that the Hebrew records might preserve a piece of accurate information was not allowed.

Further, concentration upon the camel question overshadowed another fact which may be a pointer to an opposite conclusion. It is not until the account of Joseph's administration of famished Egypt that the horse is mentioned. The advent of the horse in the Near East is set about 2300 B.C., although it is not widely attested until five centuries or so later, when there are written notices and terracotta figures.[17] These show that it was used as a pack animal as well as for riding. But it was also a very valuable creature, and one that was unsuitable for a royal person to ride (as a famous letter from Mari says), possibly becuase the art of horse-training was not well-developed (the manuals for trainers belong to the Late Bronze Age archives of Hattushas and Ashur, and the medical treatises for horses to the contemporary archives of

[15]See E. Porada, *Journal of the Walters Art Gallery* 36 (1977), pp. 1-6, for a seal of the eighteenth century B.C. From about the same period are fragments of a camel bone found at Jericho: see J. Clutton-Brock, *Proceedings of the Prehistoric Society* 45, 1979, p. 146; a few domestic horses were also present, ibid., pp. 145, 155.

[16]*The Bible BC*, p. 19. See also C. Kramer in L. D. Levine, T. C. Young (eds.), *Mountains and Lowlands, Bibliotheca Mesopotamica* 7, 1977, p. 100, n. 45.

[17]See P. R. S. Moorey, *Iraq* 32, 1970, pp. 36-50; M. A. Littauer, *Iraq* 33, 1971, pp. 24-30; S. Bokonyi, *Sumer* 28, 1972, pp. 35-38, for terracotta figures and plaques; M. Civil, *JCS* 20, 1966, pp. 121,122 and *RA* 63, 1969, pp. 104-105 for Sumerian texts, W. von Soden, *Akkadisches Handwörterbuch*, p. 1051 for Akkadian.

Ugarit).[18] From the Late Bronze Age onwards horses became the regular means of drawing chariots and of individual fast transport, as their repeated mention in the Old Testament shows. A picture of a wealthy man moving in Palestine drawn during the Late Bronze or Iron Ages might be expected to mention horses at some point, as a sign of his riches or his eminence. (Job is not credited with horses, but his home is set in the east.) Here is a case where the testimony of ancient witnesses is clear, and the patriarchal narratives are silent. In that silence we may be able to see an element that points to a greater age for the stories than those who take note of the camels alone may allow.

As to the Philistines, K. A. Kitchen has put one plausible position in his essay on this people.[19] In brief, the name may be a later replacement for an out-dated term to denote peoples from the Aegean. Once again, we could also argue that Genesis has preserved the name from a period for which, we are compelled to admit, there is no knowledge of the language or affinities of the peoples of the Aegean and Crete who were in contact with the Levant, apart from occasional material imports and the naming of Crete (Kaptara) in the Mari texts. Let us remember how the decipherment of Cretan Linear B revealed the presence of Greek speakers on the island before 1300 B.C., a presence not hinted at by any other texts and which contradicted many theories, but is now accepted. The danger of insisting upon an anachronism where our evidence is limited, and can be radically changed by a new discovery, should not be ignored. (What information is there about the cities of the Philistine region during the earlier centuries of the second millennium B.C.?)

The patriarchal narratives can be taken as products of the Israelite monarchy era, and interpreted as reflecting life in that time. Before anyone can assert that they can only derive from that period, a careful examination of them in an early second-millennium context needs to be made, and to be shown to be impossible. Is the earlier date really so unthinkable as some maintain? The narratives apparently assume that is their context, so they should be inspected on the assumption they make. There would be no hesitation in treating most texts that are excavated from ancient

---

[18]*Archives royales de Mari* 6, no. 76.

[19]D. J. Wiseman (ed.), *Peoples of Old Testament Times* (Clarendon Press, Oxford, 1973), pp. 56f.

cities in this way. The exceptions might be just those epics about heroes of the past which were handed down for centuries in Sumerian, Babylonian, Egyptian, and other scribal circles. The Epic of Gilgamesh in Akkadian, and poems about him and several other early kings in Sumerian, are stock examples. Most extant manuscripts were copied during the eighteenth and seventeenth centuries B.C., and in the seventh and sixth centuries. The literary history of some of these compositions, spanning a thousand years, is a fascinating study that has far to go and much to teach, both for the general history of world literature and for the ancient context of the Old Testament. How long before our manuscripts were made the texts were composed we do not know. The kings whom they celebrate are now believed to have lived early in the third millennium B.C. That they were real flesh and blood men is rendered likely by various later references and by the recovery of two inscriptions of a king whom the epics make slightly senior to Gilgamesh. Indeed, the attitudes and actions portrayed in some of these poems, and in various myths about the gods, were utilized thirty-five years ago as satisfactory sources for reconstructing the political development of early Sumer.[20]

It is instructive to view the changes in the convictions of scholars about the nature of Gilgamesh since the start of this century when they saw him either as indubitably a solar hero, the twelve tablets of the Akkadian epic being a clue to that (Jensen and others); or as a vegetation god who took human form, and could not be an historical person (Möwinckel).[21] Very recently the existence of stories about these kings written much closer to their traditional age has been demonstrated with the recovery of a brief text about Lugalbanda, a predecessor of Gilgamesh, amongst the tablets of Abu Salabikh, written about 2600 B.C.[22]

In connection with the Gilgamesh stories, we may note that the Sumerian texts know several independent tales, the Akkadian the single epic into which some of those tales were woven. All the tales revolve around the one hero and his city of Uruk; there is no

[20]*JNES* 2, 1943, pp. 159-172; cf. *ZA* n. F 18, 1957, pp. 91-140, both reprinted in *Towards the Image of Tammuz* (Harvard UP, 1970), pp. 132-156, 157-170.

[21]See the convenient collection of essays edited by K. Oberhuber, *Das Gilgamesh-epos* (Wissenschaftliche Buchgesellschaft, Darmstadt, 1977).

[22]R. D. Biggs, *Inscriptions from Tell Abu Salabikh* (Chicago UP, 1974), no. 327; J. D. Bing, *JANESCU* 9, 1977, pp. 1-4.

suggestion that they originated in separate places or originally told of other kings.

About 2300 B.C. the Dynasty of Akkad arose in Babylonia, founded by Sargon. The impression Sargon and his successors made was strong, lasting until the fall of Babylon to Cyrus. Yet of Sargon himself there is only a single battered and uninformative contemporary inscriptions. Others exist only in copies made five hundred years later.[23] From them the king's conquests as far as Ebla in North Syria, and the Cedar and Silver Mountains are known to us. Much more is told about Sargon in poems of the eighteenth century B.C. and other works available in much later copies. The range of his conquests is wider in these than in the inscriptions, and his campaigns are described in more detail. His grandson, Naram-Sin, is reputed to have followed Sargon's footsteps into the heart of Anatolia as he reasserted his dynasty's rule. Poems abut his feats tell of that; his own inscriptions, some contemporary, some preserved in later copies, do not name any conquests beyond northern Syria.[24]

Are the accounts of campaigns into Anatolia related by the poems later exaggerations of the achievements of Sargon and Naram-Sin? There is some reason to think they may be. During the nineteenth century B.C. there existed a network of Assyrian trading settlements in Anatolia, at Kanesh (modern Kültepe), at Hattushas (Boghazköy), at the site now called Alishar, and at other places. Thousands of tablets from Kanesh and a few from the other sites disclose the trading and business affairs of the resident Assyrians. Some indicate that they faced hostility from time to time from the native people and rulers, and had to secure their positions. Assyria was not then a military force able to defend such distant dependants, so agreements were made with the local kings. In order to strengthen their hands, the Assyrian merchants may well have claimed to be the heirs to an old-established position, owing the origin of their privileged trading posts to Sargon of Akkad, four centuries before. The account of Sargon's campaign, in the text copied or read at el Amarna by Egyptians learning Akkadian, speaks of the merchants whom he aided. By invoking a name respected by general tradition, the merchants may have hoped to strengthen their case, alleging the king had

[23]*ANET*, pp. 267-268.
[24]*ANET*, p. 268.

done more than was actually the case, to provide an aetiology of their existence. All the texts from Kanesh and the other sites belong to the same century, approximately, and so do the buildings occupied by the merchants. Consequently, the mention of Kanesh with certain other places in literary compositions dealing with Naram-Sin has been labelled an anachronism.[25]

Detection of that anachronism did not cause the modern editors of the texts to consider them valueless in their accounts of Naram-Sin's reign, being merely later retrojections; they wrote, 'It seems reasonable to conclude that the incidents recounted in the historical-literary texts . . . are basically authentic, if not in detail, and so may be properly used in reconstructing the history of Naram-Sin's reign'.[26] At a late stage in preparing their study, the editors learnt of the great archive unearthed at Ebla, an archive housed in a palace its excavator believes was destroyed either by Sargon or by Naram-Sin. They were able to add a footnote saying that the new discovery seemed to show the weakness of arguments from anachronisms.[27] Preliminary reports affirm the presence of Kanesh amongst many places named in the Ebla texts as trading with Ebla.[28] Even more recently, excavators at Kanesh have begun to uncover buildings of the age of the kings of Akkad.[29] Perhaps the stories of Sargon and Naram-Sin reaching that or neighbouring cities were not later inventions, but literary accounts of campaigns they had actually conducted.

The study of ancient near-eastern literature can supply other examples of the same thing. Repeatedly, traditional literature or records prove to report accurately events of long ago. In some cases this can now be partially seen, as with Sargon and Naram-Sin, whatever fanciful overlay there may be. In other cases supporting evidence is more meagre, yet points the same way, as with Gilgamesh. Obviously it would be wrong to claim that the existence of a king called Gilgamesh, the reality behind the stories, is established by the recovery of two brief inscriptions of a king named beside him in an epic, or that Sargon's expedition to

[25]A. K. Grayson, E. Sollberger, *RA* 70, 1976, p. 108.

[26]Ibid., p. 111.

[27]Ibid., p. 108, n. 4.

[28]G. Pettinato, *BA* 39, 1976, p. 48. A. Archi, *Biblica* 60, 1979, pp. 556-566, has issued grave cautions about the first interpretations given to the Ebla texts, throwing doubt on the identification of Kanesh (p. 563).

[29]M. J. Mellink. *AJA* 82, 1978, p. 317.

Anatolia is given historicality by the references to Kanesh at Ebla. The contribution of such discoveries is to give greater plausibility to the ancient traditional accounts, on occasion also refuting the charge of anachronism. Where there is no other evidence, where a literary text alone exists, we should be no less ready to treat it as a valuable and reliable record, unless it can be conclusively shown to be false in many matters.

If the possibility of traditional literature (including the book of Genesis) presenting reliable accounts of the past is accepted, can the patriarchal narratives be distinguished in as much as they are a series of stories revolving around one family and linked to a nation's career? A first impression might suggest that the narratives are isolated, they stand apart, and so cannot be compared with other ancient texts. In fact, this is not so. Ancient lists of kings are basic documents for the modern historian, and some served the similar basic purpose of reckoning time in antiquity. As more are recovered, another purpose appears: the celebration and cult of ancestors. There may be significance for the present study in the fact that dynastic rulers of the Late Bronze Age in the Levant traced their lines back to the nineteenth century B.C., or thereabouts, and these family trees can, in some instances, be substantiated.[30] Reference to the deeds of earlier kings in a variety of documents, and a rare text like the Inscription of Idri-mi of Alalakh, show that these king lists were far from representing the sum of the scribes' historical knowledge. The king lists are the records of royal houses, none, so far as we know, expanding to form a nation (although Kitchen has proposed that the kings of Ugarit shared a remote ancestor with the Amorite kings of Babylon and Assyria). Although they are not of exactly the same nature, they illustrate the possibility of family history being preserved, and that is exactly what the patriarchal narratives are.

In drawing upon literary sources, historical, epic, and several other types have been mentioned. Labels are freely applied to ancient documents, often through some apparent similarity to types known from other societies. Caution is needed in using these terms, for many have technical meanings that do not reach the uninitiated reader. 'Myth' is well recognized as a double-edged word, and 'saga' and 'legend' fall into the same category. 'Saga' especially has its home in the Norse world where it served a

[30]K. A. Kitchen, *Ugarit-Forschungen* 9, 1977, 131-142.

purpose different from that of the Hebrew texts. There is the danger, too, that use of these terms may pre-judge the value of the work's content, and so they are best avoided in any attempt to evaluate a text in its own setting. Again and again, incidents in the patriarchal narratives are titled 'folk elements' and thereby voided of any factual basis. Yet even a cursory consideration reveals that many are situations which could easily occur, and it may be simply because they are situations which can easily occur in large family groups in human society that they become 'folk elements'. An account of the origin of a custom or name is an aetiology; the account is not falsified or verified by that title, despite the tendency of biblical scholars to assume the former. Why may the way in which something began not have been remembered correctly?

4. TEXTS AND ARCHAEOLOGY

In attempting to set the patriarchs in an historical period, various archaeological evidences have been invoked, both in favour of an early second-milennium B.C. date, and against. Many dangers beset this practice. The patriarchal narratives tell of a family, a family comprising several hundred people, but not a vast horde. It is conceivable that a group of such size could live and move in Palestine at will whatever the current overall pattern. The evidence from one source, e.g. the Mari archives, or the changed occupation of the land after the end of Early Bronze III, cannot be made into an unyielding norm for the whole area and all its inhabitants. The objection that the patriarchal narratives name cities which were deserted until Middle Bronze II is worthless in the present uncertainty about the archaeology of Palestine between 2300 and 1800 B.C. Furthermore, a city does not have to exist as an active entity to win mention, and many of those named in Genesis are not named as inhabited places. Rather a similar question arises over Shechem (mentioned as a location in Gn. 12:6, then playing a role in the Jacob stories as a true city). From Egypt survives the oft-quoted stele of Khu-Sebek telling of an expedition to a place commonly identified as Shechem under Sesostris III (c. 1878-1843 B.C.).[31] Yet according to the excavators there was no city wall at that time around Shechem, and little

[31]*ANET*, p. 230.

remains of buildings have been found, although there were signs of construction work in Middle Bronze IIA (c. 1850-1750 B.C.).[32]

An extreme example of this way of applying archaeological evidence to the study of the Old Testament is seen in the late Y. Aharoni's essay about the Negev.[33] He argued that his excavation on Tel Beersheva proved that the patriarchal narratives included references to events 'that could not possibly have occurred prior to the thirteenth or twelfth centuries' B.C. He claimed that a well cleared by his team outside the gateway of the Iron Age I city on top of the mound was the one dug by Abraham (Gn. 21:30).

Regrettably, his arguments have to be condemned. First, there is no evidence that the mound now called Tel Beersheva was ancient Beersheba. In fact, the Roman town lay below the present city, and there was occupation there at least during the Iron Age. Secondly, the assumption that the excavated well is Abraham's well is groundless. Ancient wells are still in use at modern Beersheba which could equally be identified with Abraham's well. Thirdly, the Genesis narratives do not imply that Beersheba was a town in Abraham's day. A tract of land or a landmark can bear a name without occupation occurring, as the cases of the Cave of Machpelah, the stone of Bohen, and Ebenezer, illustrate.

5. CONCLUSION

Our study has noted several ways of studying the patriarchal narratives, and concentrated upon one aspect. The stress has been upon examining, as far as possible, the content of the stories before any literary analysis is contemplated; and in order to make that possible, we have tried to show that the patriarchal narratives are not so different from other ancient texts that this exercise can be rejected. It seems that such an approach is more likely to be fair to the text, and to involve fewer presuppositions than any others. If a theological purpose is seen to have moulded the stories, then any element can be branded as a theological construct and emptied of all other value. The religious element is present in many ancient texts, but does not lead scholars to the same conclusions. If a literary analysis is given pride of place, then its consequences for evaluating the content of the stories has to be heeded, and anyone who follows the analysis in Genesis should

[32]G. E. Wright, *Shechem* (New York, 1965), ch. 7.
[33]*BA* 39, 1976, pp. 55-76.

remember that it is partly based upon the content of the stories, so the risk of circular arguments is grave. The attitude that reads the text critically is commendable, so long as it does not stray into hypercriticism and treat the text as something to be disparaged at every turn. If there is to be a search for anachronisms, let it be balanced by a search for reliable information. Let all who read remember that the patriarchal narratives are our only source for knowledge of the earliest traditions of Israel, that traditions can be correct reflections of ancient events, and that they do not pretend to be textbooks of ancient near-eastern history or archaeology.

3
Archaeological Data and the Dating of the Patriarchs
J. J. Bimson

INTRODUCTION

If the patriarchs are taken to be historical figures, during which archaeological period can their lives and journeys most aptly be placed? Until recently, scholars assuming the basic historicity of the patriarchal narratives have favoured either Middle Bronze I[1] or Middle Bronze II as the most likely background for the movements of Abraham. A later date, in the Late Bronze Age, has also been defended, but has never had the same support. More recently, a much earlier date, in the Early Bronze Age, has been suggested. This paper will consider all four of these datings, but particular attention will be given to the MB (Middle Bronze) I and MB II periods and their problems. These problems arise from the apparent non-occupation of sites which feature in the patriarchal narratives.

In 1949, Albright was able to write that only 'a few die-hards among older scholars' had not accepted the essential historicity of the patriarchal traditions in light of archaeological data, and that it was no longer fashionable to view those traditions as artificial creations by the scribes of the monarchic period.[2] He was able to repeat this statement fourteen years later.[3] Since then, however, there has been a strong reaction against the use of archaeological

[1]In this paper the 'American' terminology will be followed in preference to Kenyon's; in the latter, the period here labelled MB I is known as the Intermediate EB-MB period. For other terms proposed for this period, see Dever, *BASOR* 210, 1973, pp. 38ff.

[2]W. F. Albright, *The Biblical Period* (Pittsburgh, 1950, reprinted from *The Jews: Their History, Culture and Religion*, ed. L. Finkelstein, Harper & Row, NY, 1949), p. 3.

[3]W. F. Albright, *The Biblical Period from Abraham to Ezra* (Harper & Row, NY, 1963), pp. 1-2.

evidence in support of the biblical traditions,[4] and Albright's comment could not be repeated with any truth today.

Scholars who prefer to see the patriarchal narratives as unhistorical products of the first millennium B.C. have justified their view in part by referring to the difficulty of locating the patriarchs in an early archaeological period.[5] In response, N. M. Sarna has rightly pointed out that an inability to place the patriarchs in a historical framework *according to the present state of our knowledge* does not necessarily invalidate the historicity of the narratives.[6] Our knowledge of the centuries around 2000 B.C. is very small, and our ignorance very great. Nevertheless, some specific suggestions can be made towards resolving the difficulties and answering the critics of historicity.

The aim of the present paper is therefore twofold: to examine the appropriateness of various archaeological periods as backgrounds to the patriarchal narratives, and to assess the arguments put forward on archaeological grounds for rejecting the view that the narratives reflect real conditions in an early period.

1. A BRIEF DISCUSSION OF ARCHAEOLOGICAL PERIODS

1.1 *The MB I background and its problems*

The view relating the patriarchs to the MB I period has been described as 'the classic formulation'.[7] It took shape in the 1930s, chiefly at the hands of W. F. Albright and N. Glueck.

In the 1920s Albright argued that the finds on the plain of Bab edh-Dhrâ, to the east of the Dead Sea, were archaeological proof for the existence of a sedentary population in that area between

---

[4]The works by Thompson and van Seters in n. 5 are characteristic of this trend. An essentially negative assessment of archaeological evidence is also found in J. H. Hayes and J. Maxwell Miller (eds.), *Israelite and Judaean History* (SCM, London, 1977). See also J. Maxwell Miller, 'Archaeology and the Israelite Conquest of Canaan: Some Methodological Observations', *PEQ* 109, 1977, pp. 87-93; E. F. Campbell and J. Maxwell Miller, 'W. F. Albright and Historical Reconstruction', *BA* 42/1, 1979, pp. 37-47.

[5]T. L. Thompson, *The Historicity of the Patriarchal Narratives* (de Gruyter, Berlin/NY, 1974), pp. 182-183; J. van Seters, *Abraham in History and Tradition* (New Haven/London, Yale UP), 1975, pp. 104-112; cf. W. G. Dever in Hayes and Miller, pp. 99-102.

[6]N. M. Sarna, *Biblical Archaeology Review* 4/1, 1978, p. 52.

[7]Dever in Hayes and Miller, p. 93.

the middle of the third millenium and the nineteenth century B.C. He believed that occupation in the region ended abruptly 'not later than 1800 B.C. at the outside', and linked this with the cataclysm described in Genesis 18-19.[8] This link suggested to Albright that 'the date of Abraham cannot be placed earlier than the nineteenth century B.C.'.[9] This fell within the dates then assigned to MB I (2000-1800 B.C.).[10]

In 1929 Albright discovered a line of Early and Middle Bronze Age mounds 'running down along the eastern edge of Gilead, between the desert and the forests of Gilead'.[11] This confirmed for him the essential historicity of the campaign waged by the eastern kings in Genesis 14, an event which he had previously considered legendary. Albright's explorations in Transjordan were continued in the 1930s by Glueck, who traced a line of MB I settlements reaching most of the length of Transjordan. From 1932 onwards, Glueck's explorations revealed that most of these sites were deserted by the end of MB I, many of them never to be reoccupied. Both Glueck and Albright linked the termination of these sites with the campaign of the eastern kings.[12]

From 1952 onwards, Glueck conducted an archaeological survey of the Negeb, and again found many MB I settlements. Arguing that the time of Abraham's journeys through the Negeb (Gn. 12:9; 13:1) must have been a period when permanent or temporary settlements and camping places flourished in the region, Glueck confidently identified MB I as the 'Age of Abraham', and coined the term 'the Abrahamitic period' as a synonym for it.[13]

Subsequently, Albright developed the theory that Abraham had been a donkey-caravaneer, trading originally between Ur and Haran, later between Damascus and Egypt. This view was first

[8]Albright, *The Archaeology of Palestine and the Bible* (Revell, London/NY, 1932, text of lectures delivered in 1931), p. 137; cf. earlier idem *BASOR* 14, 1924, pp. 5ff.

[9]W. F. Albright, *The Archaeology of Palestine and the Bible*, p. 137.

[10]Ibid., table p. 10.

[11]Ibid., p. 142.

[12]E.g. Albright, *The Archaeology of Palestine and the Bible*, [3]1935, p. 142; N. Glueck, *AASOR* XIV, 1934, p. 82, *AASOR* XV, 1935, p. 104; idem, *The Other Side of the Jordan*, ASOR, New Haven, 1940, pp. 15-16; idem, *BA* 18/1, 1955, pp. 6-9.

[13]Glueck, *BA* 18/1, 1955; *Rivers in the Desert* (Norton, NY, 1959), pp. 61-84.

presented by Albright in 1961,[14] by which time the terminal date
for MB I had been raised from c. 1800 B.C. to c. 1900 B.C..[15] In
presenting his caravaneer hypothesis, Albright had to re-argue a
date of c. 1800 B.C. for the end of MB I, because the documentary
evidence which he assembled for early donkey-caravan trading
belonged to the nineteenth century B.C.[16] Although this date was
cited by a few scholars for a time, it was soon universally rejected.
Replying to Albright, W. G. Dever and T. L. Thompson have
both noted the evidence in favour of MB II beginning earlier than
1800 B.C. In 1970, Dever argued that MB IIA could not begin
earlier than c. 1875-1850 B.C.,[17] but he subsequently described this
estimate as 'probably too conservative', and raised the date for the
transition to c. 1950-1900 B.C.,[18] and later to 2000-1950 B.C.[19]
Thompson has also shown that the low dates for MB I must be
rejected, and has dismantled in detail Albright's argument that
the first four royal tombs at Byblos (containing MB IIA pottery)
postdate the end of the nineteenth century B.C.[20] A date for the end
of MB I in the twentieth century B.C. is now the general consensus
among archaeologists.[21] The reasons for this dating need not be
examined here, and can be found in the sources cited. The point
to be noted is the implication of this date for Albright's hypothesis.
Thompson has rightly pointed out that the low chronology for
MB I is the central key to Albright's thesis. 'Once this is seen as
untenable, the rise of the caravan trade under the Twelfth Dynasty

[14]Albright, *BASOR* 163, 1961, pp. 36-54; repeated in *The Biblical Period from Abraham to Ezra* (1963), pp. 5-7, *Archaeology, Historical Analogy and Early Biblical Tradition* (Louisiana State UP, 1966), p. 22-41, *Yahweh and the Gods of Canaan* (Athlone Press, London, 1968), pp. 56-66.

[15]E.g. Glueck, *BA* 18/1, 1955, p. 9.

[16]Albright, *BASOR* 163, 1961, pp. 40-42.

[17]Dever in J. A. Sanders (ed.), *Near Eastern Archaeology in the Twentieth Century*, Glueck Festschrift (Doubleday, NY, 1970), pp. 142-144.

[18]Dever, *HTR* 64, 1971, p. 224, n. 63.

[19]Dever, *BASOR* 210, 1973, p. 38, fig. 1; cf. idem, in Cross et al. (eds.), *Magnalia Dei: The Mighty Acts of God*, Essays in Memory of G. E. Wright (Doubleday, NY 1976), pp. 6, 12.

[20]Thompson, *Historicity*, pp. 175-180; cf. Albright, BASOR 163, 1961, p. 39, n.10. See also Dever in Cross, *Magnalia Dei*, pp. 11-12 for a further criticism of Albright's arguments based on the Byblos tombs.

[21]See Dever, *BASOR* 210, 1973, p. 38, and Thompson, *Historicity*, p. 175, n. 22 for references.

pharaohs can no longer be associated with the settlements of MB I either in Palestine or the Negev'.[22]

An attempt to retain Albright's thesis and his consequent dating of Abraham to the ninteenth century B.C., while adopting the high chronology now required for MB I, would naturally place Abraham in MB II.[23] But, as will be noted below, there are problems for an MB II date for Abraham. The most reasonable course is actually to abandon the donkey-caravaneer hypothesis altogether. It has been aptly criticized as going beyond the biblical evidence,[24] and few scholars have taken it seriously.[25]

The link between Abraham and MB I has also been bolstered by the so-called Amorite hypothesis. However, this hypothesis also features in the views of some scholars who place Abraham in MB II, and will be discussed separately below.

Since an MB I dating of Abraham has been maintained independently of the donkey-caravaneer hypothesis, the justified criticisms of that hypothesis do not themselves refute the placement of Abraham in MB I. However, that dating has also been undermined in other ways, and these must be noted.

The end of occupation at Bab edh-Dhrâ can no longer be linked with the destruction of the 'cities of the plain' in Genesis 18-19 if Abraham is placed in MB I. Lapp's excavations in 1963-65 showed that the town site was abandoned at the close of EB III, c. 2400-2300 B.C.; remains from EB IV attest only squatter occupation, and a few scattered tombs are the only finds from MB I.[26]

Glueck's argument for associating the campaign of the eastern kings with the end of MB I occupation in Transjordan has been criticized by Dever. While Glueck wrote of all these sites being 'destroyed at the end of the Middle Bronze I period',[27] Dever notes: 'There is no evidence whatsoever for a "destruction" at the end of

[22]Thompson, *Historicity*, pp. 180-181.

[23]Cf. J. E. Heusman, *CBQ* 37, 1975, p. 11.

[24]E.g. K. A. Kitchen, *Ancient Orient and Old Testament* (Tyndale Press, London, 1966), p. 49, n. 71; R. de Vaux, *The Early History of Israel* (Darton, Longman & Todd, London), 1978, vol. I, pp. 225-229.

[25]Cf. the comments by K. J. Cathcart, *CBQ* 37, 1975, p. 295; also Dever in Hayes and Miller, p. 102.

[26]Thompson, *Historicity*, p. 195; Dever in Hayes and Miller, p. 101.

[27]Glueck, *BA* 18/1, 1955, p. 7.

MB I, as claimed by Glueck.'[28] Thompson also notes the lack of evidence for destructions, 'let alone the abandonment of all of the sites at any single time'.[29]

But the most serious criticisms concern the non-occupation of certain sites which feature in the patriarchal narratives. Thompson points out that Beersheba did not exist before the Iron Age, that Succoth, if identified with Tell Deir ᶜAlla as Glueck suggested, was not occupied before the Late Bronze Age, and that Salem if the same as Jerusalem, has yielded no evidence of MB I settlement; Ai (Et-Tell) was not occupied between c. 2500 B.C. and the Iron Age, while Shechem was not occupied before MB IIA.[30] J. van Seters also stresses that Shechem and Beersheba have no MB I settlements,[31] and Dever elaborates concerning the latter: 'Extensive surveys and excavations by Aharoni, Kochavi, and other Israeli archaeologists in Beersheba and vicinity have in fact revealed a conspicuous lack of MB I sites throughout the northern Negeb.'[32] Dever describes Shechem as 'the parade example' of a site which Albright listed as having MB I occupation, but where the evidence had actually been misunderstood;[33] apart from a small settlement in the Chalcolithic period, occupation began in MB IIA.[34] Dever also criticizes Albright's view[35] that Bethel was 'extensively peopled' in MB I; he has demonstrated that remains attributed to MB I in Kelso's report actually belong to the MB IIA city,[36] and that MB I occupation is 'supported by a mere handful of sherds'.[37] Dever also extends Thompson's list of problematical sites by the additon of Dothan and Hebron.[38] In his view, 'A date in MB I is ruled out for the patriarchs simply because the latest evidence shows that the main centres traditionally associated with their movements, *pace* Albright, are conspicuously lacking in MB I remains.'[39]

---

[28]Dever, *HTR* 64, 1971, p. 225, n. 64; cf. idem in Cross, *Magnalia Dei*, p. 36, n. 114.

[29]Thompson, *Historicity*, p. 192.

[30]Ibid, pp. 182-183.

[31]Van Seters, *Abraham*, p. 107; cf. pp. 111-112 on Beersheba.

[32]Dever, *HTR* 64, 1971, p. 226, n. 66; also in Hayes and Miller, p. 100.

[33]Albright, *BASOR* 163, 1961, p. 47.

[34]Dever in Sanders, *NEATC*, p. 159, n. 64.

[35]Albright, *BASOR* 163, 1961, p. 47.

[36]Dever, *Orientalia* 40, 1971, pp. 459-471.

[37]Dever in Hayes and Miller, p. 99.

[38]Ibid., pp. 99-100; on Hebron see also Dever in Sanders, *NEATC*, pp. 146-150.

[39]Dever in Hayes and Miller, p. 99.

Whether MB I can be rejected as finally as such statements suggest will be discussed below.

1.2 *The MB II background and its problems*

Several scholars prefer to assign the patriarchs generally to the first half of the second millennium B.C.[40] This places the patriarchal period within MB II.

The MB II periόd as a background to the patriarchal traditions avoids some of the difficulties we have noted concerning MB I. In MB II, Jerusalem, Shechem, Bethel, Hebron and Dothan were urban centres.[41] However, some difficulties remain. Beersheba, Succoth and Ai appear to be equally problematical in MB II. In addition, MB II raises difficulties of its own: 'To date, not a single MB IIA site has been found in all of southern Transjordan or the Negeb—one of the principal arenas of patriarchal activities in Genesis.'[42] On balance, then, MB II appears to be no more satisfactory than MB I.

1.3 *The patriarchs and the Amorite hypothesis*

The patriarchal period has been linked with both MB I and MB II on the basis of the Amorite hypothesis.

The end of EB III saw the disruption of urban life throughout Syria and Palestine. The EB III towns were destroyed, and the culture of the subsequent EB IV/MB I period was largely non-urban. This period is seen in terms of the slow sedentarization of nomadic or semi-nomadic newcomers, to whom the destruction of the EB III towns is generally attributed. A reversion to town life is attested at the beginning of MB IIA, and this has been ascribed to a further influx of newcomers. The newcomers in both periods are assumed to have been Amorites, the 'westerners' attested in Akkadian texts from the last quarter of the third millennium onwards. On the basis of a combination of textual and archaeological

---

[40]G. E. Wright, *Biblical Archaeology* (revised edn., Westminster Press/Duckworth, Philadelphia/London, 1962), p. 47; idem, *Shechem: The Biography of a Biblical City* (Duckworth, London, 1965), pp. 128-138; E. A. Speiser, *Genesis* (Doubleday NY, 1964), pp. xliii-lii; S. Yeivin in B. Mazar (ed.), *The World History of the Jewish People*, 2 (Massada, Tel Aviv, 1970), pp. 201-218; J. Bright, *A History of Israel* (revised edn., SCM London, 1972), pp. 81-85; de Vaux, *Early History*, 1, pp. 263-266.

[41]Wright, *Biblical Archaeology*, p. 47; Dever in Hayes and Miller, pp. 99-100.

[42]Dever in Hayes and Miller, p. 102.

evidence, Amorite expansions have been posited in which these people moved from Mesopotamia, through Syria and Palestine and on into Egypt. It should be noted, however, that more than the two major influxes mentioned above are envisaged, so that a number of migrations into Palestine, extending over several centuries, are in view.[43]

This picture of westward expansions by West Semitic peoples provides an attractive historical context for the migration of Abraham and his family from Ur to Haran and from there to Palestine and on into Egypt. This has been noted by Albright[44] and R. de Vaux,[45] but while Albright assumed an MB I setting for Abraham, de Vaux preferred to place his migration in MB IIA,[46] when urban society was being re-established. It must be stressed, however, that the term 'Amorite hypothesis' refers not to a possible link between Amorite movements and the migration of Abraham, but to the Amorite movements themselves.

This hypothesis, depending as it does on a large amount of *interpretation* of textual and archaeological evidence, has recently been heavily criticized by Thompson. Thompson shows that although early West Semites do appear in South Mesopotamia, including the region of Ur, there is no historical evidence for a migration from there to the north; the West Semites attested in North Mesopotamia seem to have settled there after a migration from the North Arabian desert.[47] The written materials currently available 'do no witness to a major West Semitic migration in Palestine in the early Second Millennium, and argue against any such migration from North Mesopotamia'.[48] Thompson further argues that the Amu ($^{c}\exists mw$), or 'Asiatics' who entered Egypt during the First Intermediate Period and the XIth Dynasty, were not part of any widespread nomadic movement, but people living along Egypt's eastern border.[49] Discussing the Palestinian archaeological evidence for the nature of MB I, Thompson asserts that the Amorite hypothesis has influenced the interpretation of the finds,

---

[43]De Vaux, *Early History*, 1, p. 63.

[44]Albright, *The Biblical Period*, pp. 4-5.

[45]De Vaux, *Early History*, 1, pp. 263-266.

[46]Ibid., p. 265; de Vaux's 'MB I' = MB IIA in the terminology followed here.

[47]Thompson, *Historicity*, pp. 67-88.

[48]Ibid., p. 96, summarizing the arguments of pp. 89-96; cf. pp. 89-117 discussing the Execration Texts.

[49]Ibid. pp. 118-143.

and argues strongly against the Amorite and nomadic character of the period, and against the view which attributes the disruption of urban civilization at the end of EB III to an invasion from the north.[50] Thompson also draws attention to evidence of some continuity between MB I and MB IIA, rejecting any implication of a complete break between the two cultures.[51]

In spite of Thompson's very thorough critique, Dever has continued to hold to a version of the Amorite hypothesis on the basis of archaeological material, insisting that MB I and MB IIA saw new influxes of West Semitic peoples into Palestine from Syria.[52] Dever insists, however, that the problem of locating the biblical patriarchs historically 'is a separate question and one that is likely to prejudice the discussion of MB I'.[53] Thompson has recently remarked that Dever 'seems unaware of how inseparable the migratory aspect of the old "Amorite hypothesis" is from the biblical story—indeed it is only in Genesis that any indication of a migration from the Euphrates region can be found'.[54] This deserves to be stressed. The framework into which widely scattered evidence has been drawn in the construction of the Amorite hypothesis is provided only by the biblical story of Abraham's movements, and without that framework the hypothesis is fundamentally without support. On the other hand, the migration spoken of in Genesis involves only a single family, and it is nowhere implied that that family's movements were part of a wider shift or expansion of population; therfore the movements attributed to Abraham and his family do no support the Amorite hypothesis in any case—and neither do they require the Amorite hypothesis to support their historicity.

On the basis of evidence currently available, the validity of the Amorite hypothesis remains extremely doubtful. For the reasons just stated, however, it should indeed be treated as a separate issue from discussions of the patriarchal age. As Sarna has remarked: 'If Abraham's migration can no longer be explained as part of a

[50]Ibid., p. 144-171.

[51]Ibid. pp. 163-165.

[52]Dever in Hayes and Miller, pp. 83-84, 94, 118; for Dever's earlier treatments of the Amorite hypothesis, see *NEATC*, p. 140, *HTR* 64, 1971, pp. 217-226, and *Magnalia Dei*, pp. 5, 10, 15.

[53]Dever, *HTR* 64, 1971, p. 226, n. 66; also in Hayes and Miller, p. 94.

[54]Thompson, *JSOT* 9, 1978, p. 7.

larger Amorite migratory stream from east to west, it should be noted that what has fallen by the wayside is a scholarly hypothesis, not the Biblical text. Genesis itself presents the movement from Haran to Canaan as an individual, unique act undertaken in response to a divine call, an event, not an incident, that inaugurates a new and decisive stage in God's plan of history. The factuality or otherwise of this Biblical evaluation lies beyond the scope of scholarly research.'[55]

1.4 *The LBA background*

The view propounded by C. H. Gordon places the lives of Abraham and Jacob in the fourteenth century B.C. (LB II).[56] This placement rests chiefly on the parallels which Gordon sees between patriarchal practices and the social customs reflected in the fifteenth-thirteenth century texts from Nuzi and Ugarit.

This view will not be discussed in detail here. The parallels on which it rests have been criticized by a number of scholars.[57] Without these, such a dating has nothing to support it.

Further, it is impossible to reconcile such a late date with the internal biblical chronology. Even placing the Exodus in the thirteenth century B.C. does not allow a reduction of the patriarchal age to the fourteenth century, unless the entire framework of biblical history from Abraham to the Exodus is assumed to be artificial—an assumption for which there is no real warrant.[58]

1.5 *An EBA date for Abraham*

D. N. Freedman has recently argued that the true historical setting of the Abraham narratives is the middle of the third millenium B.C., or EB III (c. 2650-2350 B.C.) in archaeological terms.[59]

[55]N. M. Sarna, *Biblical Archaeology Review* 4/1, 1978, p. 52.

[56]E.g. C. H. Gordon, *Introduction to Old Testament Times* (Ventnor, NJ, 1953), ch. 8; *JNES* 13, 1954, pp. 56-59; *Biblical and Other Studies*, ed. A. Altmann (Cambridge, Mass., 1963), pp. 5-6.

[57]M. E. J. Selman, 'The Social Environment of the Patriarchs', *Tyndale Bulletin* 27, 1976, pp. 114-136, and idem in the present work; Thompson, *Historicity*, pp. 196-297; de Vaux, *Early History*, 1, pp. 262, 265-266.

[58]Cf. the criticisms of Albright, *BASOR* 163, 1961, pp. 50-51, and de Vaux, as previous note.

[59]D. N. Freedman, 'The Real Story of the Ebla Tablets: Ebla and the Cities of the Plain', *BA* 41/4, 1978, pp. 143-164.

His arguments are based on literary and archaeological evidence, the literary material being from the recently discovered Ebla (Tell Mardikh) archives. Stating that one of the tablets from Ebla lists the five 'cities of the plain' in the same order in which they occur in Genesis 14, and that the name of one of the kings mentioned in Genesis 14 (Birsha) is preserved in almost the same form on the tablet, Freedman argues that the incidents of Genesis 14 belong in all probability to the same period as the Ebla tablet (dated in general terms to the period 2600-2300 B.C.).

Freedman's argument from archaeology concerns EBA remains in the region east of the Dead Sea. Bab edh-Dhrâ and four neighbouring sites provide evidence of settlements during the EBA, but not during the MBA. Freedman proposes identifying these settlements with the 'cities of the plain'. Discussing occupation at Bab edh-Dhrâ, Freedman notes that the last major phase of occupation is EB III, the site being finally abandoned about 2250 B.C. in EB IV. The role of all five sites as the 'cities of the plain' is confined, however, to EB III: 'All were occupied during the Early Bronze Age for varying periods of time; the only period common to all is EB III, which is also the period of the Ebla tablets.'[60]

While there is much that is superficially attractive about Freedman's hypothesis, both the literary and archaeological arguments face serious difficulties.

Reservations have recently been expressed concerning the readings of the names espoused by Freedman, and it seems that the claim that the names of all five cities occur on one tablet was in any case erroneous.[61]

Freedman himself does not insist that the king named on the tablet should be identified with Birsha, king of Gomorrah, in Genesis 14. Indeed, he admits that, although he was originally under the impression that the king named on the tablet was king of Gomorrah, he later learned that he was king of the city whose name was read as Admah. Freedman therefore suggests only that the two kings 'belong to the same era, quite possibly to the same dynasty or to related families'. The conclusion that they belong

[60]Ibid., p. 152.

[61]Cf. ibid., p. 143 insert, letter from Dahood to Freedman, See also G. G. Garner, *Buried History* 15/2, 1979, p. 4, and the anonymous report in *Biblical Archaeology Review* 5/6, 1979, pp. 52-53.

'to the same chronological horizon'[62] is completely invalidated by these qualifications. Several examples could be found of two kings reigning centuries apart, possessing the same or similar names. As one example, note Jabin, king of Hazor at the time of Joshua, and a similarly named king of Hazor attested in the Mari documents of the eighteenth-seventeenth centuries B.C.[63] Even if Joshua is dated as early as 1400 B.C., in century date for the exodus, fifteenth we still have a gap of two or three centuries between these two kings; and note, too, that an even later king of Hazor also has the same name (Jdg. 4:2).

The archaeological argument also provides little evidence for Freedman's early date. His argument here largely depends on the fact that no MB I sites have been found which can be identified as the 'cities of the plain', thus restricting the choice to the EBA sites to which he refers. The common assumption that the cities of Genesis 14 now lie beneath the southern waters of the Dead Sea, which appear to have risen considerably in comparatively recent times,[64] is dismissed rather cavalierly: 'The underwater possibility has also been investigated . . . but . . . nothing determinative or even usable has turned up. If Sodom and Gomorrah are beneath the waters of the Dead Sea, they have not been found; the hypothesis itself seems more dubious all the time'.[65] This is an unfair statement of the situation. As Albright remarked, there is no way of knowing what depth of silt may now hide the ruins from view if they lie beneath the Dead Sea, and the chances of discovering traces are very remote indeed.[66]

Unless the EBA settlements can be identified with certainty as the 'cities of the plain' (which would require four of them being shown to have suffered a simultaneous fall in the EBA; Zoar was not destroyed according to Gn. 19), Freedman's case remains weak.

If the occupation of the central Negeb is held to be important for the historicity of the patriarchal narratives, Freedman's early date faces an additional difficulty; Thompson reports 'an almost

[62]Freedman, op. cit., p. 155.

[63]Cf. Y. Yadin, *Hazor: The Head of all those Kingdoms* (OUP, London, 1972), p. 5 and references there.

[64]See Albright, *BASOR* 14, 1924, pp. 7-8; J. P. Harland, *BA* 5/2, 1942, pp. 28-31.

[65]Freedman, op. cit. p. 152.

[66]Albright, *BASOR* 163, 1961, p. 51, n. 73.

total absence of evidence for any EB exploitation of this region' until the EB IV/MB I period.[67]

A final consideration is that the biblical chronology cannot be stretched sufficiently to place Abraham in the EB III period (i.e. before 2300 B.C.). This will be apparent from the discussion of biblical chronology below. Any attempt to take the Old Testament's chronology seriously will therefore find Freedman's placement of Abraham unacceptable,[68] unless a down-dating of the EBA becomes necessary in the light of future discoveries.

1.6 Summary

Each period examined has been found to present difficulties. Two periods (LB II and EB III) are excluded by the internal biblical chronology, and in any case are weakly supported. The remaining two, MB I and MB II, face the difficulty of the non-occupation of important sites or areas. However, before the conclusion is reached that neither period provides an acceptable setting for the movements of the patriarchs, evidence for the location and occupational history of the relevant sites must be assessed in more detail.

2. INDIVIDUAL SITES DISCUSSED

2.1 Biblical and archaeological evidence compared

The aim here is to assess the exact extent of the disagreement between biblical and archaeological evidence relating to the history of occupation at relevant sites.

What follows is a list of the Palestinian topographical references contained in the patriarchal narratives. For the convenience of a later part of the discussion, the list is divided chronologically into two parts: (i) corresponding to the life of Abraham after the departure from Haran, and (ii) corresponding to the lives of Isaac and Jacob, from Abraham's death to the entry into Egypt.

Table 1
(i)

Shechem	Genesis 12:6
Bethel	12:8; 13:3
Ai	12:8; 13:3
Zoar/Bela	13:10; 14; 18-19

[67]Thompson, JSOT 9, 1978, p. 25.
[68]As noted by G. G. Garner, Buried History 15/2, 1979, p. 6.

Sodom	13:10-13; 14; 18-19
Gomorrah	13:10; 14; 18:20; 19:24, 28
Admah	14
Zeboiim	14
Ashtaroth-karnaim	14:5
Ham	14:5
Shaveh-Kiriathaim	14:5
Salem	14:18
Hebron	13:18; 23:2, 10, 18
Oaks of Mamre	13:18; 18:1
Kadesh	14:7; 16:14; 20:1
Shur	16:7; 20:1; 25:18
Beer-lahai-roi	16:14; 24:62
Gerar	20:1-18
Beersheba	21:14, 31-33; 22;19
The Negeb	12:9; 13:1; 20:1; 24:62
The land of the Philistines	21:32, 34

(ii)

Beer-lahai-roi	25:11
Gerar	26:1-20
Beersheba	26:23, 33; 28:10
Bethel/Luz	28:11-22; 35:1, 6-8, 14-16
Galeed/Mizpah	31:49
Peniel/Penuel	32:30
Succoth	33:17
Shechem	33:18-20; 34:1-31; 35:4; 37:12-14
Bethlehem/Ephrathah	35:16, 19 (+ 48:7 retrospectively)
Kiriath-arba/Hebron	35:27
Tower of Eder	35:21
Dothan	37:17
Timnah	38:13-14

Not all the places listed here can be discussed profitably. The five 'cities of the plain' have not been located, as noted above. The exact locations of Ham, Shaveh-Kiriathaim, Galeed/Mizpah, Penuel/Peniel, Beer-lahai-roi, the Tower of Eder and Timnah are unknown, except that the first four evidently lay in Transjordan. In the cases of the Tower of Eder, Galeed/Mizpah and Penuel/

Peniel, the text does not in any case require an inhabited site. The Oaks of Mamre were a cultic spot, not a settlement; the Hebron region, in which they evidently stood, will be discussed under the heading 'Hebron'. Shur was a region, not a specific locality, and the references do no indicate occupation or otherwise.

The 'land of the Philistines' and the whole question of allegedly anachronistic uses of the name 'Philistine' is discussed by A. R. Millard elsewhere in this volume.

The remaining sites will be discussed in the order in which they appear for the first time in the narrative.

2.1.1 *Shechem* When the single reference to Shechem in the Abraham narratives is compared with the several in the Jacob narratives, a distinction is apparent. In the Jacob narratives, Shechem is clearly a city, and Jacob and his sons have dealings with its inhabitants. This is the case in the very first mention of Shechem in these later narratives, where a city is specifically mentioned,[69] and Jacob sets up an altar on land bought from Hamor, its ruler (33:18-20; cf. 34:2). In contrast to this, Genesis 12:6 makes no mention of a town or settlement, and no mention of Abraham coming into contact with any inhabitants of Shechem. The reference here is in fact to the Oak of Moreh, which is described as 'the place at Shechem'.

In view of this, the possibility should be considered that no town existed at Shechem in Abraham's day, and that the use of the name is simply the narrator's way of locating the Oak of Moreh for his readers; i.e. he may be informing his contemporaries that the Oak of Moreh stood near the town of Shechem of their own day.

Turning to the archaeological evidence for occupation at Shechem, we have already noted Dever's rejection of Albright's conclusion that the site was occupied in MB I. There was, however, a city at Shechem in MB IIA.[70] If the evidence so far discovered reflects the history of occupation accurately, the time

[69]A possible reading of Gn. 33:18 is '. . . arrived at Shalem a city of Shechem' (as NIV mg.), but a direct reference to Shechem seems more probable in view of the context.

[70]Wright, *Shechem*, pp. 110ff.; idem, *Enc. of Archaeological Excavations*, 4, ed. M. Avi-Yonah and E. Stern (OUP, London, 1978), pp. 1086-1087; cf. Dever in *NEATC*, pp. 142-144; Wright's dates for MB II now need to be raised considerably; see ns. 17, 18, 19 and 21 above.

of Jacob cannot be placed earlier than MB IIA. If it is held that a city fourished at Shechem in Abraham's day, Abraham must also be placed in that archaeological period. If however, it is agreed that the narrative does not require occupation in Abraham's day, an earlier setting for Abraham is naturally possible.

Something must be said here in reply to Wright's interpretation of the archaeological remains and biblical references to Shechem. Wright suggests that the platform or *temenos* in the western part of the MB II city should be identified with the altars built by Abraham and Jacob. But Wright's assumption that the platform was an altar may well be incorrect. His assertion that it lay outside the city, as did the sacred spot mentioned in Genesis 33,[71] has been questioned by van Seters, who points out that as the wall of this phase of the city was not found, we cannot assume that the platform lay outside it. Van Seters also points out: 'There were other structures in the area—a few wall fragments, a tannur (oven) and a drain—that suggest some permanent occupation and not a completely isolated 'altar'.[72] It is therefore a reasonable assumption that the raised platform lay *within* the city. The whole notion that the platform was an altar has in fact been questioned by J. F. Ross, who finds it difficult to view it as such, and suggests it was 'merely a terrace'.[73]

Wright also assumes that in the incident in Genesis 34, Hebrew tribes took permanent possession of Shechem.[74] It should be stressed that the text refers only to the city being attacked and its buildings plundered after the slaughter of the male inhabitants; to read more into the account is unjustified. Wright uses Genesis 48:22 to support his view that Shechem became a centre for Hebrew tribes at this early period. This is a dubious argument, since it is by no means certain that Shechem is in view in this verse. The Hebrew *šᵉkem* may simply mean 'mountain-slope' here (and is so rendered in RSV; cf. NEB 'ridge of land'). Further, whereas in Genesis 34 the attack on Shechem was accomplished by Jacob's sons, the deed referred to in 48:22 was apparently accomplished by Jacob himself.[75] Also, while the deed of Genesis

[71]Wright, *Shechem*, p. 132.

[72]Van Seters, *Abraham*, p. 110.

[73]J. F. Ross, *BASOR* 180, 1965, p. 27.

[74]Wright, *Shechem*, p. 20; cf. pp. 131-132.

[75]Cf. the comment by G. Von Rad, *Genesis* (SCM London, 1961) p. 414: 'And how could he promise to one of his sons what his sons had conquered?'

34 caused distress to Jacob (verse 3), the deed of 48:22 is evidently one in which he glories; and while Amorites feature as Jacob's opponents in 48:22, the 'prince of the land' is a Hivite in 34:2. When these various differences are taken into account, it seems unlikely that a permanent capture of the city of Shechem is referred to in 48:22, and chapter 34 alone certainly does not imply such an event.

2.1.2 Bethel (Beitin)

The over-interpretation of archaeological evidence from Bethel, resulting in Albright's claim that it was 'extensively peopled' in MB I, has already been noted. However, Dever does not dispense altogether with an MB I occupation of the site. A 'handful of sherds' from MB I do attest some occupation, and Dever's remark that 'Bethel can hardly have been more than a camp-site in MB I'[76] does not pose any problem with respect to the biblical references, since they require no more than this.[77] Hence it is not necessary to limit the application of the references to the MB IIA period when there was indeed a city at Bethel.[78]

D. Livingston's argument, that Beitin may not be the correct site for Bethel,[79] should also be borne in mind. If this argument is correct, all archaeological finds at Beitin are naturally superfluous to the history of Bethel.

2.1.3 Ai (Et-Tell)

Ai is mentioned only in the Abraham narratives, where the two references most naturally imply an occupied site of some kind (though they do not absolutely demand one). The

[76]Dever in Hayes and Miller, p. 99.

[77]According to Gn. 28:19, the name Bethel was not bestowed on the site until Jacob's day, but the existence of some sort of settlement before that time is indicated by the remark that the place was called Luz before Jacob renamed it. The Hebrew ʿîr usually translated 'city' in this verse, need not indicate a permanent urban centre; cf. its use in Nu. 13:19, where it is seemingly as apt for a temporary encampment as for a fortified city.

[78]J. L. Kelso, *The Excavation of Bethel (1934-60)* = *AASOR* 39, 1968, pp. 22-23; idem, *Enc. of Archaeological Excavations*, 1, ed. M. Avi-Yonah (OUP, London, 1975), p. 192; cf. Dever as ns. 36 and 37 above, on the attribution of Kelso's 'MB I' remains to MB II.

[79]D. Livingston, 'The Location of Biblical Bethel and Ai Reconsidered', *WTJ* 33, 1970, pp. 20-44. The reply by A. F. Rainey, 'Bethel is still Beitin', *WTJ* 33, 1971, pp. 175-188, is totally unconvincing, and is well answered by Livingston, 'Traditional Site of Bethel Questioned' *WTJ* 34, 1971, pp. 39-50. See also my comments on Rainey's reply, J. J. Bimson, *Redating the Exodus and Conquest*, *JSOT* Supp. 5 (Sheffield, 1978), pp. 220-225.

problem raised by the gap in occupation between c. 2500/2400 B.C. and the Iron Age at Et-Tell must therefore be faced.

S. Yeivin has made the interesting assertion that there were omissions in the publication of pottery from the 1933-35 Marquet-Krause excavations at Et-Tell, in which he took part. Yeivin mentions several items typical of the 'Transitional Period' (= MB I), and says that this group of finds was 'carefully selected and put apart by the author because of its chronological implications', but was for some reason never included in the final publication. Yeivin says that these finds came from the corridor surrounding the citadel (also termed the 'palace' or 'temple') on the acropolis, and suggests associating them with the last phase of that building's existence, when the inhabited area of the site may have shrunk considerably. On the basis of these finds, Yeivin would extend the life of this final phase at least into the twenty-first century, and perhaps even into the twentieth/nineteenth centuries B.C.[80]

If correct, this would be a very important adjustment to the occupational history of Et-Tell. It should be noted, however, that the excavations of the joint American expedition directed by J. A. Callaway (1964-72) have not produced any evidence to support Yeivin's view,[81] though this does not automatically disprove it; the relevant evidence may all have been removed during the earlier excavations, as was most of the evidence for Iron Age re-occupation of the citadel structures.[82]

In this connection, the possibility should be emphasized that at any site discussed here which appears to lack remains from the appropriate period, there may have been scanty or sporadic occupation at the time of the patriarchs, traces of which have either been removed by erosion or simply missed by the excavators.

Finally, it should be noted that the relocation of Bethel advocated by Livingstone would automatically demand a new site for Ai as well, in which case Et-Tell has no bearing on the history of Ai. Other attempts to relocate Ai have found no archaeological

[80]S. Yeiven, *The Israelite Conquest of Canaan* (Nederlands Historisch-Archaeologisch Institute, Istanbul, 1971), pp. 51-52; cf. p. 75: 'In any case, some evidence was found there of an occupation following the end of the so-called EC period' (EC = 'Early Canaanite' = EBA).

[81]See conveniently J. A. Callaway, *Enc. of Archaeological Excavations*, 1, pp. 36-52 and references on p. 52.

[82]See Callaway, *BASOR* 178, 1965, p. 38.

support from Callaway's survey of sites in the vicinity of Et-Tell.[83] Livingston's theory, on the other hand, has yet to be tested by excavation of the two sites which he proposes for identification with Bethel and Ai.

2.1.4 *Ashtaroth-karnaim*   While this name may refer to only one site, Albright considered it to be a pairing of the names of two sites, Tell Ashtarah and Sheikh Saʾad. He identified Tell Astarah with Ashtaroth and Sheikh Saʾad with Karnaim.[84] Scholars who assume that the biblical name refers to a single site differ over which of these two tells is the probable location.[85] However, Albright reports finding evidence of EB-MB I occupation at both sites,[86] and Glueck includes these tells among those which were abandoned at the end of MB I.[87]

2.1.5 *Salem*   If this place is to be identified with Jerusalem, as is perhaps indicated by Psalm 76:2, the reference in Genesis 14 would have to be related, on present evidence to MB II; Kenyon's excavations on the eastern spur produced no remains of MB I date.[88]

It should be remembered, however, that Kenyon's excavations of the early city were very limited indeed, and the recently renewed excavations may change the picture.[89] A Cypriote bowl of MB I date was discovered in earlier excavations on the Ophel,[90] and this may indicate occupation in that period; it is also possible, however, that the bowl remained in use into the MB II period.

The possibility should also be considered that the Salem of Genesis 14 is not to be identified with Jerusalem. This identification may read too much into the fact that the name occurs in

[83]See ibid., p. 16, n. 4; idem, *JBL* 87, 1968, p. 315, and *BASOR* 196, 1969, p. 5.

[84]Albright, *BASOR* 19, 1925, pp. 14-15.

[85]Cf. S. Cohen, IDB, Abingdon, NY, 1962, 1, p. 255.

[86]Albright, *BASOR* 19, 1925, pp. 15-16, idem, *The Archaeology of Palestine and the Bible*, 1932, p. 142.

[87]Glueck, *Rivers in the Desert*, Q1968, p. 73-75.

[88]E.g. K. M. Kenyon, *Digging up Jerusalem* (Benn, London, 1976), p. 78.

[89]See H. Shanks, *Biblical Archaeology Review* 3/4, 1977, p. 25, and Y. Shiloh, 'City of David: Excavation 1978', *BA* 42, 1979, pp. 165-171.

[90]R. Amiran, *IEJ* 10, 1060, p. 225; B. Mazar in *Jerusalem Revealed* (Israel Exploration Soc., Jerusalem, 1975), p. 3; cf. Kenyon, *Digging up Jerusalem*, pp. 80-81.

parallel with Zion in Psalm 76:2. The name is not used there as an alternative toponym for, or abbreviation of Jerusalem, but as 'a poetic and religious appellation'.[91] It may be significant that Salem is not mentioned in connection with Abraham's visit to Moriah in Genesis 22, while Moriah is identified with, or placed in close proximity to Jerusalem, in 2 Chronicles 31:1 (where 'Mount Moriah' is identified with the temple hill north of pre-Solomonic Jerusalem). It has been suggested that the identification of Salem with Jerusalem would suit the route taken by Abraham on his return from Damascus to Hebron after rescuing Lot and his family.[92] However, although Abraham is certainly in the region of Hebron again by Genesis 18, the time of this chapter is evidently many years after the time of chapter 14 (cf. 16:3, which takes us to Abraham's eighty-fifth year, and 17:1, where he is said to be ninety-nine); hence there is no reason to assume that Abraham was returning directly to Hebron from Damascus when he encoutered Melchizedek at Salem. If he was not travelling towards Hebron, but simply southwards down the Jordan Valley, Salem could have been a more easterly location than later Jerusalem, and may indeed have been located in the Valley, as certain early Christian writers suggested.[93]

2.1.6 *Hebron* Wright attempts to dispense with references to Hebron in the patriarchal narratives, commenting: 'We are informed only by two explanatory notes that Mamre is Hebron, indicating that although Abraham settled there, the city itself was not yet in extistence'.[94] Unfortunately, this approach will not do in the case of Genesis 23:10, where we have mention not only of a city of Hebron but also of a city gate, indicating a walled urban settlement. It was in the gate of the city that the transaction between Abraham and Ephron over the Cave of Machpelah was carried out.

The archaeological evidence from Jebel er-Rumeideh would confine the time of Abraham to MB II, since excavations there

[91]G. A. Barrois, *IDB*, 4, p. 166.

[92]Cf. D. J. Wiseman in *NBD* (Tyndale Press, London, 1962), p. 1124.

[93]Cf. Barrois, *IDB*, 4, p. 166; for other views on the location of Salem, see ibid. and Wiseman as previous note. Albright, *BASOR* 163, 1961, p. 52, would amend Gn. 14:18 to read: '. . . Melchizedek, a king allied to him. . .', assuming a haplography.

[94]Wright, *Biblical Archaeology*, p. 47.

have revealed a fortified town of MB II date, but no such remains from MB I.[95] Dever's investigations of the Hebron area discovered 'several isolated MB I cemeteries and even some seasonal settlements in the Hebron hills, but no trace of occupation anywhere in the immediate vicinity of Hebron'.[96] So far, therefore, there are no MB I finds from the Hebron region which would correspond to the indications of Genesis 23.

However, the MB I traces found by Dever in the general area of Hebron may indicate that evidence of something more than seasonal settlements still awaits discovery somewhere in the area. Albright suggested in 1932 that biblical Hebron lay under the modern town in the valley, and not on the hill er-Rumeideh.[97] In 1961 he repeated the view that Hebron 'almost certainly lies under the remains of later times, buried deep under modern el-Khalil'.[98] Only excavation can prove the validity or otherwise of this suggestion, and present-day occupation probably rules out adequate excavation for the foreseeable future. But for the present, the clear indication of a walled town in Genesis 23 is unsupported by archaeological evidence if Abraham is placed earlier than MB II.

2.1.7 *Kadesh* Of the two possible sites for biblical Kadesh (-barnea), the springs of Ain Qudeis and Ain el Qudeirat (roughly 8 km apart), the latter is considered the more likely, having much more abundant water and vegetation.[99] Alternatively, it has been

---

[95]P. C. Hammond, *RB* 73, 1966, pp. 566-569; *RB* 75, 1968, pp. 253-258. Excavations at Ramat el-Khalil, the traditional site of Mamre, 3 km. north of Hebron, produced some early MB II pottery, but none from MB I. For the ancient sources which identify Ramat el-Khalil as the site of Mamre, and a report of the excavations, see A. E. Mader, *Mambre*, 2 vols. (Freiburg in Breisgau, 1957); for a brief summary, see conveniently S. Applebaum, *Enc. of Archaeological Excavations*, 3, pp. 776-778.

[96]Dever in Hayes and Miller, p. 100; see Dever in *NEATC*, pp. 146-150 for details of the finds.

[97]Albright, *The Archaeology of Palestine and the Bible*, 1932, p. 208, n. 16.

[98]Idem, *BASOR* 163, 1961, p. 48; cf. A. Negev (ed.), *Archaeological Encyclopedia of the Holy Land* (Jerusalem, 1972), p. 142.

[99]Y. Aharoni, *Antiquity and Survival* II, 2/3, 1957, pp. 289-290; idem in B. Rothenberg, *God's Wilderness: Explorations in Sinai* (Thames & Hudson, London, 1961), p. 122; see Kitchen in *NBD*, p. 687, for further sources and discussion.

suggested that Kadesh-barnea was 'the name of a *fairly extensive region* embracing *among others* the spring of Ain el Qudeirat'.[100]

During a survey of the Sinai Peninsula undertaken in the winter of 1956-57, Israeli archaeologists discovered many temporary and permanent settlements around the oasis of Ain el Qudeirat and in the neighbouring region, dating from the Palaeolithic, MB I, Israelite, Persian and Roman-Byzantine periods. MB I finds were numerous and included an agricultural settlement on the hill overlooking the spring.[101] No MB II finds were made in the region. Unless such finds still await discovery, the archaeological evidence suggests an MB I setting for the references in Genesis 14, 16 and 20.

2.1.8 *Gerar*   Y. Aharoni suggested locating Gerar at Tell Abu Hureira, and this location was adopted by Albright and Glueck.[102] The site is unexcavated, but pottery of both MB I and MB II has been found on the tell.[103]

Dever notes that the identification of this site with Gerar is unproven and disputed, and hence casts doubt on the relevance of these finds.[104] However, even though the exact location of Gerar remains uncertain, a location somewhere in the region of the Wadi Gaza is definitely indicated,[105] and surface finds attest MB I and MB II occupation at several sites along the Wadi Gaza. While Dever describes the MB I settlements in this region as 'apparently small unwalled villages similar to those of the central Negeb',[106] Thompson describes the settlements as 'very large and stable,

[100]Rothenberg, *God's Wilderness*, p. 39, n. 2; cf. p. 45, where Rothenberg suggests that Kadesh-barnea comprised the region of Ain el Qudeirat, Ain Qadeis, El Qusaima and El Muweilah.

[101]Rothenberg, *God's Wilderness*, pp. 33-46; Albright, *BASOR* 163, 1961, p. 37; M. Dothan, *IEJ* 15, 1965, p. 134; Glueck, *Rivers in the Desert*, ²1968, p. 74; cf. idem, *BA* 18/1, 1955, p. 6, and *BASOR* 159, 1960, p. 6.

[102]Aharoni, IEJ 6, 1956, pp. 26-32; cf. F. M. Cross and G. E. Wright, *JBL* 75, 1956, p. 213; Albright, *BASOR* 163, 1961, pp. 47-48; Glueck, *Rivers in the Desert*, ²1968, p. 75.

[103]Albright, *BASOR* 163, 1961, pp. 47-48; Y. Aharoni in D. Winton Thomas (ed.), *Archaeology and Old Testament Study* (Clarendon, Oxford, 1967), p. 389.

[104]Dever in Hayes and Miller, p. 100.

[105]Cf. Aharoni, *IEJ* 6, pp. 26-32 for data relevant to the location. The Naḥal Gerar forms the northern arm of the Wadi Gaza.

[106]Dever in Hayes and Miller. p. 100.

showing occupation during all periods of the Bronze Age',[107] a contradiction which well illustrates the uncertainty and subjectivity involved in the interpretation of archaeological evidence.

Since Gerar must be located in this general area, there is no reason to doubt the authenticity of the reference to a king and people of Gerar in Genesis 20 and 26, regardless of whether the incidents of these chapters are placed in the MB I or MB II period. The problem of the Philistines referred to in chapter 26 (cf. the phrase 'land of the Philistines' in chapter 20) is discussed by A. R. Millard elsewhere in this volume. The fact that the narrative speaks of a 'king' of Gerar does not necessarily imply a large fortified settlement, since semi-nomadic peoples were also ruled by kings.

2.1.9 *Beersheba* Tel Beersheba (Tell es-Seba^c) completely lacks pre-Iron Age remains. It does not therefore bear on the question of whether the patriarchal narratives relate better to MB I or MB II. But it raises a more serious problem, casting doubt, as some see it, on the authenticity of the patriarchal traditions.[108]

Two possibilities deserve consideration. The first is that the references to Beersheba in the patriarchal narratives do not actually require a settlement on the site at the time in question. Sarna has argued thus in reply to van Seters: 'The biblical passages refer only to a well and a cultic site. . . . No king or ruler is mentioned, and no patriarch ever has dealings with the inhabitants of Beersheba. The only description of Beersheba as a "city" in the patriarchal narratives is a late editorial note (Gn. 26:33) which clearly has nothing to do with the narrative context, and which views the material through the eyes of a later age.'[109] In 1967, Aharoni held the view that the absence of early archaeological evidence does not contradict the patriarchal narratives, which, he then suggested, have only the *area* of Beersheba in mind, not a town.[110]

However, Aharoni later expressed a more negative view, arising from the discovery that the well on the heights of the mound at Tel Beersheba post-dated the period of the Israelite settlement

[107]Thompson, *JSOT* 9, 1978, p. 25.
[108]Van Seters, *Abraham*, pp. 111-112; Dever in Hayes and Miller, p. 100.
[109]Sarna, *Biblical Archaeology Review* 3/4, 1977, p. 9.
[110]Aharoni in Winton Thomas, p. 389.

(thirteenth-twelfth centuries B.C. in his view). The patriarchal narratives specifically refer to Abraham digging a well at Beersheba (21:30): 'Since the digging of this well did not ante-date the settlement period, it therefore seems certain that neither can the patriarchal narratives associated with Beersheba refer to an earlier period.'[111] Aharoni concludes that the patriarchal narratives are compilations of many traditions originating in different periods.

This argument overlooks the possibility that the well dug by Abraham may not be the well on the mound at Tel Beersheba. In the vicinity of modern Beersheba (Bir es-Saba^c), about two miles west of Tel Beersheba, there are a number of wells. Excavations at Bir es-Saba^c in 1953, 1962, 1966 and 1968 uncovered Chalcolithic and Iron Age II remains beneath those of the Roman-Byzantine period. R. Gophna, who carried out the 1962 excavations, comments: 'As a result of the excavations . . . it now seems certain that a large settlement flourished there at least during Iron Age II. This settlement existed at the old traditional site, near the wells. The fortified town uncovered by the excavations of Tel Beersheba was built in the time of the Monarchy as an administrative center.'[112] It is therefore possible that if there *was* a settlement at Beersheba in Abraham's day, it was located at the site of Bir es-Saba^c, and that remains from the patriarchal period still await discovery beneath unexcavated parts of the modern town.

There is certainly no reason to identify the well dug by Abraham with the one at Tel Beersheba. Hence the late date of this well, and the absence of MBA traces from the tell, are irrelevant to the historicity of the patriarchal narratives.

2.1.10 *The Negeb*   We have already noted that no MB II remains have come to light from the Negeb, while in the preceding MB I period the region was occupied with numerous unwalled settlements.

Thompson speaks of 'several hundred new settlements, with a number of very large villages' appearing during the EB IV/MB I period in the central Negeb. These occur in two main zones, environmentally distinct. The largest number of settlements and dwellings, and all of the large villages, lie on the north-western slopes of the central hills; they were supported by agriculture

[111]Aharoni, *BA* 39/2, 1976, p. 71; cf. pp. 62-65.
[112]R. Gophna, *Enc. of Archaeological Excavations*, 1, p. 159.

based on wadi terracing, which kept arable fields productive with the aid of run-off water. Remains of groups of round stone huts have been found in the areas of Ramat Maṭred, Har Romem, Naḥal Ṣin and the upper Naḥal Nisànà. Long-term winter grazing is possible in these regions, and Thompson believes these settlements were oriented to animal husbandry.[113] Therefore it seems that at this time the settlement of the central Negeb was based on a mixed ecomony of agriculture and grazing.

As Glueck noted in the 1950s, these MB I settlements provide an excellent background to Abraham's movements through the Negeb with flocks and herds (12:9-10; 13:1). It is also notable that the patriarchs practised cultivation, either occasional patch cultivation or the more intensive form attested by the wadi terracing; Genesis 26:12 refers to Isaac sowing and reaping in the region of Gerar (where, incidentally, agriculture is aided by plentiful and stable ground water).[114]

It has been argued by Y. Aharoni and A. F. Rainey that the Negeb's MB I settlements are actually irrelevant to the setting of the patriarchs. These scholars have argued that in the Old Testament the term 'Negeb' has a much more restricted application than in modern usage, and that the biblical Negeb was a narrow E-W band extending only about 20 km north and south of Beersheba. They point out that the MB I sites of the modern central Negeb lie outside this area, and that no MB I sites have been found within the limits of the *biblical* Negeb.[115]

Whatever the limits of the Negeb as envisaged in the patriarchal narratives, the argument of Aharoni and Rainey overlooks some important biblical data. Abraham is said to have dwelt for a time 'between Kadesh and Shur' (Gn. 20:1), and Isaac is found at one point journeying from Beer-lahai-roi, and later dwelling there, after Abraham's death (24:62; 25:11; cf. 16:14 on location). These references leave no doubt that Abraham and Isaac journeyed through, and occasionally settled in, the region in which many MB I sites have been found. In 1955 Glueck described the region in which MB I sites had been discovered as extending from a site 28 km SE-SSE of Beersheba to a site 22 km SE of Ain el-Qudeirat

---

[113]Thompson, *JSOT* 9, 1978, pp. 25, 18-19.

[114]Ibid., p. 25.

[115]Aharoni, *BA* 39/2, 1976, p. 55; Rainey, 'The Negeb in Biblical Studies', *The Tyndale Paper* 22/3, 1977, p. 2 (transcribed from a tape of a public lecture).

(Kadesh-barnea),[116] and MB I sites have since been discovered further west, along what was perhaps the biblical 'Way of Shur'.[117]

Therefore, even if Abraham's movements through the Negeb on his way to and from Egypt are disregarded, his and Isaac's sojournings there do fit ideally into the MB I period, when agricultural settlements in the Negeb are well attested.

2.1.11 *Succoth*   Tell Deir ʿAlla, with which Succoth was identified by Glueck, has no stratified remains from before the LBA. This becomes irrelevant, however, if Franken is correct in abandoning Glueck's view.[118] Thompson remarks that Franken's reasons for rejecting this identification are primarily that Tell Deir ʿAlla did not exist before the LBA, thus implying a circular argument.[119] This overlooks Franken's other reasons for rejecting the identification, the most striking being evidence that the River Jabbok once ran to the north of the tell, putting it on the wrong side of the river to be Succoth in Gad.[120]

But even if the identification with Succoth is maintained, it should be noted that, although Franken's excavations have revealed no trace of MB remains, Glueck reported finding a small quantity of pottery 'which can definitely be assigned to MB IIA' during his surface explorations (pottery characteristic of Tell Beit Mirsim G-F).[121]

[116]Glueck, *BA* 18/1, 1955, p. 6.

[117]Rothenberg, *God's Wilderness*, pp. 58ff.; Albright, *BASOR* 163, 1961, p. 37. Cf. also Glueck, *BASOR* 179, 1965, pp. 6ff. on more MB I Negeb sites discovered after 1960. Dever's remark (*HTR*, 64, 1971, p. 226, n. 66; cf. in Hayes and Miller, p. 100) that the MB I culture 'cannot be easily reconciled with the *milieu* apparently required for the Patriarchal period', because the Negeb's MB I sites are mostly well away from caravan routes, is irrelevant if it is not insisted that Abraham and Isaac were donkey-caravaneers; the biblical references imply nothing about proximity to caravan routes, and speak of these two patriarchs *dwelling in* the region of the modern Negeb as well as travelling through it.

[118]H. J. Franken, *Excavations at Tell Deir ʿAlla*, 1 (Brill, Leiden, 1969), pp. 4-8.

[119]Thompson, *Historicity*, p. 183, n. 65.

[120]Franken, op.cit., p. 5.

[121]Glueck, *BASOR* 90, 1943, p. 15. Glueck reports finds of MB IIA sherds from other sites in the northern half of the east side of the Jordan Valley, ibid., pp. 7, 17; he reports MB I sherds from some sites, pp. 7, 17, 19, 22, but none from Tell Deir ʿAlla, p. 15.

Hence either Tell Deir ᶜAlla is not Succoth, in which case its occupational history is not relevant to the reference in Genesis 33; or the identification is correct, in which case there is slight but sufficient indication of temporary settlement in MB IIA. Glueck found no pottery there from MB I.

2.1.12 *Bethlehem*   M. Avi-Yonah has argued that since Bethlehem has no springs, and a regular water supply is dependent on cisterns, this restricts the establishment of the town proper to the period when cisterns were being used in the mountainous areas of the country, i.e. in the LBA.[122]

It is possible, however, that a settled sited is not in view in the references to Bethlehem (Ephrath) in Genesis 35. A cultic spot may be intended, thought there is admittedly no other biblical evidence that Bethlehem was of cultic significance at that time. It is also possible that the name 'Ephrath' is being used retrospectively by the writer in order to indicate to his contemporaries the location of Rachel's death and burial.

The possibility of sporadic settlement before the LBA should not be ruled out, and excavation of the mound which lies east of the Church of the Nativity, with Bronze and Iron Age surface pottery, may reveal evidence of such.

In view of these possibilities, the present lack of evidence for MBA occupation does not prove that the references in Genesis 35 are anachronistic; nor can it stand against the authenticity of the incident which provides their context.

2.1.13 *Dothan*   Excavations at Tel Dothan have uncovered no evidence from MB I, but have revealed an urban centre of the MB II period.[123]

2.2 *Summary, and a possible solution*

The main difficulty which emerges from the above is that some sites mentioned in the patriarchal narratives show occupation in MB I but not in MB II, while others have produced remains from MB II but not MB I. However, this need not be an insurmountable obstacle to locating the patriarchal age against these archaeological

[122]Avi-Yonah, *Enc. of Archaeological Excavations*, 1, p. 200.
[123]J. P. Free, *BASOR* 152, 1958, pp. 14ff.; Dever in Hayes and Miller, p. 100.

periods, and it certainly cannot be used to disprove the historicity of the narratives. The following three points must be borne in mind.

First, non-occupation of a site cannot be proved conclusively by a lack of finds. Traces of scanty or short-lived occupation may have been removed in subsequent periods, either by erosion or by building activities; or they may simply have been missed by the excavators, since only a small proportion of any site can be explored in detail. While it would be less reasonable to appeal to this possibility in the case of the complete lack of MB II finds throughout the Negeb, it should always be borne in mind in cases of individual sites.[124]

Secondly, the chronological distinction made between MB I and MB II styles of pottery should not be taken to mean that the two archaeological ages never overlapped. The MB I-MB IIA transition did not occur suddenly, or simultaneously at all sites. As Thompson remarks: 'There never was a time when the EB IV/MB I culture no longer existed and MB IIA had not yet begun. Nor is every EB IV/MB I corpus of pottery earlier than every MB IIA corpus.'[125] It is therefore possible that MB IIA finds from one site overlap chronologically with MB I finds elsewhere, and vice versa.

Finally, there is the possibility that the time covered by the patriarchal narratives actually spanned the transition between MB I and MB II. It is this third possiblity which offers the most satisfactory solution to the difficulties noted above.

It may be significant that in Table I, Ai, Kadesh, the Negeb and north Transjordian sites occur only in the first half of the list, corresponding to the lifetime of Abraham. Kadesh and the Negeb we have seen were occupied in MB I but not in MB II. If Et-Tell is assumed to be the site of Ai, the sherds noted by Yeivin may indicate occupation there in MB I but no later. The evidence discovered by Albright and Glueck for MB I occupation in north Transjordan may justly be noted in connection with Genesis 14, without reviving Glueck's claim that the eastern kings 'gutted every city and village ... from Ashtaroth-Karnaim in southern Syria through all of Transjordan and the Negev.'[126] We have seen

---

[124]See Kitchen's remarks on apparent gaps in occupation, *The Bible in its World* (Paternoster, Exeter, 1977), pp. 11-14.

[125]Thompson, *Historicity*, p. 164, n. 104.

[126]Glueck, *Rivers in the Desert*, ²1968, p. 11.

that the archaeological evidence does not attest sudden destructions, or even the simultaneous abandonment of all the MB I sites; but neither does Genesis 14 imply that this MB I civilization was (in Glueck's phrase) 'savagely liquidated';[127] the narrative speaks only of the subjection of the people of Transjordan and the Negeb to the rule of the eastern kings (14:5-7).[128]

In short, it seems that the sites and areas mentioned only in the Abraham narratives (or Abraham-Isaac narratives in the case of the Negeb) were exclusively MB I sites, though Ai cannot be included with certainty.

The only references to Succoth and Dothan occur in narratives concerning Jacob; similarly, those references to Shechem which clearly speak of a city belong in the Jacob narratives, the reference in Genesis 12:6 being open to another interpretation. We have seen that these places were occupied in MB II but not in MB I (i.e. if Succoth = Tell Deir ᶜAlla, otherwise we can cay nothing of its history at all); indeed, in MB II Shechem was a large urban centre, just as we find implied by the Jacob narratives.

The possibility suggested by these correspondences is that while the time of Abraham belongs in MB I, the time of Jacob belongs in MB II.

A site which does not lend itself to this scheme is Hebron, a walled town in Abraham's time, but not attested archaeologically as such until MB II. With the exception of this one site, the above suggestion harmonizes the biblical and archaeological evidence more satisfactorily than does a purely MB I or MB II setting for the patriarchal period. The anomaly of Hebron may be resolved by further excavations, either by the discovery of a walled town of MB I date in the valley, or by indications of MB I beginnings for the remains on Jebel er-Rumeideh currently attributed to MB IIA.

Generally speaking, a shift is certainly observable in the focus of patriarchal movements; in the Abraham and Isaac narratives, the Negeb as far south as the region between Kadesh and Shur is included in the patriarchs' wanderings, whereas the family of Jacob, after their return from Paddan-Aram, *do not frequent this area at all*, but instead are found in central Palestine, often in the

---

[127]Ibid.

[128]No occupation of northern Transjordan is implied for the time of Jacob; Jacob travels through Gilead on his southward journey from Paddan-Aram (Gn. 31), but apparently has no contact with any inhabitants of the region.

vicinity of Shechem. This shift corresponds to the depopulation of the Negeb at the end of MB I, and the rise in central Palestine of urban centres such as Shechem in MB II.

3. THE MB I–II TRANSITION AND THE BIBLE'S CHRONOLOGY

It has already been stated that the end of MB I is not dated between 2000 and 1900 B.C. Several scholars prefer a date nearer to 2000 and 1900 B.C.[129] A correlation of the lives of Abraham and Isaac with MB I therefore requires the life of Abraham to be dated largely, if not entirely, before 2000 B.C.

This is an earlier dating than is currently popular, but it does have the suppport of the chronological framework of the Old Testament. Linking the patriarchal age with later history are two periods whose lengths are given in summary. The period spent in Egypt is given as 430 years in Exodus 12:40 (400 years in Gn. 15:13), and the period from the Exodus to the building of the first temple is given as 480 years in 1 Kings 6:1. Both these periods of time have been shortened by critical treatments, the sojourn in Egypt to as little as 130 years,[130] the period between the Exodus and Solomon to about 300 years or less, placing the Exodus in the thirteenth century B.C. A short sojourn, or a thirteenth-century date for the Exodus, would place Abraham in MB II, while a combination of both would place him in the LBA. However, other biblical material does not allow these periods to be shortened so drastically. If both periods are taken at face value, and if the patriarchal period itself is allowed the time required by the biblical chronology, Abraham's life does indeed fall almost entirely before 2000 B.C.

[129]See n. 21. On the basis of Carbon-14 dates, J. Mellaart has recently proposed a high chronology for Egypt before the Second Intermediate Period, and for parallel eras of Mesopotamian history, requiring mid-3rd millennium dates for MB I (Mellaart, 'Egyptian and Near Eastern Chronology: a dilemma?', *Antiquity* 53/207, 1979, pp. 6-18). Several lines of data argue against Mellaart's chronology: for example, only seven generations separate the Hittite king Suppiluliumas I, who reigned in the fourteenth century, from Mursilis I, making it unlikely that the latter should be placed in the eighteenth century; Mellaart's twentieth-century date for Shamshi Adad I of Assyria requires a gap of 200 years in the Assyrian king list, for which there is no evidence.

[130]H. H. Rowley, *From Joseph to Joshua* (OUP, London, 1950), p. 164.

3.1 The sojourn in Egypt

The figure of 430 years found in Exodus 12:40 has been adequately defended by K. A. Kitchen and T. C. Mitchell.[131] Attempts to reduce the figure on the basis of the genealogy of Moses in Exodus 6:14-20 overlook other genealogical material which points to the genealogy in Exodus 6 being incomplete, indicating only family, clan and tribe. The prediction of an Exodus 'in the fourth generation' in Genesis 15:16 cannot be cited in support of a short sojourn because of the possibility that *dôr* here does not indicate a generation but a longer period of time, as do related terms in early Assyrian sources and in Syriac.[132]

The LXX reduces the sojourn from 430 years by inserting the phrase 'and in the land of Canaan' in Exodus 12:40. Thus it reads: 'And the sojourning of the children of Israel, which they sojourned in the land of Egypt and in the land of Canaan, was four hundred and thirty years.' It is commonly assumed that this refers to the 430 years elapsing between Abraham's arrival in Canaan and the Exodus. This understanding leaves only 215 years for the sojourn, a figure which a number of scholars have adopted.[133] Quite apart from the possibility that the LXX does not preserve the original reading, it seems rather unlikely that this is how it should be understood. Abraham, Isaac and Jacob would hardly be described as 'children of Israel', as this view assumes they are. Before the birth of Jacob's sons, there were no 'children of Israel' to dwell in Canaan. It is worth noting that the biblical material makes Joseph thirty-nine years old when Jacob and his other sons entered Egypt (Gn. 41:46, 53; 45:6), and Joseph was born sometime before Jacob left the household of Laban. The biblical chronology therefore allows approximately thirty years between the arrival of Jacob and his sons in Canaan and their descent into Egypt. If the sojourn in Egypt is taken as 400 years, as in Genesis 15:13, the sojourn of 'the children of Israel' in both Egypt and Canaan would be about 430 years in all. It seems far more likely

[131]K. A. Kitchen and T. C. Mitchell in *NBD*, p. 214; Kitchen, *Ancient Orient and Old Testament*, pp. 53-56.

[132]Albright, *BASOR* 163, 1961, pp. 50-51; Kitchen, *Ancient Orient and Old Testament*, p. 54 with n. 99.

[133]E.g. C. F. Burney, *Israel's Settlement in Canaan*, 1919, pp. 87-89, 95; M. Anstey, *The Chronology of the Old Testament*, repr. 1973, pp. 65-66.

that this is the meaning of the LXX reading than that Abraham and Isaac are supposed to be involved. This argument is not intended to suggest that the LXX is original and correct; the additional phrase may have been inserted by the LXX translators in order to remove the 30-year difference between Exodus 12:40 and the 400 years of Genesis 15:13. (The difference is not in fact problematical; as Kitchen has noted, the 400 years of Gn. 15:13 are simply a round figure in prospect, the 430 being more precise in retrospect.)[134]

In short, neither the LXX nor other biblical material relating to the time of the sojourn contradicts the figure of 430 years found in Exodus 12:40.

3.2 *The 480 years of 1 Kings 6:1*

I have discussed elsewhere the extra-biblical evidence on which a thirteenth-century date for the Exodus has been based, suggesting that it does not support that date so strongly as has been commonly supposed, and proposing instead a date in the fifteenth century B.C.[135] The arguments normally advanced for a thirteenth-century date for the Exodus will not be reviewed here, but some points will be noted against the reduction of the figure in 1 Kings 6:1.

Kitchen states that because the Old Testament is ancient near-eastern literature, 'Ancient Oriental principles must be applied' in understanding the figure of 480 years.[136] He suggests that the figure results from the totalling of a number of partly concurrent periods, producing a figure which is too long in absolute years. As 'a parallel problem' Kitchen cites the list of kings which the Turin Canon preserves for Egypt's XIIIth-XVIIIth Dynasties. The Turin Canon places some 170 kings in this period; their reigns total 'at least 520 years', but the astronomically fixed dates for the XIIth and XVIIIth Dynasties allow them 'a maximum period of only 240 years at most'. The problem has been resolved by the conclusion that the dynasties involved were all partly contemporary. But one may question whether this really illustrates the situation behind the 480 years of 1 Kings 6:1. The Turin Canon

---

[134]Kitchen, *Ancient Orient and Old Testament*, p. 53.
[135]J. J. Bimson, *Redating the Exodus and Conquest* (see n. 79).
[136]Kitchen, as n. 134, p. 73.

does not provide an over-all total for the reigns which it lists, while 1 Kings 6:1 gives no hint whatever of being an aggregate of several lesser figures. The parallel is therefore somewhat artificial.

Secondly, Kitchen's own defence of the 430 years of Exodus 12:40 shows that he does not consider the application of ancient near eastern principles to be truly obligatory; they are applied in the case of 1 Kings 6:1 simply in order to reconcile the figure of 480 years with a thirteenth–century date for the Exodus arrived at on other grounds—the same grounds which I have elsewhere shown to be questionable.

Other writers have argued for a reduction of the 480 years on the assumption that the figure is a round number representing twelve generations.[137] However, a critical examination of this assumption shows it to be unfounded.[138]

Against a reduction of the 480 years we may note that Judges 11:26 gives the time between the Israelite occupation of Trans-jordan and the days of Jephthah as 300 years. To argue that this figure too results from the totalling of concurrent periods is surely a case of special pleading. Also, a period in the order of 480 years between the Exodus and the time of Solomon is indicated by one of the genealogies for this period (1 Ch. 6:33-37),[139] though admittedly some scholars do not accept this material as listing descent in a straight-forward historical manner.[140]

3.3 *The date of the patriarchal age*

The 480 years of 1 Kings 6:1 has its lower end fixed at the fourth year of the reign of Solomon, for which a date of 967 B.C. seems probable.[141] This figure, and the 430 years of Exodus 12:40, together place the descent into Egypt at about 1877 B.C. This date should not be considered exact, since some small leeway must be

[137]E.g. Bright, *History*[2], p. 121.
[138]See Bimson, as n. 79, pp. 81-86.
[139]See ibid., p. 96, for a brief discussion of this material.
[140]E.g. E. L. Curtis and A. A. Madsen,*The Books of Chronicles*, ICC, Edin-burgh, 1910, pp. 134ff.; K. Möhlenbrink, *ZAW* 52, 1934, pp. 202ff.; R. J. Coggins, *Chronicles* (C.U.P., 1976), pp. 42-45.
[141]Cf. E. R. Thiele, *The Mysterious Numbers of the Hebrew Kings* (Grand Rapids, Michigan, 1965), pp. 39-52; Kitchen and Mitchell in *NBD*, pp. 217, 219; R. K. Harrison, *Introduction to the Old Testament* (Tyndale Press, London, 1970), pp. 184-185, 189; Kitchen, *The Third Intermediate Period in Egypt* (Aris & Phillips, Warminster, 1972), pp. 74-75, p. 493; cf. Hayes and Miller, pp. 678-683.

allowed for the dating of Solomon's reign, and the figures of 430 and 480 may themselves be round estimates. However, adopting the date of 1877 B.C. as an approximate baseline, the lives of the patriarchs are dated as follows by the chronological material in Genesis:

Table 2

Approx. date B.C.	Event	Ages	Ref.
2092	Abraham's migration from Haran	Abraham 75	12:14
2067	Isaac born	Abraham 100	21:5
2031	Sarah dies, aged 127	Abraham 136	23:1
2007	Jacob born	Abraham 160 Isaac 60	25:26
1992	Abraham dies	Abraham 175 Isaac 75	25:7
1887	Isaac dies	Isaac 180 Jacob 120	35:28-9
1877	Jacob and family move to Egypt	Jacob 130	47:9

This dating scheme places Abraham's life almost entirely before 2000 B.C., and therefore in MB I: part of Isaac's life, before his move from Beer-lahai-roi to Gerar (cf. 25:11 and 26:1), is also allowed to fall within MB I, before the depopulation of the Negeb. It is tempting to speculate that the famine which drove Isaac from the southern Negeb to Gerar was part of the change in conditions which led to the depopulation of the Negeb as a whole at the end of MB I.[142] Jacob's life after his return from the household of Laban falls satisfactorily within MB II.

This scheme of dating relies on the ages attributed to the individual patriarchs by Genesis, and many scholars would reject this information as unreliable and the ages as impossible. Thompson remarks: 'That Abraham lived 175 years has to be taken seriously,

[142]For recent attempts to reconstruct times of climatic change during the third to second millennia B.C., see B. Bell, 'The Dark Ages in Ancient History: I. The First Dark Age in Egypt', *AJA* 75, 1971, pp. 1-26; idem, 'Climate and the History of Egypt: The Middle Kingdom', *AJA* 79, 1975, pp. 223-269.

but it is nonsense from an historical critical perspective.'[143] He also says of the data discussed above: 'It does not appear that we can use any of the extant chronological systems to arrive at an absolute date for the patriarchal period. They were not constructed

---

[143]Thompson, *Historicity*, p. 13. It would be quite wrong to insist that the ages reached by Abraham, Isaac and Jacob are intrinsically impossible; see A. Leaf and J. Launois, *National Geographic* 143/1, 1973, pp. 93-118, discussing remarkable examples of longevity among peasant communities of the Caucasus Mountains, Hunza (Kashmir) and Vilcabamba (Equador), where ages of between 130 and 150 are not uncommon. (The article actually mentions one alleged 168-year-old!) It is not impossible that environmental conditions in the third to early second millennium B.C. were such as to allow great ages to be reached frequently in the ancient near east. (For a recent ingenious attempt to provide a scientific framework for biblical longevity and its abatement, see D. W. Patten and P. A. Patten, 'A Comprehensive Theory on Aging, Gigantism and Longevity', *Catastrophism and Ancient History* 2/1, 1979, pp. 13-60.) Extra-biblical sources do not generally provide data which allow us to check this possibility, but some evidence is at least consistent with it. The Egyptians considered a lifespan of 110 years to be the ideal, and it seems reasonable to suggest that this notion arose at a time when men sometimes reached such an age without the ravages of extreme senility. Janssen lists references to this ideal, the earliest example dating back to the Egyptian Old Kingdom (third millennium B.C.): J. M. A. Janssen, 'On the Ideal Lifetime of the Egyptians', *Oudheidkundige Mededelingen uit het Rijksmuseum van Oudheden te Leiden* 3, 1950, pp. 33-44, discussed by J. Vergote, *Joseph en Égypt* (Louvain, 1959), pp. 200-201. An Egyptian pharaoh of the Old Kingdom, Pepi II, is given a *reign* of over 90 years by both Manetho (99 years) and the Turin Canon (90+x years), which implies a life somewhat in excess of a century (though Africanus admittedly adds: 'Began to reign at the age of six and continued to a hundred'). Such a lifespan could, of course, have been exceptional. No other reigns of that order are recorded, though Manetho's lists for the first six dynasties (see conveniently A. Gardiner, *Egypt of the Pharaohs* (OUP, 1961), pp. 430-436 attribute reigns in excess of forty years to some dozen kings, and reigns of sixty years or more to five of them; on the other hand, neither the Turin Canon nor the monuments support any of these figures, apart form the long reign of Pepi II mentioned above and the Turin Canon actually contradicts some of them. The latter source does, however, give Inyotef II and Menthotpe I of Dyn. XI reigns of forty-nine and fifty-one years respectively (and perhaps gives forty-four years to Pepi II's predecessor Merenre in Dyn. VI; Gardiner, op. cit., p. 436; on Dyn. XI see p. 438). The monuments confirm long reigns (30, 44, 35, 33 and 45 years) for five kings of Dyn. XII (ibid., p. 439). Although long reigns undeniably occur in later dynasties too (fifty-four years for Tuthmosis III, sixty-seven years for Ramesses II, 54 years for Psammetichus I, 44 years for Amasis), there does seem to be a slightly greater concentration of them in this early period, i.e. at least in Dyns. XI-XII, and perhaps in earlier dynasties too if some of Manetho's figures are reliable. This may point to long lifespans at this period (third-early second millennium); further research is needed to throw more light on the situation.

from the point of view of the historical critical method, and it is methodologically unsound to treat them as if they were'.[144] The above results show, however, that it is precisely the dating of the patriarchal age by the internal biblical chronology which provides the best solution to the problem of archaeological background. But the above survey of the chronological material has not been undertaken with the aim of supporting the biblical chronology; the aim was rather to show that the biblical chronology is simply compatible with the placement of the patriarchal period suggested by the bulk of the archaeological evidence.

CONCLUSION

Discussions of the dating of the patriarchal age in relation to archaeological periods have tended to disregard the length of the patriarchal age itself. The result is that an 'either/or' choice has been presented by discussions of the appropriateness of MB I and MB II. This is particularly true of Dever's treatment,[145] which, by stressing that neither period is an appropriate background to the patriarchal age as a whole, reinforces the negative conclusions of Thompson and van Seters concerning the historicity of the patriarchal narratives.

This paper has tried to contribute to the debate by emphasizing the length of the patriarchal age as envisaged in Genesis, thus showing that it was quite long enough to span the major changes in patterns of settlement which occurred during the transition from MB I to MB II. Such a setting is in accord with the biblical dating of the patriarchs.

Without pretending that this removes every trace of disharmony between the patriarchal narratives and archaeological evidence, it can be said that it offers by far the most complete solution to the problems raised in this area by recent scholarship. Remaining traces of disharmony, e.g. concerning Hebron, and possibly Ai, can be explained in a variety of ways, the most likely cause being our ignorance of the correct location of the early settlements. Such problems should certainly not be treated as proof of the unhistorical nature of the narratives, in view of the limitations of archaeological evidence and the uncertainties surrounding its

[144]Thompson, *Historicity*, pp. 15-16.
[145]Dever in Hayes and Miller, pp. 99, 102.

interpretation. From the point of view of the Palestinian archaeological evidence, there is certainly no reason to reject an early setting for the events of the patriarchal narratives, and ideally those events should be placed within the twenty-first to nineteenth centuries B.C.

4
Comparative Customs and the Patriarchal Age
M. J. Selman

1. CONSTRUCTION OF A NEW CONSENSUS

1.1 *The rise of the consensus*

In the first major publication of the cuneiform texts from ancient Nuzi,[1] C. J. Gadd reported a brief suggestion of Sidney Smith that text no. 51 in Gadd's collection offered a 'very remarkable parallel' to the incident of Rachel's theft of the household gods as described in Genesis 31.[2] Smith's comment, however, was not seen at the time as being of much importance. The prevailing scholarly view ascribed little historical value to the patriarchal narratives, whether one followed Wellhausen (who believed that they provide 'no historical knowledge of the patriarchs, but only of the time when the stories about them arose in the Israelite people'),[3] or Gunkel (who identified the stories about the patriarchs as saga, a genre essentially different from historical writing). Although Gunkel recognized that saga may well contain historical data, he concluded that no adequate means existed of distinguishing between what is reliable history and what is not.[4] Yet despite this background, Smith's proposal became the harbinger of a succession of important studies linking the patriarchal narratives with various collections of Mesopotamian and Syrian cuneiform texts dating mainly from the second millennium B.C.

The appearance of this comparative wealth of newly excavated material led eventually to a widespread consensus, at least in the

---

[1] *RA* 23,1926, pp. 49-161. Although the majority of Gadd's collection of texts came from nearby Arrapha (pp. 50-52), they are sufficiently homogeneous with those from Nuzi to be treated together.

[2] Ibid., p. 127.

[3] J. Wellhausen, *Prolegomena to the history of Israel* (A. & C. Black, Edinburgh, 1885), pp. 318-319.

[4] H. Gunkel, *The Legends of Genesis* (Schocken, New York, 1964), pp. 1-12; idem, *Genesis* (Vandenhoeck & Ruprecht, Göttingen, [2]1902), XI-XVI.

English-speaking world, that a reliable historical setting could be established for the biblical patriarchs. A quotation from G. E. Wright expresses clearly the new conclusions that had been reached. Writing in 1960, he said, 'We shall probably never be able to prove that Abram really existed, that he did this or that, said thus and so, but what we can prove is that his life and times, as reflected in the stories about him, fit perfectly within the early second millennium, but imperfectly within any later period.'[5] The greatest influence in confirming and consolidating this position has probably been J. Bright's *History of Israel*,[6] where it is claimed that 'one is forced to the conclusion that the patriarchal narratives authentically reflect social customs at home in the second millennium rather than those of later Israel'.[7]

In the space of little more than three decades a fundamental change had thus taken place in the scholarly assessment of the biblical patriarchs. A whole series of reasons was advanced in favour of this new understanding, including such wide-ranging subjects as personal names, movements of peoples, political alliances, religious ideas and practices, and social customs.[8] In every case, a prominent though not necessarily pre-eminent position was accorded to the evidence of the social customs, for the patriarchal practices had been shown to be parallel in many cases

[5]G. E. Wright, *Biblical Archaeology* (Westminster Press, Philadelphia; Duckworth, London, ²1962), p. 40.

[6]J. Bright, *History of Israel* (Westminster Press, Philadelphia, 1959; SCM, London, 1960). The chapter on the patriarchs in the second edition of 1972 is slightly more cautious, but the major conclusions remain unaltered. All references in footnotes will be to the second edition.

[7]Ibid., p. 79.

[8]For more details concerning the main arguments, see, e.g., J. Bright, *History*, pp. 78ff.; W. F. Albright, *The Biblical Period from Abraham to Ezra* (Harper, New York, 1963), pp. 1-9; idem, *Yahweh and the Gods of Canaan* (Athlone, London, 1968), pp. 47-95; H. H. Rowley, 'Recent discoveries and the Patriarchal Age', *BJRL* 32, 1949-1950, pp. 44-79 (= *The Servant of the Lord and Other Essays* [Blackwell, Oxford, ²1965], pp. 281-318); R. de Vaux, *RB* 53, 1946, pp. 321-348; 55, 1948, pp. 321-347; 56, 1949, pp. 5-36; C. H. Gordon, *Introduction to Old Testament Times* (Ventnor Publ., Ventnor, NJ), 1953, pp. 100f.; idem. *Journal of Bible and Religion* 21, 1953, pp. 238-243; R. T. O'Callaghan, *CBQ* 6, 1944, pp. 391-405; G. E. Wright, op. cit., pp. 40-52; K. A. Kitchen, *Ancient Orient and Old Testament* (Tyndale, London, 1966), pp. 41-53; R. Martin-Achard, *Actualité d'Abraham* (Delachaux, Neuchatel, 1969); A. Parrot, *Abraham et son temps* (Delachaux, Neuchatel, 1962) (= *Abraham and his Times* [Fortress, Philadelphia, 1968]).

to those known from a variety of places and periods in the ancient near east. Arguments concerning these customs, therefore, played a major part in the modern reconstruction of the Patriarchal Age, and without such considerations, the case for patriarchal historicity, quite apart from any question of a date for the Patriarchal Age, would be seriously weakened.

1.2 *Variant presentations of the consensus*

Although one may rightly speak of a consensus about the establishment of a historical setting for the patriarchs, significant variations can be discerned in both the arguments employed and the conclusions reached on the subject of social customs. W. F. Albright, for instance, proposed that Abraham's relationship with Eliezer (Gn. 15:1-6) could be explained by adoption practices at Nuzi, a view that was developed in two stages.[9] In the fuller expression of this theory, Albright understood adoption at Nuzi as a means whereby an adopter could obtain credit from his adoptee who was in reality a moneylender, in order to buy supplies, donkeys, and other equipment for caravaneering or related activities. This understanding was particularly attractive in that Damascus was an important caravan centre and it was therefore quite appropriate that Eliezer, apparently a 'Damascene',[10] should be cast in the role of a moneylender. Albright's reconstruction, the sole instance of a Nuzi custom employed by him in his interpretation of the patriarchs, was in fact only a part of his larger theory which portrayed Abraham as a donkey-caravaneer of the Middle Bronze I period.[11] This view of Abraham was based more on archaeological considerations than on customary law, but neither Albright's theory as a whole, nor his use

[9]W. F. Albright, *The Archaeology of Palestine and the Bible* (Revell, New York, 1932), pp. 138 and 209, n. 25; idem, 'Abram the Hebrew: A New Archaeological Interpretation', *BASOR* 163, 1961, pp. 36-54. See also, idem, *The Biblical Period from Abraham to Ezra* (Harper, New York, 1963), pp. 7-8; *Yahweh and the Gods of Canaan* (Athlone, London, 1968) p. 58.

[10]Gn. 15:2. For the textual problems of Gn. 15:2-3, see M. Weippert, *Bib* 52, 1971, p. 420, n. 1; and especially H. L. Ginsberg, *BASOR* 200, 1970, for the difficulties involved in Albright's translation 'Damascene' (quoted in M. F. Unger, *Israel and the Arameans of Damascus* (J. Clarke, London, 1957), p. 114, n. 21.

[11]W. F. Albright, 'Abram the Hebrew: a New Archaeological Interpretation', *BASOR* 163, 1961, pp. 36-54.

of Nuzi adoption practices in illuminating Eliezer's role, has met with much acceptance.[12] From the biblical side, there is the problem that the picture of Abraham as Eliezer's financial dependant and as a trader between Damascus and Egypt remains purely hypothetical. Similarly, in the Nuzi 'sale adoptions', to which Albright appeals for support, there is no evidence that adoptees functioned as moneylenders or adopters as merchants. If any comparison is possible between the Nuzi texts and Genesis 15, it must be on the basis of the real adoption texts and not the so-called 'sale adoptions'.[13]

Although Albright's use of social customs in determining the background of the patriarchs is slender and hypothetical, the same cannot be said of C. H. Gordon. Gordon gave particular attention to the Nuzi texts as a source of comparison for the patriarchal narratives. In an influential and comprehensive article published in 1940,[14] well over twenty biblical passages were illuminated by the Nuzi material, the majority concerning the patriarchal narratives. His conclusion that the Nuzi texts 'tie in so closely with the patriarchal narratives that it is generally agreed that a close sociological relationship exists between the two sets of texts'[15] provided the dominant reason for his being able to establish a clear historical background for the patriarchs. Because of this strong emphasis on the social background, and in the light of other material from El Amarna and especially from Ugarit, Gordon argued that the Patriarchal Age should be set in the fourteenth century B.C., although this date was significantly later than that proposed by the majority of scholars who were equally confident of the historicity of the patriarchs.[16] Gordon also found support

[12]For a detailed refutation of Albright's interpretation of Abraham, see M. Weippert, *Bib* 52, 1971, pp. 407-432.

[13]For the interpretation of these texts, see E. Chiera and E. A. Speiser, *JAOS* 47, 1927, pp. 36-40; E. Cassin, *L'adoption à Nuzi* (Maisonneuve, Paris, 1938), pp. 1-48; H. Lewy, *OrNS* 11, 1942, pp. 15-32; N. B. Jankowska, in I. M. Diakonoff (ed.), *Ancient Mesopotamia* (USSR Academy of Sciences, Moscow, 1969), pp. 235-252; T. L. Thompson, *Historicity of the Patriarchal Narratives* (BZAW 133), (De Gruyter, Berlin and New York, 1974), pp. 209-212.

[14]C. H. Gordon, 'Biblical customs and the Nuzi tablets', *BA* 3, 1940, pp. 1-12.

[15]A. Altmann (ed.), *Biblical and Other Studies* (Harvard UP, Cambridge, Mass., 1963), p. 5.

[16]C. H. Gordon, *JNES* 13, 1954, pp. 56-59; *Biblical and Other Studies*, pp. 5-6; *Introduction to Old Testament Times*, pp. 102ff. See also T. L. Thompson, *Historicity*, p. 201.

from within the Old Testament, on the basis of several genealogical texts which seemed to indicate a comparatively short
period between the time of the patriarchs and the exodus.[17] He did
not, on the other hand, take full account of the individual year
reckonings of the patriarchs nor the biblical tradition of a gap of
some four centuries between these two eras.[18]

A third distinctive approach was that of E. A. Speiser, whose
work enjoyed as much influence as Gordon's and who was, if
anything, even more confident about the relevance of the Nuzi
customs for the biblical patriarchs. He proposed more that twenty
cases where the Nuzi texts elucidated the book of Gensis alone,
mainly in the sphere of family law.[19] Many of Gordon's examples
were accepted, but Speiser advocated in addition the existence of
parallels to Isaac's deathbed blessing[20] and the custom of wife-
sister marriage.[21]

Two features of Speiser's argument are worthy of note here.
First, he was more cautious than either Albright or Gordon about
positing a date for the patriarchs, though like them he believed
that there was sufficient evidence to confirm the biblical picture
of a patriarchal era, even if the latter was not necessarily accurate
in every detail. In the absence of any direct synchronism between
the patriarchal narratives and other texts, Speiser accepted that
the patriarchal period 'must technically be put down as prehistoric'.[22] He did nevertheless advocate what had become a widely
accepted setting for the patriarchs in the second quarter of the
second millennium B.C. By this he meant the latter part of the Old
Babylonian period from Hammurapi onwards,[23] a date that was
different again from those of Albright and Gordon.

---

[17]Jos. 7:1; Nu. 26:5ff.; cf. Gn. 15:16.

[18]Gn. 15:13; Ex. 12:40; cf. Gn. 15:16. Both H. H. Rowley (*From Joseph to
Joshua*, Oxford UP, London, 1950, pp. 57-77) and O. Eissfeldt (CAH 2/2, 1975,
p. 312) have proposed a similar date for the patriarchs on grounds similar to
those of Gordon, though Eissfeldt gives little weight to the extrabiblical material.

[19]E. A. Speiser, *Genesis* (Anchor Bible, Doubleday, New York, 1964).

[20]Gn. 27:1ff. 'I Know Not the Day of my Death', *JBL* 74, 1955, pp. 252-256.

[21]Gn. 12:10-20; 20:1-18; 26:6-11. 'The wife-sister motif in the patriarchal narratives', in A. Altmann (ed.), *Biblical and Other Studies*, pp. 15-28 (reprinted in
J. J. Finkelstein and M. Greenberg, ed., *Oriental and Biblical Studies*, University
of Pennsylvania, Philadelphia, 1967, pp. 62-82.

[22]*Genesis*, xliii.

[23]Ibid., xliv.

The second significant feature of Speiser's approach concerns his interpretation of the manner in which some of these customs were recorded in Genesis. In his view, the compilers of the biblical traditions had handed down only the bare facts, without reference to the real reasoning and motivation that lay behind the present accounts of the customs. The original social background had become blurred in the biblical text. Indeed, the original background could no longer be recovered from the Old Testament in some cases, and could be restored only through the cuneiform data of Nuzi. These textual variations led Speiser to two complementary hypothetical solutions: (a) that there had been a lengthy period of oral transmission behind the written sources J, E, and P, and (b) that the traditions of individual practices had been handed down through a common international antecendent, labelled conveniently as 'T'.[24] Thus in several crucial instances, Speiser was comparing Nuzi customs not with Genesis, whose compilers no longer understood the practices they recorded, but with some hypothetical pre-biblical tradition whose existence and content were determined only by the few specific examples quoted by Speiser.[25]

1.3 Methods and conclusions of the consensus

Despite these variations, the common ground of these writers and many others who participated in the new consensus was far stronger than their differences in approach. For instance, the method by which parallel examples of social customs were established showed little real divergence. In many cases, one or two biblical passages, usually with only an incomplete record of a particular custom, were compared with a small number of cuneiform texts. Although Speiser in particular attempted to widen the basis of comparison as much as possible, in most instances only a very limited amount of comparative material was employed, often amounting to a single text or even part of a text.[26] It was almost

---

[24]Ibid., xxxvii-xliii.

[25]See also T. L. Thompson, *Historicity*, p. 202. Apparently van Seters' rather general objections are also directed at Speiser's method (J. van Seters, *Abraham in history and tradition*, Yale UP, New Haven and London, 1975, pp. 67-68).

[26]In many cases too, general works on the patriarchal period quoted only a small number of cuneiform texts in their comparisons, of which the majority were usually from Nuzi (cf. M. J. Selman, *TB* 27, 1976, pp. 116-117).

invariably assumed, in addition, that the examples used were typical for their date and location, although this can by no means be taken for granted. Thus the unsuspecting reader of general works on the patriarchal period gained little knowledge of the wider context out of which the claimed parallels arose, even though he was frequently given the strong impression that the case for the patriarchs's historicity was almost beyond dispute.

In practice, there were three distinct ways in which non-biblical data were employed in the setting up of such parallels. First, there were straightforward cases in which the cuneiform material simply provided extra examples of practices already known in Genesis. These included the supposed introductory formula used in death-bed dispositions, 'and now I have grown old (Gn. 27:2),[27] the sale of a birthright to another brother (Gn. 25:29-34),[28] or the father-in-law's restriction ensuring that his daughter would not be displaced by a second wife (Gn. 31:50).[29] The second method amplified the biblical material by furnishing a more detailed background, as in the case of the Old Babylonian shepherding contracts and Genesis 31,[30] or the various examples of a barren wife providing her husband with her slavegirl in order to raise up children (Gn. 16:1-4; 30:1-13).[31]

The third method yields the largest number of examples, but many of them are also the most controversial cases. In such instances, the extrabiblical data has been employed not only to provide a fuller background for the biblical material, but also to offer an explanation for the existence of a biblical practice which is only poorly understood. Examples include Laban's adoption of Jacob (Gn. 29-31),[32] the adoption of Eliezer by Abraham (Gn. 15:1-4),[33] and the practice of wife-sister marriage (Gn. 12:10-20; 20:1-18; 26:6-11).[34] In these and other similar cases, the attempts to

---

[27]E. A. Speiser, *JBL* 74, 1955, pp. 252-256, cf. C. H. Gordon, *BA* 3, 1940, p. 8.

[28]C. H. Gordon, ibid., p. 5.

[29]C. H. Gordon, *BASOR* 66, 1937, p. 26; cf. M. J. Selman, loc. cit., p. 130.

[30]J. J. Finkelstein, *JAOS* 88, 1968, pp. 30-36; cf. R. Frankena, *OTS* 17, 1972, pp. 58-59.

[31]C. H. Gordon, *RB* 44, 1935, p. 35; cf. M. J. Selman, loc. cit., pp. 127-129.

[32]C. H. Gordon, *BASOR* 66, 1937, pp. 25-27; *BA* 3, 1940, pp. 5-7; *Introduction to Old Testament Times*, pp. 115-118; *Biblical and Other Studies*, p. 6.

[33]W. F. Albright, *The Archaeology of Palestine*, pp. 138 and 209, n. 25; C. H. Gordon, *BA* 3, 1940, pp. 2-3; M. J. Selman, loc. cit., pp. 125-127.

[34]E. A. Speiser, *Biblical and Other Studies*, pp. 15-28. But cf. also, C. J. Mullo Weir, *Transactions of the Glasgow University Oriental Society* 22, 1967/8,

fill in the gaps in our understanding of the biblical evidence have not always met with much success. Two major difficulties have arisen. First, on some occasions (as in the case of wife-sister marriage or the function of household gods/teraphim as a title to an inheritance) a proposed custom has now been found to be without support in the non-biblical texts, and therefore cannot be employed as a means of elucidating a biblical passage. In such instances, the interpretation of the problems in Genesis must be sought in other directions. The second problem concerns those cases where the cuneiform material has been compared with a hypothetical pre-biblical form of the biblical text. This procedure, which was used particularly by Speiser[35] though it was unconsciously pioneered by Gordon in his novel interpretation of the Jacob-Laban narratives,[36] inevitably makes any comparison established on the basis of it equally hypothetical, and is therefore of only minimal use in any discussion of patriarchal historicity.

There are two main conclusions for our understanding of the biblical patriarchs. First, the re-establishment of the Patriarchal Age has become readily and widely accepted. Indeed, for Bright, 'so massive is the evidence for it that we cannot begin to review it all'.[37] Nevertheless, one ought to be aware at this juncture of two matters which should encourage a slightly more cautious attitude: (1) Although the modern understanding of the patriarchs has been modelled on the biblical pattern, it has actually been constructed with the materials of modern historical research. Despite the existence of much relevant cuneiform evidence, there remains no direct extrabiblical reference to the patriarchal clans. The basis of the modern consensus, therefore, is indirect, extrabiblical evidence as it can be shown to correspond with biblical material. When it is subsequently discovered that some of the bricks in this

pp. 14-25; D. Freedman, *Journal of the Ancient Near Eastern Society of Columbia University* 2/2, 1970, pp. 77-85; T. L. Thompson, *Historicity*, pp. 234-248; M. J. Selman, loc. cit., pp. 119-121; S. Greengus, *HUCA* 46, 1975, pp. 5-31; H. Shanks, *Biblical Archaeology Review* 1/3, 1975, pp. 22-26.

[35]See above, pp. 95-96.

[36]C. H. Gordon's frequently quoted statement that the Jacob-Laban narratives have taken on 'an entirely new meaning in light of the Nuzi documents' (*BASOR* 66, 1937, p. 25), and his treatment of Genesis 29-31 in ibid., 25-27; cf. also J. Bright, *History*, p. 79.

[37]J. Bright, *History*, p. 76.

reconstructed edifice do no fit at all in their supposed contexts, it is therefore not necessarily the Old Testament which is at fault. On the contrary, it is some of the modern stones rather than the ancient ones which (it has now been discovered) do not fit in the work of reconstruction. (2) In the modern re-establishment of the Patriarchal Age, it is readily assumed that, while the comparisons which have been made comprise only a relatively small and random collection of examples, they actually represent a much greater wealth of material yet to be uncovered and interpreted. This will also increasingly confirm the picture of the Patriarchal Age currently being drawn. Whether such an assumption is justified continues to be a matter of debate, but it is important to understand that the conclusions about historicity are much more wide-ranging than the historically demonstrable comparisons which form their base. From the point of view of the historian who assigns no independent historical value to the patriarchal narrative, the social background is only beginning to be drawn, while those scholars who are more positive about the reliability of Genesis 12-50 need to be aware of the limits as well as the benefits of cuneiform data, especially as it relates to social customs.

The second conclusion about the Patriarchal Age is that many scholars are confident that a definite historical setting can be found for it, even though the details cannot be precisely fixed. Despite the lack of agreement, as shown by the varying results of Albright, Gordon, and Speiser,[38] there is in fact greater unanimity than is sometimes acknowledged on the date of the Patriarchal Age. All these scholars, for instance, concur in placing the patriarchs in the second millennium B.C. at a period prior to the exodus. There is also clearly a majority view that places the Patriarchal Age between the twentieth and sixteenth centuries B.C.,[39] i.e. in the Middle Bronze II period,[40] against which the opinions of Albright and Gordon are notable exceptions. Significantly too, since certain Israelite customs as found mainly in the legal portions of the Old Testament are contradictory to those

[38]See also the criticisms of J. van Seters (*Abraham*, pp. 8-9), and W. G. Dever, in J. H. Hayes and J. M. Miller (ed.), *Israelite and Judean History* (SCM, London, 1977), pp. 91-96.

[39]J. Bright, *History*, p. 83.

[40]W. G. Dever, *Israelite and Judean History*, p. 95.

recorded in the patriarchal narratives, the weight of external evidence is supported by inner-biblical testimony.[41]

The lack of precision can be explained by a number of factors. First, many of the problems arise from the difficulties in interpreting the biblical chronology concerning the patriarchs, in particular the information contained in the genealogies. The Late Bronze Age dates of Gordon, Eissfeldt, and Rowley rely heavily on the existence of four or five generations between the patriarchal and exodus eras as suggested by certain genealogical texts, but it is now well known that ancient near-eastern genealogies were not compiled on the principle of completeness and are therefore unhelpful for dating purposes.[42] Secondly, the indirect nature of extrabiblical data also contributes to imprecise dating, a problem that is not altered by the exact dates found in some of the relevant cuneiform tablets. Finally, since social customs are often extremely difficult to limit chronologically, they too are of little advantage in finding a precise setting for the patriarchs. The lack of exactness therefore does not mean that no real consensus exists. Rather, those who have aligned themselves with this viewpoint have accepted that the Patriarchal Age can be historically determined from external as well as from internal sources, and in so doing, they stand poles apart from the positions of Wellhausen and Gunkel which they inherited.

2. THE DESTRUCTION OF THE CONSENSUS

The position described above was never universally recognized. Initially, opposition was cautious, and even the most sceptical

[41]Three clear cases of conflict between the pentateuchal laws and patriarchal custom can be distinguished: (1) the patriarchal birthright appears to have included the major part of the father's property (Gn. 25:5-6), whereas in Dt. 21:15-17 the eldest's share is strictly defined as a double share (or perhaps 'two-thirds', cf. M. Noth, *Die Ursprünge des alten Israel*, Arbeitsgemeinschaft für Forschung des Landes Nordrhein-Westfalen, Köln, 1961, pp. 19-20. J. van Seters *Abraham*, p. 92); (2) marriage to two sisters is forbidden in Lv. 18:18, contrary to Jacob's union with Leah and Rachel (Gn. 29:15-30); and (3) Abraham's marriage to his half-sister Sarah (Gn. 20:12) would be prohibited according to Lv. 18:9, 11; 20:7; Dt. 27:22; cf. Ezk. 22:11; 2 Sa. 13:13. For a recent investigation into the relationship between Old Testament law and Israelite practice, see H. McKeating, 'Sanctions against Adultery in Ancient Israelite Society', *JSOT* 11, 1979, pp. 57-72.

[42]See e.g., R. R. Wilson, *Genealogy and History in the Biblical World* (Yale UP, New Haven and London, 1977), pp. 33-36, 65-69, 126, 162-163, 197; K. A. Kitchen, *Ancient Orient and Old Testament* (Tyndale, London, 1966), pp. 36-39.

writers appeared to accept the validity of at least a few of the proposed comparisons. Gradually, however, the momentum was increased through an unco-ordinated series of attacks which were launched against individual proposals. They did not at first call into question the whole theory, but led eventually to the full-scale challenges of Thompson and van Seters.[43] Since the appearance of these two works, the entire concept of a historical Patriarchal Age has been seriously questioned and vigorously debated, and much of the old consensus now lies in ruins.

2.1 Cautious acceptance

Three stages can be discerned in the build up to the present position as represented by Thompson and van Seters. First, there were those such as de Vaux and Mullo Weir who, while recognizing that real advances had been made, were noticeably cautious in accepting the prevailing view. Indeed, the hesitancy of both tended to increase, although their conclusions developed in different directions. De Vaux in particular became much more reserved in his later writings, both in his assessment of the value of comparative customs and in his conclusions about even the basic character of a Patriarchal Age. In an initial series of articles published between 1946 and 1949,[44] however, de Vaux appeared enthusiastic, acknowledging that the patriarchal narratives had preserved 'a treasure-store of exact reminiscences' concerning Israelite origins.[45] His approach to the question of comparative social customs was more muted, concluding that most of the analogies were imperfect, and in some cases rather uncertain.[46] But in his later work, especially in his *Early History of Israel*, initially published in French in 1971,[47] de Vaux saw the extra-biblical customs as being of value only in bringing the patriarchal narratives into the general social and legal pattern of the ancient

---

[43]T. L. Thompson, *Historicity of the Patriarchal Narratives* (BZAW 133, De Gruyter, Berlin and New York, 1974); J. van Seters, *Abraham in History and Tradition* (Yale UP, New Haven and London, 1975).

[44]R. de Vaux, 'Les patriarches Hebreux et les découvertes modernes', *RB* 53, 1946, pp. 321-348; 55, 1948, pp. 321-347; 56, 1949, pp. 5-36.

[45]*RB* 53, 1946, p. 328.

[46]See, for example, his comments on the adoptions of Eliezer and Jacob, and the interpretation of Laban's household gods, *RB* 56, 1949, pp. 34-35.

[47]*The Early History of Israel* (Darton, Longman & Todd, London, 1978), translated from *Histoire ancienne d'Israel* (Gabalda, Paris, 1971). See also *RB* 72, 1965, pp. 5-28.

near east, and he rejected many of the standard examples of Gordon and Speiser.[48] The customs gave no help in determining either the historicity or the date of the patriarchs,[49] and 'very few real points of contact and similarity between the biblical and extrabiblical data can now be established at all'.[50]

The work of Mullo Weir[51] is in many ways parallel to the earlier contributions of de Vaux, acknowledging that near-eastern social customs helped to a certain extent to validate Israelite tradition.[52] The distinctiveness of his position was his emphasis on customs for which parallels existed from a wide range of locations in the ancient Near East. For Mullo Weir, the customs practised by the Nuzians were not greatly different from those of their Semitic neighbours, and since many Mesopotamian customs were probably observed in Palestine, it was not surprising that significant contacts existed with the Nuzi texts as well as with material from other sources. Thus, in his view, the basis of comparison was not a heavy dependence on the single site of Nuzi but a much wider foundation altogether. Potentially at least, the Patriarchal Age was being made more secure without the doubtful advantage of a direct relationship with Nuzi tied around its neck.

2.2 No Patriarchal Age

The responses of Noth and von Rad were at first very different, though Noth's position became closer to those just described, especially to that of de Vaux.[53] Neither Noth nor von Rad was able to speak with any confidence of a Patriarchal Age,[54] but both did accept the validity of at least a few parallels with the social

[48] For example, the following customs were seen as irrelevant for Genesis 12-50; the use of household gods as a title to an inheritance, the parallels to Jacob's purchase of birthright, the adoptions of Eliezer and Jacob, the practice of errēbu and wife-sister marriages.

[49] R. de Vaux, *Early History*, 1, pp. 241-256.

[50] Ibid., p. 259.

[51] C. J. Mullo Weir, 'Nuzi', in D. W. Thomas (ed.), *Archaeology and Old Testament Study* (Oxford UP, London, 1967), pp. 73-86.

[52] Ibid., p. 83.

[53] For the view that Noth and Bright stand closer to each other than is often represented, see J. A. Soggin, *BA* 23, 1960, pp. 95-100; R. de Vaux, *Bible et Orient* (Éditions du Cerf, Paris, 1967), pp. 175-185, = *The Bible and the Ancient Near East*, (Darton, Longman & Todd, London, 1972), pp. 111-121.

[54] Cf. M. Noth, *VTS* 7, 1959, p. 267.

customs of Nuzi.[55] On the basis of connections with Nuzi and the Amorites of the Mari texts, Noth acknowledged that 'the beginnings of Israel are rooted in historical presuppositions which are proved by archaeological discoveries to be located in the middle of the second millennium B.C.'[56] But Noth was unable to go beyond this, for two main reasons. The comparisons dealt not with historical events but with relationships and ways of life, and both he and von Rad gave priority to the results of literary criticism and tradition history in the study of the patriarchal narratives. Even though von Rad emphasized the historical origins of the patriarchal sagas, their historicity rested in the 'community's experience of faith', and it was not possible to discover what historical events lay behind individual incidents.[57] The effect of near-eastern social customs therefore was to shed only little light on the biblical patriarchs.[58]

2.3 Challenges to individual customs

This extreme caution was gradually followed by a series of challenges to what had become the standard interpretation of certain patriarchal customs. This development was initiated by Greenberg, who in 1964 questioned whether the household gods of Nuzi and Laban's family had anything to do with a title to an inheritance.[59] It was his opinion that the possessor of such images was probably the head of the family unit, and that theft of the gods could not achieve for Rachel or Jacob privileges legally conferred by bequeathal.[60] Within a few years, Mullo Weir published a similarly devastating and detailed assault on Speiser's theory of wife-sister marriage,[61] and like Greenberg, he argued

[55]M. Noth, 'Hat die Bibel doch Recht?', in W. Schneemelcher (ed.), *Festschrift für G. Dehn* (Neukirchener Verlag, Neukirchen, 1957), pp. 7-22; G. von Rad, *Genesis*, (SCM, London, ³1972), pp. 184, 191, 192, 310.

[56]M. Noth, *VTS* 7, 1959, pp. 269-270.

[57]G. von Rad, *Genesis*, pp. 30-42.

[58]M. Noth, *VTS* 7, 1959, p. 270.

[59]M. Greenberg, 'Another look at Rachel's theft of the *teraphim*', *JBL* 81, 1962, pp. 239-248.

[60]Ibid., pp. 241-245; cf. M. J. Selman, loc. cit., pp. 123-124; R. Frankena, *OTS* 17, 1972, p. 56; H. Vorländer, *Mein Gott* (AOAT 23, Butzon & Bercker, Kevelaer, 1975), pp. 64-65, 178; T. L. Thompson, *Historicity*, pp. 272-278; J. van Seters, *Abraham*, pp. 93-94; R. de Vaux, *Early History*, 1, pp. 251-253.

[61]C. J. Mullo Weir, 'The Alleged Hurrian Wife-Sister Motif in Genesis', *Transactions of the Glasgow University Oriental Society* 22, 1967/8, pp. 14-25.

that both the Nuzi and Old Testament evidence had been mis-interpreted. Subsequent studies have confirmed that wife-sister marriage is nothing more than a modern invention.[62] Two articles by van Seters which appeared at about the same time as Mullo Weir's contribution emphasized what had now become a definite trend. First of all, he questioned whether the Nuzi adoption and marriage contract HSS 5 67[63] had any relevance for the patriarchal practice of an infertile wife providing a slavegirl for her husband,[64] and argued that the Nuzi tablet 'is so different from anything in the Old Testament that to use it as a parallel is more misleading than helpful'.[65] In the second article, van Seters contended that the concept of *errēbu* marriage, which had been used as a means of interpreting Jacob's marriages, did not exist even in its supposed Mesopotamian contexts,[66] labelling the whole idea as an 'academic fiction'.[67] The notion of Jacob's adoption was simultaneously discarded.

In most of these cases, it was argued that the supposed parallel customs had non-existent foundations in cuneiform texts, and they were therefore quite useless as a means of interpreting poorly understood patriarchal practices. The case of the barren wife and her slavegirl was different, however, for van Seters proposed that better parallels could be found in texts dating from the first millennium B.C. In the same connection, Abraham's purchase of the cave at Machpelah (Gn. 23) had also been recently compared with 'dialogue contracts', which were particularly prominent in

[62]For references, see above, n. 34.

[63]E. A. Speiser, *AASOR* 10, 1930, No. 2; J. B. Pritchard, *ANET*, p. 220; text only in E. Chiera, *Excavations at Nuzi*, 1 (Harvard Semitic Series, 5, Harvard UP, Cambridge, Mass., 1929, No. 67).

[64]J. van Seters, 'The problem of childlessness in Near Eastern law and the patriarchs of Israel', *JBL* 87, 1968, pp. 401-408; cf. M. J. Selman, loc. cit., pp. 127-129; R. Frankena, loc. cit., pp. 56-57; C. J. Mullo Weir, *Archaeology and Old Testament Study*, p. 75; T. L. Thompson, *Historicity*, pp. 253-269; G. von Rad, *Genesis*, p. 191; R. de Vaux, *Early History*, 1, pp. 244-245.

[65]J. van Seters, *JBL* 87, 1968, p. 405.

[66]J. van Seters, 'Jacob's Marriages and Ancient Near Eastern Customs: a Re-examination, *HTR* 62, 1969, pp. 377-395; cf. R. de Vaux, *RB* 56, 1949; idem, *Early History*, 1, pp. 246-247; R. Frankena, loc. cit., pp. 54-56; G. von Rad, *Genesis*, p. 310; T. L. Thompson, *Historicity*, pp. 269-280; M. J. Selman, loc. cit., pp. 124-125.

[67]J. van Seters, *HTR* 62, 1969, p. 388.

the Neo-Babylonian period.[68] Van Seters' preference for later parallels was not therefore just a lone voice crying in the wilderness.

2.4 *Total rejection*

The real explosion in patriarchal studies came a few yars later
with the appearance of the books by Thompson and van Seters.[69]
Both writers challenged the modern concept of a Patriarchal Age
so comprehensively that in the view of one commentator, 'it is
doubtful whether the theory for an early dating of the patriarchal
period can ever again be decently resurrected. Certainly it can
never be revived in its present form.'[70] Thus the question whether
any reliable historical memory of a Patriarchal Age exists at all is
now again in the forefront of discussion, in which the social
customs are still of primary significance, even though in some
quarters this subject has given way to more strictly archaeological
concerns.[71]

The objections of Thompson and van Seters to the earlier
consensus are considerable, and their questions concerning the
customs will be discussed in detail below. Initially, however, it is
important to recognize that they are united only in opposing the
consensus and that their own solutions are greatly at variance
with each other. For Thompson, 'the quest for the historical
Abraham is a basically fruitless occupation',[72] since he understands Genesis as a 'collection of literary traditions'[73] and stories
which are best compared with other tales and literary motifs.[74]
His work is a conscious attempt to turn the clock back more than
half a century to the methods of Gunkel, Gressmann, and Galling;

---

[68]H. Petschow, *JCS* 19, 1965, pp. 103-120; G. M. Tucker, *JBL* 85, 1966,
pp. 77-84; cf. J. J. Rabinowitz, *Journal of Juristic Papyrology* 13, 1961, pp. 131-
135. This interpretation of Gn. 23 involved a rejection of Lehmann's view that
Abraham's purchase should be understood against the background of Hittite law
(*BASOR* 129, 1953, pp. 15-18).

[69]For reference, see above, n. 43.

[70]S. M. Warner, *JSOT* 2, 1977, p. 50, with full approval from J. M. Miller,
ibid., p. 62.

[71]Especially T. L. Thompson, *JSOT* 9, 1978, p. 2-43.

[72]T. L. Thompson, *Historicity*, p. 315.

[73]Ibid., p. 3.

[74]See D. Irvin, *Mytharion* (AOAT 32, Butzon & Bercker, Kevelaer, 1978), to
which Thompson frequently refers, cf. *Historicity*, pp. 202, 246, 293.

though of course Thompson's own approach is presented in modern form, and is not intended to be a mere repetition of earlier work.[75] Van Seters, on the other hand, accords a comparatively small place to oral tradition, preferring to understand the Abraham narratives as very largely the work of exilic and post-exilic authors. Building on the position of his earlier articles, he attempts to find a historical background for Abraham in the late monarchy and afterwards by the use of arguments concerning social customs, nomadism, etc., which have traditionally been employed as a basis for a second-millennium setting.

3. CURRENT DISCUSSION

The contributions of Thompson and van Seters have sparked off a lively discussion covering many important matters in the interpretation of the patriarchal way of life. In addition to a rigorous examination of individual customs, much debate has focused on questions of methodology. Two such issues, relating to the relationships between historical and literary approaches and between external and internal evidence, are of such a fundamental nature that they must be considered before other matters which relate more specifically to the customs.

3.1 *Historical and literary approaches*

The relationship between historical and literary approaches to the interpretation of the patriarchal narratives was raised by Thompson very early in his book, where he asserts that 'no part of Genesis can be assumed to be history unless its literary character can first be shown to be historiographical'.[76] Thus the primary use of archaeological data to determine historicity in the patriarchal narratives is inadmissible for Thompson, who gives priority instead to literary investigation. Yet he maintains no consistency on this crucial issue, and indeed, there is evidence of confusion in his approach. For he also says of the social customs: 'If the presentation of these parallels is as valid and as unique as has been claimed, the thesis that the stories do go back to a period

---

[75]T. L. Thompson, *Historicity*, p. 3, n. 6. Thompson's approach naturally involves a much greater use of archaeological material than that of these earlier scholars, but his interpretation of the patriarchal narratives follows closely their convictions concerning the unhistorical character of Genesis.

[76]T. L. Thompson, *Historicity*, p. 3.

prior to that of the Conquest must undoubtedly be accepted, and that at least a position similar to that of Martin Noth, that the patriarchal narratives do have at least an historical core, must be seen not only as historically possible but as likely.'[77] On the basis of this statement, which is equally as clear as the one quoted above, the archaeological data on their own are valid for establishing at least a minimum historical value for Genesis 12-50.

That Thompson's dilemma is no superficial oversight but a deepseated difficulty is confirmed at other points in the book. On the one hand, he chastises Wright and Albright for forming hypotheses about the patriarchs 'on the basis of unexamined biblical texts', which means here that they have given insufficient weight to form criticism and the history of traditions.[78] Yet on the other hand, he spends considerable energy in rebutting arguments based on archaeological data, even though such matters are supposedly of secondary importance in the literary investigation of the narratives. Even when he explains his own view that the patriarchal narratives are literature and not history, Thompson's interpretation is preceded by a much more lengthy discussion of the archaeological data.[79] By attempting therefore to discount the historicity of the patriarchal narratives mainly on the basis of archaeological and historical rather than literary arguments, Thompson tacitly acknowledges that both approaches are equally necessary. Even if it is argued that the main purpose of Thompson's book is to discuss the archaeological data commonly used to support the concept of a Patriarchal Age, positive reasons for a purely literary interpretation are remarkable for the brief space allotted to them.

This vital matter has also been taken up by others. J. M. Miller,[80] for instance, has underlined his basic agreement with Thompson's position by asserting that 'critical historians now have unavoidable grounds for suspicion that the very idea of a patriarchal age originated as a literary construct'.[81] Miller is

[77]Ibid., p. 201.

[78]Ibid., pp. 6-7.

[79]See e.g., *Historicity*, pp. 246-248 on the motif of 'Despoiling the Egyptians' in Gn. 12; p. 293 on the motif of 'The success of the Unpromising' in Gn. 27; and pp. 311-314 on the unhistorical genealogies of Gn. 11:10–12:9.

[80]J. M. Miller, 'The Patriarchs and Extra-biblical sources: a Response', *JSOT* 2, 1977, pp. 62-66.

[81]Ibid., p. 64.

concerned to defend form criticism as a method of primary importance in interpreting Genesis, and argues that the results of form critical study on the patriarchal narratives have led to 'a strong suspicion that this picture is historically untrustworthy'.[82]

A different approach, however, has been taken by J. T. Luke,[83] who objects to the either/or method of Thompson and van Seters, which in this context means either a literary or an historical/archaeological approach. Both methods of study are necessary, and since the Old Testament is a part of ancient near-eastern literature, the separation of these enquiries is evidence of an 'arbitrary methodological territorialism'.[84] Luke emphasizes that the obvious historiographical intent of the patriarchal narratives must be taken into account, and that in any case a late date is not a necessary consequence of their form-critical investigation.[85]

There can be no doubt of the importance of a proper literary study of Genesis 12-50 alongside a historical and archaeological approach, and one must not ignore the equally significant theological interests of the book. A balanced method does not put aside any evidence which may be of relevance, and takes fully into account the varied concerns which have produced the biblical Patriarchal Age. It is also quite clear, as recognized by Thompson and Miller, that the form-critical results of such writers as Gunkel, Noth, von Rad, or Irvin have led to an unfavourable appreciation of the historical value of the narratives, but such results cannot intrinsically prove or disprove their historical value. Miller can speak only of suspicion, and even Thompson counters the consensus on archaeological rather than on literary grounds. Indeed, these negative conclusions have been arrived at precisely because form criticism has often been employed in isolation from historical concerns, but as Luke has rightly recognized, such a one-sided approach is to 'preclude the outcome of this dispute by dictating the rules'.[86] Literary study of the patriarchal narratives certainly indicates their historiographical interests,[87] and some of these historical factors can now be tested by cuneiform and other

---

[82]Ibid., p. 64.
[83]J. T. Luke, 'Abraham and the Iron Age: Reflections on the New Patriarchal Studies', *JSOT* 4, 1977, pp. 35-47.
[84]Ibid., p. 36.
[85]Ibid., pp. 37, 39.
[86]Ibid., p. 37.
[87]Cf. ibid., p. 37.

archaeological material, as has been recognized by some of the form critics.[88]

3.2 Internal and external evidence

On a separate but related issue, it has recently been argued that the Old Testament itself must be the primary source for establishing a Patriarchal Age, and that external sources have only a secondary function. Although this question is not raised by Thompson or van Seters, since both use external data to support their own hypotheses, it has been brought to the fore by Talmon in a general discussion of the 'comparative method',[89] and by Warner[90] and Miller[91] directly in relation to the patriarchs. According to Talmon, when any item is considered for comparison, the biblical context should be understood first. All biblical features, including social customs, should be interpreted by inner-biblical parallels (if available) before any use is made of extra-biblical material. If external data are employed, then preference should be given to societies which lie in the same 'historical stream' as biblical Israel, though Talmon is also careful to underline the dictum of the anthropologist W. Goldschmidt that 'there is always an element of falsification when we engage in institutional comparisons among distinct cultures'.[92] This reminder of the fundamental importance of the biblical context is indeed timely, but the article as a whole gives the impression that external comparisons are of relatively minor value, and tends to overlook the fact that when they are properly used, they neither

[88]See above, nn. 55, 56, for the view of von Rad and Noth. A literary investigation of the historical characteristics of the patriarchal narratives is certainly overdue and likely to be most instructive, but in the absence of such a work, the following include some recent contributions in this area: J. Bright, *History*, pp. 73-76; K. A. Kitchen, *The Bible in its World* (Paternoster, Exeter, 1977), pp. 61-65; R. de Vaux, *Early History*, 1, pp. 161-185; R. C. Culley, in J. W. Wevers and D. B. Redford (ed.), *Studies on the Ancient Palestinian World* (Toronto UP, Toronto, 1972), pp. 102-116.

[89]S. Talmon, 'The "Comparative Method" in Biblical Interpretation— Principles and Problems', *VTS* 29, 1977 (publ. 1978), pp. 320-356.

[90]S. M. Warner, 'The Patriarchs and Extra-biblical Sources', *JSOT* 2, 1977, pp. 50-61.

[91]J. M. Miller, 'The Patriarchs and Extra-biblical Sources: a Response', *JSOT* 2, 1977, pp. 62-66.

[92]S. Talmon, loc. cit., p. 356, quoting W. Goldschmidt, *Comparative Functionalism* (California UP, Berkeley, 1966), p. 131.

submerge the Old Testament's distinctiveness nor cast it loose from its historical mooring.

Warner has applied similar restraints to the interpretation of the patriarchal narratives. He believes that 'to determine any major part of the period's profile from sources which do not mention the patriarchs is nonsense',[93] and sees the role of extra-biblical sources as being 'very secondary'.[94] Similarly, Miller insists that it is the Bible which must fix the 'historicity' and 'approximate chronological context' of the Patriarchal Age, if that is possible.[95]

It is right, of course, to recognize the limits of external evidence, but one must not lose sight of the fact that the Old Testament data themselves also have certain limitations. The book of Genesis, for instance, is not a general historical work on the pre-exodus era, in contrast to many modern histories of Israel, but is primarily concerned with the relationship between one small clan and their God. The emphasis on the family interest and the consequent lack of concern for contemporary international politics and religion mean inevitably that some 'major parts of the period's profile' are dealt with at best tangentially and sometimes not at all. The modern historian, however, who is concerned to reflect as fully and accurately as possible all the elements of the period he is describing, including political, military, economic, sociological, religious, and other features, will certainly find that though his interests overlap with those of the compiler of Genesis, they do not always coincide. If therefore he is going to attempt to describe a Patriarchal Age according to the patterns of modern historical writing, he will be bound to use material external to the Old Testament. Furthermore, the lack of agreement in current scholarship about the interpretation of the pre-exodus chronology of the Old Testament makes Miller's insistence that the Bible should fix the chronological setting seem rather naive in the present context. In the light of a range of opinions which is unable to decide whether there is a short or long gap between the end of Genesis and the beginning of Exodus, or even whether the gap is a real

[93]S. M. Warner, loc. cit., p. 52.
[94]Ibid., p. 55, cf. p. 52.
[95]J. M. Miller, loc. cit., p. 63.

one at all,[96] it is surely reasonable to look for data from outside the Old Testament which might help to resolve the difficulty.

Nevertheless, one must admit that some external data have been used in an unsuitable manner. Some suposed parallels have fitted awkwardly with the biblical text, and on some occasions have even been imposed hastily and uncritically on their cuneiform contexts. Many of these examples fall within the third category of parallels described earlier,[97] where the nonbiblical material is used to explain poorly understood or nonexistent features in the biblical description or where comparison has been made with a hypothetical prebiblical tradition. Even in the case of parallels which still stand, however, it is important to remember that no complete picture of a custom is found in the patriarchal narratives, and that while it is natural to want to supply the gaps, it is essential for the end result to conform to the biblical context and not to do violence to it.

One ought to ask finally what are the consequences of this new 'Back to the Bible' plea. It has to be admitted that there is currently little agreement among scholars as to the Old Testament's concept of the patriarchs and the era in which they lived, and that on the basis of internal evidence alone there exists considerable confusion about the way in which Genesis 12-50 should be interpreted. While form critics generally have argued that little reliable historical memory has been preserved in the patriarchal narratives, they have hardly been able to put any agreed alternative in its place.[98] Thompson has also recently acknowledged that even the criteria for distinguishing oral from written tradition are not clear, and that oral tradition itself, which

---

[96]See above, pp. 98-101. On this problem, see the rather inconclusive discussions of H. H. Rowley, *From Joseph to Joshua* (Oxford UP, London, 1950), pp. 57-77, and T. L. Thompson, *Historicity*, pp. 9-16, 298-314. Cf. also W. M. Clark's statement of 'a non-existent consensus as to when the ancient Hebrews dated the patriarchs' (J. H. Hayes and J. M. Miller, eds., *Israelite and Judean History*, SCM, London, 1977, p. 122), and his own assessment of the main alternatives to a Middle Bronze date for the patriarchs (ibid., pp. 145-148).

[97]See above, pp. 97-98.

[98]See for example, the chapter by J. A. Wilcoxen on 'Narrative' in J. H. Hayes (ed.), *Old Testament form Criticism* (Trinity UP, San Antonio, 1974), pp. 57-98, and the strong criticism of Gunkel and his dependents by S. M. Warner, *VT* 29, 1979, pp. 325-335.

is sometimes employed as a last resort in the absence of other evidence, is actually absent from the Old Testament which contains at most only representations of oral traditions.[99] The position concerning literary criticism offers little improvement. The documentary hypothesis of the Pentateuch remains after all a hypothesis, and has probably never suffered such a severe challenge as it is undergoing at the present time.[100] In any case, form and literary criticism are not to be regarded as alternatives to each other or to the use of external data. The external material has often actually been added to rather than displaced the conclusions of form and literary critical study. As Weeks has pointed out, some proposed parallels have actually been dependent on the documentary hypothesis and a prior period of oral transmission whose existence depends mainly on ingenuity and guesswork.[101] Form criticism too has been heavily dependent on the use of external criteria, both in the delineation of the basic categories in Old Testament narrative and the identification of individual motifs, whether using Germanic and Icelandic oral tradition or ancient near-eastern stories as a basis for comparison.

It is certainly right at this time to give stress to a proper exegesis of the Old Testament, which has sometimes been in danger of being swamped by comparative material in the interpretation of the Patriarchal Age. But it is precisely because the methods of internal biblical study have not produced satisfactory answers to questions about the patriarchs that external data is both admissible and necessary. Once again, the either/or approach, whether emphasizing internal or external sources, exhibits a tendency to lead into what too often turns out to be a cul-de-sac, but the controlled use of both groups of material opens up a more profitable route towards the interpretation of the patriarchs.

3.3 Specific customs

Thompson and van Seters have both given detailed criticisms of the ways in which near-eastern social customs, and especially

[99]T. L. Thompson, *JAOS* 98, 1978, pp. 83-84.

[100]R. Rendtorff, *Das überlieferungsgeschichtliche Problem des Pentateuch* (*BZAW* 147), (De Gruyter, Berlin and New York, 1977); idem, *VTS* 28, 1975, pp. 158-166 (= *JSOT* 3, 1977, pp. 2-10); H. H. Schmid, *Der sogenannte Yahwist* (Theologischer Verlag, Zurich, 1976); J. van Seters, *Abraham*, pp. 123-313.

[101]N. K. Weeks, *Abr-Nahrain* 16, 1976, pp. 79-80.

those of Nuzi, have been compared with patriarchal narratives. The reason for this careful attention has been well expressed by van Seters: 'Many scholars have seen in these patriarchal customs the strongest criterion for considering the Genesis stories to be of great antiquity.'[102] Their rejection of the consensus view has both reflected and magnified the growing dissatisfaction with some of the claimed parallels which has been manifested in the works of Greenberg, Mullo Weir, van Seters, Tucker, and Petschow,[103] and which has been continued more recently by Greengus, Weeks, Clark and de Vaux.[104] The common conclusion of Thompson and van Seters is that the Nuzi texts have no special interest for the patriarchal narratives,[105] although their alternative proposals vary widely. Van Seters believes that much better parallels could be established with first-millennium texts. Thompson, however, while acknowledging that some customs fit very well into the general context of ancient near-eastern family law and that such comparisons are 'quite helpful', insists that the patriarchal customs are not in conflict with later Old Testament practice, that there is no reason why they should not be of Palestinian origin, and that they cannot be dated to any specific period in ancient near-eastern history.[106] On the basis of this and other factors, he also concludes that 'there is nothing historically known which can directly associate the narratives with the historical and archaeological data of the second millennium'.[107]

The objections of Thompson and van Seters place the claimed parallels into three distinct groups: those which are rejected entirely, those which are to be interpreted against a general ancient near-eastern background, and those for which the best parallels are found in texts of the first millennium B.C. Both

[102]J. van Seters, *Abraham*, p. 65.

[103]See above, pp. 103-105.

[104]S. Greengus, *HUCA* 46, 1975, pp. 5-31; N. K. Weeks, *Abr-Nahrain* 16, 1976, pp. 73-82; W. M. Clark, in J. H. Hayes and J. M. Miller (eds.) *Israelite and Judean History* (SCM, London, 1977), p. 143; R. de Vaux, *Early History*, 1, 1978, pp. 241-256.

[105]See Thompson's approval of van Seters' conclusions on the negative value of the Nuzi texts, *JAOS* 98, 1978, p. 78 (for van Seters' own reaction to Thompson, see *Abraham*, x). Note also the author's conclusion on the special relationship with Nuzi, *TB* 27, 1976, p. 135.

[106]T. L. Thompson, *Historicity*, p. 294.

[107]T. L. Thompson, *JSOT* 9, 1978, p. 4.

scholars place some customs in the first group, but the second group belong mainly to Thompson and the third entirely to van Seters.

3.3.1 *Rejected parallels*   Abraham's inheritance relationship with his slave Eliezer is not easy to interpret, not least because of the translation difficulties of Genesis 15:2-3. Many have attempted a solution through positing Abraham's adoption of Eliezer on the basis of analogies from Nuzi and elsewhere. Yet a major difficulty in the way of this interpretation is that in cuneiform texts an adoptee who had been allocated an inheritance never forfeited that inheritance even if the adopter subsequently had sons of his own, whereas Eliezer's inheritance rights are not mentioned after the birth of Isaac (cf. Gn. 25:5-6). This weakness is recognized by Thompson and van Seters, while for Thompson Eliezer's slave status is a further problem. Van Seters sees greater relevance in certain inner-biblical parallels, particularly Proverbs 17:2 where a slave can inherit alongside the brothers.[108] There is no doubt that Eliezer's lack of an inheritance poses a real difficulty, but it is not necessarily an insuperable one. Although Proverbs 17:2 may in the end provide the better comparison, one should equally not overlook the several cuneiform examples of slave adoption, and especially an Old Babylonian text from Larsa which suggests that a man without sons could adopt his own slave.[109]

(2) Speiser's strange interpretation of Nahor's marriage to his niece Milcah (Gn. 11:29) as an example of the type of adoption described in a 'tablet of daughtership and daughter-in-lawship' (*ṭuppi mārtūti u kallatūti*) has been severely criticized by Thompson. He argues rightly that texts of this kind are not concerned with the marriage of nieces, but that the main purpose was the adoption of a girl in order to give her in marriage to someone else, and thus to receive the marriage payment (*terḫatu*) from her

    [108]T. L. Thompson, *Historicity*, pp. 203-230; J. van Seters, *Abraham*, pp. 85-87.
    [109]M. J. Selman, loc. cit., pp. 125-127. For the real adoption of a slave as distinct from adoption for the purposes of manumission, see e.g., J. Köhler and A. F. Ungnad, *Hammurabis Gesetze* (Pfeiffer, Leipzig, 1904-1923), Nos. 22, 23; J. Köhler and F. E. Peiser, *Aus dem babylonischen Rechtsleben* (Pfeiffer, Leipzig, IV, 1898), pp. 13-14; R. H. Pfeiffer, *Excavations at Nuzi*, 2 (HSS 9, Harvard UP, Cambridge, Mass., 1932), No. 22.

husband.[110] One might note in addition that Speiser's emphasis on the earlier death of the girl's father is quite irrelevant both to this type of adoption and to Genesis 11:29.

(3) Another of Speiser's theories, that of wife-sister marriage, has gained much greater notoriety than the previous example, but is just as unconvincing. Although Thompson and van Seters are united in their rejection of Speiser's view,[111] they were preceded by some years by the little-known article of Mullo Weir (referred to earlier) which very effectively challenged the wife-sister marriage.[112] Mullo Weir's conclusions have also been confirmed by other contributions over the last few years.[113]

(4) A similar reaction has also emerged towards a related theory of Speiser's, namely his interpretation of Rebekah's marriage (Gn. 24) as a sistership adoption. Again, it is alleged that Speiser has misunderstood the purpose of this practice, which like daughter-ship adoption, is to adopt a girl in order to give her in marriage to someone else. It is generally agreed also that Rebekah's consent (Gn. 24:57), on which Speiser placed so much emphasis, was given not to the arrangement of her marriage but to the time of her departure from Paddan-Aram.[114]

(5) Recent interpretation of the significance of household gods at Nuzi and among Laban's family has moved away from seeing the gods as a title to an inheritance, following Greenberg's strong denial of the earlier view.[115] Thompson and van Seters have also acknowledged the force of Greenberg's arguments.[116] In their view, the Nuzi evidence has been wrongly understood and uncritically applied to the account of Rachel's theft, and even apart from this, the Old Testament story on its own gives no indication that either Jacob or Rachel had any interest in inheriting Laban's estate. And yet this was the earliest and the parade example of a

[110]T. L. Thompson, *Historicity*, pp. 230-234.

[111]T. L. Thompson, *Historicity*, pp. 234-248; J. van Seters, *Abraham*, pp. 71-76.

[112]See above, n. 61.

[113]For references, see above, n. 34.

[114]T. L. Thompson, *Historicity*, pp. 248-252; J. van Seters, pp. 76-78; cf. M. J. Selman, loc. cit., pp. 121-123.

[115]See above, n. 59.

[116]T. L. Thompson, *Historicity*, pp. 272-278; J. van Seters, *Abraham*, pp. 93-94; cf. also the references in n. 60.

Nuzi parallel to a patriarchal custom, as indicated by Speiser, 'perhaps the outstanding example of an exclusively Hurrian custom which the patriarchal account records, but which became incomprehensible later on in Canaanite surroundings'.[117]

(6) The closely related hypothesis of Jacob's adoption by Laban and his *errēbu* marriage have also come in for severe criticism. The adoption is opposed because the Old Testament evidence is contrary to such a proposal, but Jacob's *errēbu* marriage is rejected by Thompson because no brideprice (*terḫatu*) was paid in such instances, whereas van Seters, following his earlier view, denies even the existence of this type of marriage.[118]

(7) Two Nuzi texts are somtimes quoted as further examples of the sale of birthright as carried out by Esau (Gn. 25:29-34). One of them, HSS 5 99,[119] is rightly rejected by Thompson as being unrelated to the question of the transfer of birthright. Thompson and van Seters have both criticized the value of the second, JEN 204,[120] for interpreting Esau's action on the grounds that there is no means of knowing whether the seller made a good or bad deal. Thompson also notes two further fundamental difficulties: that the identity of the firstborn in JEN 204 is unknown, and that it is not future inheritance rights that are being sold, but only that the land in question happens to be inherited. Both scholars, however, do recognize that this text is one example of several instances where part of an inheritance is transferred from one brother to another, though only van Seters sees them as being analogous with the biblical passage.[121]

(8) The patriarchal blessings of Isaac and Jacob are unique in ancient literature, but Speiser has argued that the account in Genesis 27 has certain legal features comparable with those mentioned in some Nuzi documents. Speiser understood the phrase 'and now I have grown old' (verse 2) to be an introductory legal formula, but this is countered by Thompson on the grounds that

---

[117]E. A. Speiser, *Biblical and Other Studies*, p. 24, n. 40.

[118]T. L. Thompson, *Historicity*, pp. 273-280; J. van Seters, *Abraham*, pp. 78-81. See also the references above, n. 66.

[119]E. A. Speiser, *AASOR* 10, 1930, No. 18 (text only in E. Chiera, *Excavations at Nuzi*, 1 (HSS 5, Harvard UP, Cambridge, Mass., 1929), No. 99.

[120]E. Cassin, *L'adoption à Nuzi* (Maisonneuve, Paris, 1938), pp. 230ff.; H. Lewy, *OrNS* 9, 1940, pp. 369-370 (text only in E. Chiera, *Joint expedition with the Iraq Museum at Nuzi*, 2, Geuthner, Paris, 1930, No. 204).

[121]T. L. Thompson, *Historicity*, pp. 280-285; J. van Seters, *Abraham*, p. 93.

it occurs in only one Nuzi text and even that is not a final death-bed disposition. The upholding of an oral statement in a lawcourt is also not supported, since the claim made in the tablet AASOR 16 56[122] is recognized by the court on the basis of the witnesses' testimony and not on the grounds of any intrinsic legality of an oral statement. Both Thompson and van Seters argue in any case that the patriarchal blessing is not a legal phenomenon. According to the latter, Esau could have received redress at law, while Thompson asserts that in a real situation one would expect Isaac to reverse his decision on discovering the deception. These comments, however, appear to confuse the patriarchal blessing, occurring only in Genesis 27 and 48, where the words of blessing were immutable, with the more obviously tangible benefits of inheritance which were subject to legal procedures.[123]

In addition to these examples from the sphere of family law, a small number of other practices are often mentioned in this same context, of which two well-known cases are briefly included here. Abraham's purchase of a burial ground from a 'son of Heth' (Gn. 23) has sometimes been interpreted against the background of Hittite law, but this is challenged by Thompson and in a more detailed fashion by van Seters. According to van Seters, the main problem is that this interpretation 'must supply the story with the missing point of comparison and then reconstruct the rest to agree with it'.[124] The missing parts in the Genesis account are any reference to feudal service associated with the property, and an indication that the seller's entire holdings are involved, while the assumed connection between the Hittites and Hebron is also questioned. In place of this view, van Seters prefers certain later texts as a means of interpreting the chapter.[125] The second example concerns Jacob's shepherding arrangements with Laban in Genesis 31:38ff., which have been compared with certain Old Babylonian shepherding contracts. Van Seters' objections to the validity of this comparison are based on the fact that such contracts are not confined to any particular period, and that the unique non-cultic

[122]R. H. Pfeiffer and E. A. Speiser, *AASOR* 16, 1936, No. 56.

[123]T. L. Thompson, *Historicity*, pp. 285-293; J. van Seters, *Abraham*, pp. 94-95.

[124]J. van Seters, *Abraham*, p. 99.

[125]J. van Seters, *Abraham*, pp. 98-100; T. L. Thompson, *Historicity*, pp. 295-296; cf. M. R. Lehmann, *BASOR* 129, 1953, pp. 15-18; G. M. Tucker, *JBL* 85, 1966, pp. 77-84; H. Petschow, *JCS* 19, 1965, pp. 103-120.

pi^cel use of the verb $ḥāṭa^ɔ$ in Genesis 31:39 should be compared not with Old Babylonian $ḫīṭum$, 'loss', but with the more general Akkadian verb $ḫâṭu$, 'to weigh out (money), to pay compensation'. It must be said, however, that van Seters' arguments lack conviction, for several reasons. The Hebrew verb $ḥāṭa^c$ must be repointed as a qal form, it is related morphologically to $ḫīṭum$ but not to $ḫâṭu$,[126] and the meaning 'loss' is much more suitable in the context than van Seters' tentative alternative.[127]

Many of these objections of Thompson and van Seters can certainly be sustained. The various marriage theories of Speiser and most of Gordon's proposals concerning the relationship between Jacob and Laban are clearly wide of the mark, can now be seen to be founded more on the shifting sands of enthusiasm than on the solid rock of accuracy. Even among the ruins of these parallels, however, some of the extrabiblical data is still relevant to Genesis 12-50. The various examples of the sale of an inheritance within the family provide a useful general background to Esau's transaction with Jacob, and the Old Babylonian herding contracts exhibit genuine points of contact with the patriarchal narratives. Two issues which must continue to be left open are the adoption of Eliezer and the relevance of feudal duties to Abraham's purchase of a burial ground.[128]

3.3.2 *Parallels of a general character* Despite Thompson's generally negative assessment of the value of Nuzi family law for the patriarchal narratives, he does conclude that real contacts exist: 'Positively, it can be said that many of the customs in Genesis, that cannot be directly related to known literary motifs, fit very well into the general context of ancient near-eastern family law, and a comparison of these stories with this legal material is quite helpful in understanding the intention of these narratives.'[129] The following list contains his main suggestions which are in agreement with this conclusion.

---

[126]W. von Soden, *Akkadisches Handwörterbuch* (Harrassowitz, Wiesbaden), I, 1965, p. 350.

[127]J. van Seters, *Abraham*, pp. 95-98, commenting on J. J. Finkelstein, *JAOS* 88, 1968, pp. 30-36; cf. also R. Frankena, *OTS* 17, 1972, pp. 58-59. Thompson is aware of Finkelstein's proposals, but he makes no comment on them (*Historicity*, p. 279, n. 360).

[128]See K. A. Kitchen, *The Bible in its World*, p. 71; H. A. Hoffner, *TB* 20, 1969, pp. 33-35.

[129]T. L. Thompson, *Historicity*, p. 294.

(1) Various practices in Genesis associated with a wife's slave-girl are mentioned in extrabiblical texts. The inclusion of a female slave within a dowry as in the marriage accounts of Leah, Rachel, and probably Rebekah has several extrabiblical parallels.[130] Similarly, the practice of Sarah, Rachel, and Leah who each provided their husbands with a slavegirl in the face of their own barrenness (Gn. 16:1-4; 30:1-13) is mentioned occasionally else-where, though sometimes the girl was obtained especially for the purpose while on other occasions she already belonged to the wife. The ambiguous position of the inheritance prospects of the sons resulting from a union of this kind is also well documented. The variations that exist in these customs, particularly within the cuneiform material, are to be explained by the demands of indi-vidual situations rather than by any chronological or geographical factors.[131]

(2) A clause restricting a man from taking a second wife as mentioned in Genesis 31:50, sometimes appears in cuneiform marriage contracts, though again with variable details. In Genesis 31, however, this forms part of a legal 'covenant' between Jacob and Laban, made after the birth of Jacob's children but before the final parting of the two men. For Thompson, this is the one aspect of the supposed parallels between Genesis 29-31 and the Nuzi text Gadd 51[132] which stands up to scrutiny, but it can be accepted only in 'a very limited and a very vague sense',[133] since these two cases belong to a group of references stretching from Sumerian texts in the late third millennium B.C. to the Graeco-Egyptian papyri of the second and first centuries B.C.[134]

(3) Although Thompson rejects Speiser's sistership theory as an explanation of Rebekah's marriage, he does draw attention to the fact that the arrangement of the marriage by Rebekah's brother Laban is paralleled by a number of instances where a brother takes responsibility for his sister's welfare. These include three cases of the arrangement of his sister's marriage, twice in the Old Babylonian period and once in the Neo-Babylonian.[135]

---

[130]Gn. 29:24, 29; cf. 24:59, 61. T. L. Thompson, *Historicity*, pp. 264, 270-271; J. van Seters, *Abraham*, p. 84.

[131]T. L. Thompson, *Historicity*, pp. 260-269.

[132]C. J. Gadd, *RA* 23, 1926, No. 51.

[133]T. L. Thompson, *Historicity*, p. 269.

[134]Ibid., pp. 260-270; J. van Seters, *Abraham*, p. 84.

[135]Ibid., pp. 249-250, especially n. 36.

(4) A dominant feature of the discussion relating to the privileges of the eldest son has been the fairly frequent assertion that both at Nuzi and in patriarchal society, birthright could be arbitrarily bestowed on any son. This conclusion is partly confirmed by Thompson, who speaks of a father's discriminating power in dividing an inheritance. However, he seems to have confused two separate issues, for the wide-ranging examples cited by Thompson actually refer to those who would not inherit in the normal course of succession rather than to any variation in the status of the eldest son. There is considerable evidence inside and outside the Old Testament that the alteration of any heir's inheritance rights was an extremely serious matter, and was certainly not subject to a father's arbitrary decision.[136] This, however, was a different matter from providing special gifts for a wife, son, or daughter, which stood outside the main inheritance arrangements, or from making special arrangements in unusual circumstances, such as when a man died intestate, or when he had only daughters, as in the case of Zelophehad's family (Nu. 27:8-11). These latter arrangements to which Thompson refers do not materially affect the special position of the eldest son.[137]

Thompson's view that neither the patriarchs nor the citizens of Nuzi were isolated from the rest of the ancient Near East as far as family law is concerned is an accurate assessment, though it is not a unique position. This was recognized by Mullo Weir in 1967, and by others more recently,[138] but differing conclusions have been drawn from this common basis. Weeks, for example, who recognizes that 'the parallels which remain valid are the more general ones',[139] is very pessimistic about being able to establish any real external confirmation of the patriarchal narratives. Thompson is equally certain that such contacts provide us with neither a historical background nor a 'constitutive legal structure'

---

[136]Cf. e.g., the Laws of Hammurapi paras. 168-169, where disinheritance was allowed by a court only after a second serious offence, or the experience of Reuben who lost his birthright after immoral sexual behaviour with his father's concubine (Gn. 35:22; 49:3-4).

[137]T. L. Thompson, *Historicity*, pp. 285, 290-293.

[138]See above, p. 102, also M. J. Selman, loc. cit., pp. 125-131; N. K. Weeks, *Abr-Nahrain* 16, 1976, pp. 73-82; R. de Vaux, *Early History*, I, pp. 241-256. pp. 241-256.

[139]N. K. Weeks, loc. cit., p. 78 (though only a single example, that of the wife's substitute slavegirl, is actually mentioned).

for the patriarchs, and they certainly cannot help in establishing a separate Patriarchal Age.[140] Indeed, he has recently asserted that the earliest possible date for determining anything at all about the patriarchs is that of the earliest known existence of Israel, namely the beginning of the Israelite monarchy in the tenth century B.C. Anything earlier is pre-Israelite, when basic traditions may have existed for millennia![141] Thus although Thompson makes the positive suggestion that this general legal background is helpful in interpreting some aspects of the patriarchal stories, it is only a minor gain. We can at most learn something only of the time in which the stories were written, and nothing at all about the patriarchs and their world.

But these pessimistic conclusions do not necessarily follow from the general nature of the social customs. No a priori reason exists why the patriarchal clans themselves should not have practised these customs, since the parallels that can be established are concrete historical examples in individual family settings. It can even be said that whereas J. Bright saw the patriarchal customary law as being at home only among the population of Nuzi,[142] that background should now be extended to include the general customary law of the ancient Near East. Although the number of Thompson's contacts is relatively meagre, it should also be recognized that even at the present time the list can be significantly extended, as will be indicated below.[143] That it is the approach of Mullo Weir and de Vaux rather than that of Gordon and Speiser which is now seen to be more accurate should not lead us to draw hasty conclusions that the historicity of the patriarchs has thereby been disproved. Rather, it has been put on a wider and therfore more stable foundation.

3.3.3 *Parallels with first-millennium texts*   (1) In his examination of the wife-sister episodes in Genesis, van Seters draws attention to Egyptian marriage contracts of the sixth century B.C. where a wife is occasionally referred to as a man's 'sister', even though there is clearly no blood relationship. He suggests that these terms of affection help to explain the patriarchs' actions,

---

[140]T. L. Thompson, *Historicity*, pp. 294-296, 321-324.
[141]T. L. Thompson, *JSOT* 9, 1978, p. 5.
[142]J. Bright, *History*, p. 86.
[143]See below, pp. 135-138.

and notes that similar usage is found twice in the Apocrypha, but his interpretation is open to objection. It encounters the difficulty of importing an explanation into the patriarchal narratives for which there is no supporting point of contact, while the factual note of Genesis 20:12 renders the comparison unnecessary. The most serious problem, however, is that in Genesis 12 an Egyptian Pharaoh does not understand what according to van Seters is a custom of his country and time![144]

(2) The same Genesis passages include the description of adultery as 'great sin' (Gn. 20:9; cf. 26:10). This phrase, as van Seters notes, was similarly used in a Ugaritic text of the late thirteenth century B.C. and in Egyptian marriage contracts from the ninth to sixth centuries B.C.[145] He appears to ignore his own evidence, however, since the Ugaritic reference requires that it cannot be regarded as purely first-millennium usage. This expression was apparently not restricted geographically or chronologically in the ancient Near East.

(3) Whereas in Thompson's understanding of Rebekah's marriage (Gn. 24) it is the brother's action which is significant, the more relevant parallels for van Seters are those cases from the Old and Neo-Babylonian periods where the marriage is the joint responsibility of the bride's mother and brother.[146] In fact, no great distinction should be drawn between those instances where a brother acts alone and those where he acts with his mother. It was quite usual in ancient near-eastern marriage contracts for a father, mother or brother to take the responsibility, even though in most cases it was the duty of the girl's father. Rather, one should note the continuity through the millennia of the way in which the arrangement of marriages is described, and not attempt hairline distinctions which were probably dictated by family circumstances. As for Rebekah's father, his inactivity is not to be identified automatically with his absence, and he cannot simply be relegated to a scribal gloss without good reason.

(4) For the interpretation of Laban's daughters' complaint that their father had 'sold' them (Gn. 31:15), van Seters turns to a

[144] J. van Seters, *Abraham*, p. 75.

[145] Ibid., p. 76; cf. W. L. Moran, *JNES* 18, 1959, pp. 280-281; J. J. Rabinowitz, *JNES* 18, 1959, p. 73.

[146] J. van Seters, *Abraham*, p. 77.

Neo-Assyrian example of purchase marriage, a practice which is unusual in this period. This particular text also closely resembles a slave sale transaction. Van Seters acknowledges, however, that the girls' complaint can also be explained against the background of other texts from the Old Babylonian period, Nuzi, and Elephantine, where on occasion a father would withhold from his daughter a part of the bride payment which was normally handed on as a dowry. Nevertheless, he stresses that a date in the late Israelite monarchy is an entirely possible setting for the Genesis passage.[147] In the light of the earlier evidence, however, it is impossible to be so emphatic about the relevance of the Neo-Assyrian text. The existence of purchase marriage among the patriarchs is unlikely and cannot be proved from this one verse. Furthermore, the phrase ʾākal kesep ('to consume money') in Genesis 31:15 also appears in identical contexts at Nuzi in its Akkadian equivalent (kaspa akālu), which suggests that the biblical reference may well belong with van Seters' rejected alternative.[148]

(5) An alternative to the discarded Nuzi parallels to Esau's sale of his birthright is proposed by van Seters. He notes that the ability to transfer inheritance rights, even before they were received, was in evidence in the Neo-Babylonian and Achaemenid periods, and although he does not make clear whether all these cases took place between brothers, he does mention one damaged tablet where it is possible that a two-thirds portion, that is, a birthright, was in fact transferred from one brother to another. Unfortunately, it is impossible to be certain about this particular text, but of course the transfer of inherited property was known in several periods, not restricted to the first millennium.[149]

(6) Finally, one must take note of van Seters' own interpretation of the customs relating to a wife's slavegirl. He has insisted repeatedly that the best parallel to the biblical practice is found in a Neo-Assyrian text from Nimrud, whereas this text actually illustrates the long continuity of the custom in the ancient Near East.[150] It contains one of the few examples of a wife who

[147]Ibid., p. 84.

[148]M. J. Selman, loc. cit., pp. 131-133.

[149]J. van Seters, *Abraham*, p. 93; cf. above, p. 116.

[150]J. van Seters, *JBL* 87, 1968, pp. 401-408; *Abraham*, pp. 68-71; A. K. Grayson and J. van Seters, *OrNS* 44, 1975, pp. 485-486.

provided her husband with a slavegirl for the purpose of producing children for the husband and wife, in contrast to the usual procedure where the husband made his own choice of a second wife or a concubine. This text thus stands closely alongside the Nuzi text HSS 5 67[151] and a small number of other second-millennium references, as well as the biblical instances of Sarah, Rachel, and Leah. Van Seters' distinction between the children of the wife and those of the husband is artificial and unrealistic,[152] and misses the emphasis of this group of texts which is to protect the position of the chief wife. His statement that in both the Neo-Assyrian text and the biblical references the wife retains full control over the slavegirl is also erroneous. The Nimrud tablet clearly states: 'If she hates (her), she may sell her,'[153] whereas Sarah's maid could only be expelled by Abraham who was himself hesitant until he received divine enouragement (Gn. 21:9-14). Van Seters' estimate of the value of this text is therefore somewhat misplaced.[154]

Mention must be made here of attempts to trace the structure of Neo-Babylonian 'dialogue documents' in certain passages in the patriarchal narratives. According to van Seters, not only does Abraham's purchase in Genesis 23 reflect the structure of these texts, but Laban's herding negotiations with Jacob also fall into the same pattern.[155] While it is quite possible that these patriarchal negotiations are patterned on contractual procedures, it is very difficult to discern with any accuracy the form of the 'dialogue documents' in Genesis. These texts had a fairly precise structure, quite different from the extensive dialogue in the narratives of Genesis. In Genesis 23, for example, Tucker argues that the 'dialogue document' form begins at verse 16, but this is a purely arbitrary point at which to divide the narrative, and in any case, the dialogue between Ephron and Abraham ceases at verse 15! Furthermore, the 'dialogue document' is not restricted to the late Assyrian period onwards, as asserted by van Seters, but is attested early in the second millennium.[156]

[151]For details, see above, n. 63.

[152]J. van Seters, *OrNS* 44, 1975, p. 486.

[153]1,46 (collation of J. N. Postgate, *OrNS* 44, 1975, p. 485).

[154]See also M. J. Selman, loc. cit., pp. 127-130; K. A. Kitchen, op. cit., p. 71.

[155]J. van Seters, *Abraham*, pp. 97-100.

[156]D. J. Wiseman, *Bibliotheca Sacra* 134, 1977, p. 130, n. 29, with reference to *CT* 45, 1964, No. 60; cf. also T. L. Thompson, *Historicity*, p. 296; H. Petschow, *JCS* 19, 1965, pp. 103-120; K. A. Kitchen, op. cit., p. 71.

Van Seters' conclusion that the chronological data of the social customs 'all point to the mid-first millennium rather than to the earlier period'[157] cannot be supported. In practically every case, equally appropriate material is available from earlier periods. This is not to be discarded in favour of the later texts, but in fact confirms that the evidence of parallel customs fits well into the general family background of the ancient Near East.

3.4 Interpretation of extrabiblical evidence

Many of the difficulties which have been encountered in this whole area have been occasioned by the nature of the information in the cuneiform sources, which too often is scattered and isolated from material which could help to set it in a proper and meaningful context. Comparisons have been constructed on the basis of individual texts whose availability is determined more by the chance of archaeological discovery than anything else and which have little connection with each other either in time or location. These factors have also been commented on by Thompson and van Seters, though as before, their emphasis has varied. Van Seters' protest has centred upon the apparent preference for second-millennium sources against what he sees as the almost complete exclusion of later texts. While it is acknowledged that this has resulted partly from the greater volume of texts from the earlier period, he alleges that the primary cause is the direct influence of Old Testament studies which has led to a 'prejudicial treatment' in favour of the second millennium.[158]

While van Seters therefore sees the problem as an imbalance which he seeks to correct, Thompson regards the issue as much more deep-seated. For him all the texts used are unrepresentative, and modern scholarship has failed to take into account 'the enormous lack of data for the history of the Second Millennium'.[159] Thompson's statement gives the impression that the task of writing any meaningful history, even of the comparatively well-documented early second millennium, is almost hopeless. But one does not need to be so pessimistic. Our information is steadily increasing, and what is more important, so is our appreciaton of its significance. Thus the 300 Nuzi texts on family law have come

[157] J. van Seters, *Abraham*, p. 121.
[158] Ibid., 10, pp. 66-67.
[159] T. L. Thompson, *Historicity*, pp. 7, 320.

under increasing scrutiny,[160] for instance, and the city of Sippar in the Old Babylonian period, has recently been subjected to an in-depth demographic study.[161] Other sites too, particularly in the Old Babylonian period, can provide significant information, and material from a range of locations in different periods is now available.

It must be admitted that we have fewer sources from the first millennium, so that care must be exercised in assessing the value of the larger quantity of earlier material, and these later texts cannot be ignored in any comparative study of social customs. Van Seters' own approach, however, which amounts to an almost complete overriding of the greater number of second-millennium texts in favour of later material, is no improvement on the position he seeks to criticize. While the current situation is thus far from ideal, and full account needs to be taken of the variations in the evidence, there is even now much to be gained.

The best use of extrabiblical material will involve the recognition that the evidence has certain limitations. Of primary impor-tance should be the study of any custom in its own context, and no meaningful comparison can take place until a thorough investigation of this kind can be carried out. Such a contextual approach will need to take account of at least three separate stages. In the first place, any text that appears to be significant for comparative purposes needs to be examined as to its own literary characteristics, its purpose, date and geographical location. Secondly, it must be related with other material on the same subject from the same site, and finally compared with similar texts from a variety of sites and periods in the ancient Near East. The worth of an individual cuneiform tablet can only really be appreciated by gaining this kind of synchronic and diachronic perspective, though even then it may not be possible to distin-guish much development of a custom.

Variations will certainly be apparent, but current evidence suggests that this is probably due more to individual require-ments than to anything else. Two examples of this variation will

---

[160]For a very full bibliography on Nuzi up to 1972, see M. Dietrich, O. Loretz, and W. Mayer, *Nuzi-Bibliographie* (AOATS 11, Butzon & Bercker, Kevelaer, 1972). The author also hopes to make available soon the results of a compre-hensive study of Nuzi social customs.

[161]R. Harris, *Ancient Sippar* (Nederlands Historisch-Archaeologisch Instituut, Istanbul, 1975).

indicate the real significance of the contextual approach. The custom by which an infertile wife gave her slavegirl to her husband has been compared with a number of cuneiform texts, including one notable tablet from Nuzi, HSS 5 67.[162] In the light of a wider appreciation of this text, it becomes clear that it was in fact untypical of Nuzi practice. For whereas in this text and in Genesis, the wife presented her own slavegirl to her husband, in five other cases the husband could take a second wife and in four he could take a concubine of his choice. It is also apparent, however, that practices similar to that described in HSS 5 67 are found occasionally in texts of the Old Babylonian and Neo-Assyrian periods, and it is these texts which form the closest background to the biblical passages.[163] Similar variation, even within the same site at the same period, can be traced in the larger inheritance share of the eldest son. In Nuzi and at Larsa in the Old Babylonian period, although the normal practice was for the eldest son to receive a double share, there are also references to an equal division of the inheritance, but at Kutalla in the Old Babylonian period, one eldest son received a double share and another only an extra 10%.[164] The same differences are also evident in examples of the first millennium,[165] whereas the norm in Middle Babylonian Nippur was an extra 10% for the eldest son.[166]

Thompson has helpfully pointed out that 'contracts are not customs',[167] or in other words, one cannot automatically assume that any single text should be taken as representative for its time and place. Some attention therefore should be given to the function of cuneiform contracts. It has been concluded, for instance, that many Old Babylonian marriage contracts depict 'abnormal family situations',[168] and that 'wills were drawn at Nuzi only in unusual circumstances'.[169] This suggests that many contracts were used only when there was the possibility of some dispute or difficulty

---

[162]See above, pp. 119, 123-124.

[163]M. J. Selman, loc. cit., pp. 127-130.

[164]L. Matouš, *Archiv Orientalni* 17, 1948, pp. 153-155; J. Klíma, *Untersuchungen zum altbabylonischen Erbrecht* (Orientalisches Institut, Prague, 1940), p. 32.

[165]J. van Seters, *Abraham*, pp. 91-92.

[166]R. T. O'Callaghan, *JCS* 8, 1954, pp. 137-141.

[167]T. L. Thompson, *JAOS* 98, 1978, p. 78.

[168]S. Greengus, *JAOS* 89, 1969, p. 512; cf. R. Harris, *JNES* 33, 1974, p. 368.

[169]J. S. Paradise, *Nuzi Inheritance Practices* (University microfilms, Univ. of Pennsylvania, 1972), p. 12.

or where some abnormal problem was involved, a conclusion which is also supported by the accounts of customs in the patriarchal narratives. On the other hand, this does not mean that the contracts contain only exceptions, since in many cases they quite clearly confirm the usual principle and practice or else reapply the common practice where some unusual element was involved. They can still therefore be employed as a legitimate source for the study of customs.

3.5 *Interpretation of biblical material*

If we need to emphasize correct procedures in the interpretation of nonbiblical texts, perhaps we need even more to stress that the exegesis of Old Testament passages should not be overstretched. The stories of the patriarchs are found, after all, in the Old Testament and not outside it, and the patriarchal social customs must be seen first of all in their Old Testament context. This means, for instance, that Eliezer's status as heir may be an example of the exercise of *patria potestas* by Abraham, as suggested by a similar though not necessarily identical case in Proverbs 17:2 (despite the existence of appropriate extrabiblical material), or that David's treatment of Uriah, Bathsheba's husband, provides the best analogy to the anticipated actions of the Egyptian and Philistine kings towards the wives of Abraham and Isaac.

It is most important to recognize the limitations of the biblical accounts of patriarchal customs and the consequent dangers of over-enthusiasm in attempting to fill the gaps in our understanding. Additional explanatory material from outside the Old Testament is at best hypothetical, and it is the wrong use of this data which has occasioned many of the problems that have arisen in connection with the parallels, and which has caused a number of them to be rejected. In these cases, the meaning of the text has actually been clouded and confused by the nonbiblical data, which has thus done a disservice to correct exegesis. Furthermore, the Patriarchal Age which has been built up from some of these supposed parallels has not always been based upon the biblical record, but has sometimes owed more to the ingenuity of modern 'parallelologists'.

An important feature of the biblical picture is that the biblical tradition as a whole places the patriarchs in the period prior to the sojourn in Egypt and the exodus. This has recently been recognized by Warner, who notes that the genealogies, the chronological data, and the historical narratives of the Old Testament are all consistent in this respect.[170] Since this tradition is firmly entrenched, at the very least the concept of a pre-exodus patriarchal era becomes a working hypothesis, and it is therefore quite legitimate and reasonable on the basis of the date generally agreed for the exodus to look for contacts in the early and mid second millennium.[171] Thus while van Seters' protest that the first-millennium cuneiform material had not received a fair treatment in the overall study of ancient near-eastern family law is probably justified, the preference for comparing second-millennium sources with the patriarchal narratives is not due to prejudice but is based on a recognition of the biblical scheme. Unless this pattern is rejected as being entirely unhistorical, it is in the earlier material that contacts might initially be expected to be found, although any proper study of the chronological setting of a Patriarchal Age must include consideration of alternative periods.

Thompson has also alleged that the real implications of the second-millennium parallels for the documentary hypothesis of the Pentateuch have been ignored. Two issues in particular are mentioned: that it is assumed that the original tradition, rooted in historical events and passed on orally, somehow remained intact for over 800 years, and that the independent character of most of the Genesis pericopes is overlooked.[172] In practice, however, it can hardly be said that the existence of social parallels has greatly affected the documentary hypothesis as a whole. Most of those who have accepted the validity of the parallels have simply attached their results to a modified form of the documentary hypothesis, without any great alteration to either the archaeological or the literary interpretation of the Pentateuch. The only major effect has been the positing of a basic historical tradition,[173] which in Speiser's view could sometimes be at variance with the

---

[170]S. M. Warner, *JSOT* 2, 1977, p. 59.

[171]The earlier date for the exodus proposed by J. J. Bimson (*Redating the Exodus and Conquest*, JSOT Suppl. 5, Sheffield, 1978), does not affect the principle involved here.

[172]T. L. Thompson, *Historicity*, pp. 7-8.

[173]G. E. Wright, *ExpT* 71, 1960, p. 294; W. F. Albright, *CBQ* 25, 1963, pp. 1-11; J. Bright, *History*, pp. 68-76.

present form of the biblical text,[174] but which was linked to the various sources of the documentary hypothesis by the unprovable assumption of a long period of oral transmission. It is thus the preliterary stage rather than the sources themselves which have been most affected, but although this has signified an alternative approach to that of Gunkel, Noth, and von Rad towards the history of tradition, it has never been worked out in any detail. Only a few writers have used the archaeological data as a whole, including the social parallels, as a direct challenge to the documentary hypothesis.[175]

There are two points in particular where the evidence from social customs affects the conclusions of literary study. First, the historical nature of the comparative material means that the disciplines of literary and form criticism must reckon with the fact that some parts of the patriarchal narratives are at home in historical texts outside the Old Testament. If any literature is studied in isolation from historical data, it will soon be concluded that it is unhistorical, but the continued existence of social parallels requires that this historical dimension can no longer be excluded from a consideration of the origins of the patriarchal narratives. Secondly, the conclusions of internal literary hypotheses cannot override the objective information of the cuneiform tablets, where the latter can be shown to be of relevance to the patriarchal narratives. The cuneiform texts are preserved as original documents, whose date and place of origin are often accurately known, and which provide an incidental, unconscious, and therefore valuable insight into family life in the ancient Near East. Where these extrabiblical texts are genuinely applicable to particular biblical contexts, such objective data can be of real value, even though it cannot of course replace internal literary investigation.

3.6 Guidelines for comparison

A significant element in the current discussion has been the attempt by several writers to provide specific guidelines for comparing external evidence with the patriarchal narratives. Lists of

---

[174]E. A. Speiser, *Genesis*, xxxvii-xliii.

[175]C. H. Gordon, *Ugaritic literature* (Pontifical Biblical Institute, Rome, 1949), pp. 6f.; idem, *Christianity Today* 4/4, 1959, pp. 131ff.; R. K. Harrison, *Introduction to the Old Testament* (Tyndale, London, 1970), pp. 79-80, 515-516, 531-541;

rules have been contributed by Clark,[176] Luke,[177] and Warner,[178] in addition to the general comments of Talmon on the 'comparitive method'.[179] While all of them are useful, however, none can be said to treat the patriarchal comparisons comprehensively. Warner and Talmon have concentrated so heavily on the importance of the biblical data that insufficient attention is given to the positive value of external texts, Clark seems to have little concern for the actual process of comparison and deals with the whole matter very briefly, while Luke, whose approach is the most satisfactory, gives scant consideration to the interpretation of the sources in their own contexts. In addition, apart from Talmon, who is not greatly concerned with the patriarchal narratives, the proposals are almost entirely theoretical, and the absence of concrete examples makes some of them difficult to evaluate.

In what is probably an attempt to avoid the danger of giving undue weight to parallels which appear initially attractive but which subsequently are shown to be superficial or even inaccurate, Warner argues that the primary role of the nonbiblical sources is 'a negative, falsifying one' and not 'a positive, verifying one'.[180] He proposes that the most one can expect of these sources is that any suggested reconstruction of the patriarchs will not be falsified by them. This approach, however, is as unsatisfactory as the method which Warner seeks to avoid, for its effect is to ignore data that may be extremely valuable, and to overlook the positive contribution that can be made by external sources. Luke's proposal that one should consider how far a given interpretation fits with known facts is a better procedure, and does not involve arbitrary assessments of the value of any piece of evidence, internal or external.[181]

Both Warner and Clark make the important if somewhat obvious point that the extrabiblical evidence should be examined in its

---

K. A. Kitchen, *The Bible in its World*, pp. 19-36, 56-74; E. M. Yamauchi, *The Stones and the Scriptures* (IVP, London, 1973), pp. 21-41; K. A. Kitchen, *Ancient Orient and Old Testament* (Tyndale, London, 1965), pp. 17-34, 41-56, 112-135.

[176]W. M. Clark, in *Israelite and Judean History*, 1977, p. 143.

[177]J. T. Luke, *JSOT* 4, 1977, pp. 36-37.

[178]S. M. Warner, *JSOT* 2, 1977, pp. 51-57.

[179]S. Talmon, *VTS* 29, 1977, (publ. 1978), pp. 320-356.

[180]S. M. Warner, loc. cit., pp. 52-55.

[181]J. T. Luke, loc. cit., p. 37.

widest context and thus demonstrate an inner consistency,[182] but only Talmon draws attention to the maxim that comparisons are best attempted only with those 'cultures lying within a given historic stream', that is, where there is historical, geographical and cultural affinity.[183] On a similar matter, Luke requires that arguments concerning cultural contacts and transmission of a custom must be plausible.[184] One might also add that such contacts should take account of the linguistic and sociological relationship between the cultures concerned. Thus those writers who were sceptical about the apparently one-sided reliance of the patriarchal customs on a Hurrian milieu were justified in their attitude, and there should be similar caution about placing too much weight on a purely Hittite interpretation of Genesis 23. This also means, of course, that the practices of the modern Bedouin and the oral literature of mediaeval Europe are of even more marginal interest for the patriarchs.

A conflict is discernible between Warner and Thompson as to whether differences in the form of texts allows any real comparison of their content. Thompson is extremely pessimistic,[185] whereas Warner not only accepts that any type of extrabiblical data can be used to 'elaborate' the patriarchal narratives, but also asserts that it is better to make a check from sources which do not share the same interest.[186] While comparisons of both form and content can be made, most are actually based on the content of texts, on the reasonable grounds that the same custom can appear in such different forms as narratives, law collections, or private records. It is probable too that myths and epics of Ugarit and Sumer contain valuable information about the social structures of the human societies which produced the stories.[187] However, attempts to find Mesopotamian literary forms such as the 'dialogue documents' or the sistership adoption contracts in Genesis 23 and 24 respectively have met with a considerable lack of success.

[182]S. M. Warner, loc. cit., p. 56; W. M. Clark, *Israelite and Judean History*, p. 143.

[183]S. Talmon, loc. cit., pp. 326, 356, quoting M. J. Herskovitz, *Comparative Studies in Society and History* 1, 1958/9, p. 3.

[184]J. T. Luke, loc. cit., pp. 36-37.

[185]T. L. Thompson, *Historicity*, pp. 294, 320-321.

[186]S. M. Warner, loc. cit., pp. 56-57.

[187]See A. van Selms, *Marriage and Family Life in Ugaritic Literature* (Luzac, London, 1954); A. F. Rainey, *OrNS* 34, 1965, pp. 10-22; T. Jacobsen, *JNES* 2, 1943, pp. 159-172.

Another difficulty concerns the extent to which the sheer number of parallels influences our conclusions about the reality of a Patriarchal Age. In criticizing Albright and Bright for their emphasis on the quantity of contacts, Warner has asserted: 'A plethora of historical data makes the task of reconstructing a historical period more difficult.'[188] A similar position is taken by Miller and Thompson, the latter attacking what he calls 'meaningless mathematical criteria' such as the 'balance of probability'.[189] Such criticisms, however, overreach their target by some distance, for the implication of Warner's bland statement is that it would be better to have as few sources as possible. The objections really focus on two issues which have come to light as the extrabiblical evidence about the Patriarchal Age increases. First, attention must be given to the quality as well as to quantity of material, a point which is actually recognized by Warner in his plea for distinguishing between the essential and the non-essential.[190] Then one must also recognize that a relatively large amount of comparative material will not always improve our understanding of the biblical picture unless it has a ready point of contact with the knowledge that we already possess. In this connection, Warner's requirement of 'a very high degree of correlation between the biblical and the extra-biblical sources'[191] is unrealistic, since conditions of this nature cannot be defined or quantified.

Any comparison of social customs therefore will have to take the following issues into account: (1) All relevant nonbiblical material should be properly investigated in its own context, and it may have a positive or a negative function as far as our modern understanding of the patriarchs is concerned. (2) Comparisons are best drawn from those civilizations which stand in the same historic stream as ancient Israel, though links with their non-Semitic neighbours are by no means ruled out. (3) The means of transmission between the cultures concerned, including linguistic and sociological contacts, must be examined. (4) The different forms of texts are not necessarily a hindrance to a comparison of their contents. (5) The quality of the contacts is at least as important as their quantity. (6) There must be some basic link

[188]S. M. Warner, loc. cit., p. 51.
[189]J. M. Miller, loc. cit., pp. 62-63; T. L. Thompson, *Historicity*, p. 7.
[190]S. M. Warner, loc. cit., p. 51.
[191]Ibid., p. 55; cf. Luke's reference to the exactness of the similarities, loc. cit., p. 37.

between the customs involved if the contact is to be established at all, especially if the biblical custom is being explained by non-biblical material.

A brief comment should also be inserted here concerning the implications of comparative social customs for the date and historicity of the patriarchs. It has been recognized for some time that social customs often continued for many centuries and even millennia in the ancient Near East with few variations, and that it is extremely difficult to trace chronological developments. The unsuitability of customs for the dating of the patriarchs has been recognized in several quarters, and the position was well summarized in 1961 by Freedman: 'The conclusion to be drawn is rather that the MB pattern of social custom and practice survived basically unchanged for centuries in certain localities in the Near East; and Nuzi, at least, cannot be used as determinative for dating. Caution must be exercised in using cultural and social patterns for dating purposes; since these are our principal clues in the case of the Patriarchal Age, considerable flexibility in fixing the chronology is advisable.'[192] If in rare circumstances a custom is to be used for chronological purposes, it must be shown to have been displaced by other practices in other periods, and its relationship to similar contemporary customs established so that variations with the same period can be correctly interpreted.

As for the issue of historicity, the most that can be achieved by a study of the social customs is to set the general historical background in a sharper focus than would otherwise be the case. The customs form only one element in a consideration of the Patriarchal Age, and since in the nature of the case their witness is indirect, they cannot by themselves determine the matter of historicity. Nevertheless, the evidence is such that some patriarchal customs can be set against an objective historical background in the general context of ancient near-eastern family law.

4. CONCLUSION

When the biblical and nonbiblical material is subject to proper control, the way is still open for the social customs of the patriarchal narratives to be legitimately illustrated and supported from a variety of historical contexts in the ancient Near East. The

[192]D. N. Freedman, in G. E. Wright (ed.), *The Bible and the Ancient Near East* (Routledge and Kegan Paul, London, 1961), p. 205.

following list includes those examples which remain valid in the light of the conditions for comparison discussed above.

(1) The practice of granting a birthright, that is, additional privileges to an eldest son, is mentioned several times in the patriarchal narratives (Gn. 25:5-6; 25:32-34; 43:33; 49:3-4; cf. 48:13-20) and was widespread in the ancient Near East. As in the Old Testament, so elsewhere the privileges and their proportion in comparison with those of the younger sons could vary considerably. The double portion, well known in texts from the Old Babylonian to the Neo-Babylonian period, is clearly found in the Old Testament only in Deuteronomy 21:15-17.[193]

(2) In Genesis 25:23, the Hebrew term for the eldest son is not the usual $b^e\underline{k}\hat{o}r$ but $ra\underline{b}$, which is used here only in this sense. The cognate Akkadian word, $rab\hat{u}$, is also used by itself of the eldest son, but so far has turned up only in tablets of the mid-second millennium, from Nuzi, Alalah, Ugarit, and Middle Assyria.[194] Since the texts from Babylonia and those of the Neo-Assyrian period use different terminology, such as $aplu(m)\ rab\hat{u}(m)$ ('eldest heir')[195] or $maru(m)\ rab\hat{u}(m)$ ('eldest son'),[196] it appears that this biblical datum has some chronological significance.[197]

(3) The alteration of a man's inheritance prospects was never subject to a father's arbitrary decision, whether it involved the loss of the birthright privilege or total disinheritance, but was brought about in every case by serious offences against one's own family.[198] Thus Reuben's sexual offences against his father's concubine (Gn. 35:22; 49:3-4) can be linked with behaviour of similar gravity elsewhere, such as taking legal action against one's parents,[199] the

---

[193]See above, pp. 120-121.

[194]E.g. E. A. Speiser, *AASOR* 10, 1930, No. 4:12, 14 (= *HSS* 5 7), No. 21:6 (= *HSS* 5 72); D. J. Wiseman, *The Alalakh Tablets* (British Institute of Archaeology in Ankara, London, 1953), No. 87:7, 92:19-20; J. Nougayrol, etc., *Ugaritica V* (Geuthner, Paris, 1968), RS 17.36:5; G. R. Driver and J. C. Miles, *The Assyrian Laws* (Clarendon, Oxford, 1935), B 1:3, 11.

[195]E.g. J. Köhler and A. F. Ungnad, *Hammurabis Gesetze* (Pfeiffer, Leipzig, 1904-1923), No. 95; J. Köhler and A. F. Ungnad, *Assyrische Rechtsurkunden* (Pfeiffer, Leipzig, 1913), No. 41:96a.

[196]E.g. M. Schorr, *Urkunden des altbabylonischen Zivil- und Prozessrechts* (Hinrichs, Leipzig, 1913), No. 12:8.

[197]Cf. E. A. Speiser, *Genesis*, pp. 194-195.

[198]See above, p. 120.

[199]E. A. Speiser, *AASOR* 10, 1930, No. 4 (= *HSS* 5 7); F. Thureau-Dangin, *Syria* 18, 1937, pp. 249ff., RS 8.145.

usurping of a father's authority,[200] or the despising of one's parents.[201] The seriousness of disinheritance is indicated in the laws of Hammurapi where such action could be undertaken only after a second offence of sufficient importance and with the permission of a court of law.

(4) A man's ability to sell inherited property is documented at different periods in the ancient Near East, though at the present time no clear case is known of an eldest son who, like Esau, sold either his inheritance or his rights to an inheritance.[202]

(5) While the inheritance relationship between Abraham and Eliezer may find its explanation in Proverbs 17:2, the examples of adoption of slaves, and the specific case of the Old Babylonian letter from Larsa (where it is suggested that a man without sons could adopt his own slave), are also very apposite to this situation. It is precisely the custom of the adoption of one's own slave that is found only in the Larsa letter and in Genesis 15.[203]

(6) The adoption of Ephraim and Manasseh by their grandfather (Gn. 48:5) may be compared with a similar adoption of a grandson at Ugarit.[204] Furthermore, the phrase, 'they are mine' (Gn. 48:5) is almost identical to the usual ancient near-eastern adoption formulae, as found for instance in the Laws of Hammurapi para. 170.

(7) The custom of bearing 'upon the knees' has frequently been interpreted as an adoption rite since the time of Stade, who supported his view with parallels from various farflung locations including Homeric Greece, Old Germany, and the modern Bedouin.[205] The practice is mentioned five times in the Old Testament, of which three references occur in the patriarchal narratives.[206] A study of all these passages reveals no clear connection with

[200]Keret 2:vi:54-57.

[201]F. Thureau-Dangin, loc. cit., RS 8.145.

[202]See above, p. 123, cf. e.g. C. F. A. Schaeffer, *Palais royal d'Ugarit*, 6 (Imprimerie Nationale, Paris, 1970), No. 40; M. San Nicolò, *Babylonische Rechtsurkunden* (Bayerischen Akademie der Wissenschaften, Munich, 1951), No. 11.

[203]See above, p. 114. For the Larsa letter, see M. David. *Symbolae biblicae et mesopotamicae F. M. T. de Liagre Böhl dedicatae* (Brill, Leiden, 1973), pp. 90-94.

[204]I. Mendelsohn *IEJ* 9, 1959, pp. 180-183.

[205]B. Stade, *ZAW* 6, 1886, pp. 143-156.

[206]Gn. 30:3; 48:12; 50:23; Jb. 3:11-12; Is. 66:12.

adoption, however, an impression which is confirmed by similar references in two Hurrian myths and several Neo-Assyrian blessings. Rather, both the biblical and extrabiblical passages have associations with birth, name-giving, breast-feeding, and fondling of a child, and seem to indicate some kind of recognized welcome or acceptance of a newborn child into the family which could be carried out by parents, grandparents, or even great-grandparents.[207]

(8) The gift of a female slave as part of a dowry, a practice mentioned three times in the patriarchal narratives, is well known in the ancient Near East at various periods.[208] If the marriage proved to be infertile, the husband normally took matters into his own hands, but on certain occasions, the wife was able to present one of her slavegirls, sometimes specially purchased, to her husband to produce children for their own marriage. The parallels to the biblical references (Gn. 16:1-4; 30:1-13) for this rare custom are found so far in the Hammurapi Laws, and in single instances from Nuzi and Nimrud.[209] In each case, the authority over the children resulting from this union belonged not to the slavegirl who bore them but to the chief wife.[210] According to two examples from Old Babylonian texts,[211] the inheritance prospects of the sons of any concubine were uncertain until the sons were officially adopted, and similar recognition may also have been required for the sons of Hagar, Bilhah, and Zilpah in order to secure their full inheritance status.[212]

[207]H. A. Hoffner, *JNES* 27, 1968, 199 and 201, n. 27; S. Parpola, *Letters from Assyrian scholars* (AOAT 5/1, Butzon & Bercker, Kevelaer, 1970), No. 72:r.12-15; No. 186:16-17.

[208]E.g. J. Köhler and A. F. Ungnad, *Hammurabis Gesetze*, Nos. 2; 3; 9; M. Schorr, *Urkunden* (*UZP*), No. 77; M. San Nicolò and H. Petschow, *Babylonische Rechtsurkunden aus dem 6. Jahrhundert v. Chr.* (Beck, Munich, 1960), Nos. 2, 3.

[209]Laws of Hammurapi, paras. 144, 163; E. A. Speiser, *AASOR* 10, 1930, No. 2 (= *HSS* 5 67); J. N. Postgate, *Fifty Neo-Assyrian Legal Documents* (Aris & Phillips, Warminster, 1976), No. 14. Cf. also M. Schorr, *Urkunden* (*UZP*), No. 77, where a girl is purchased as a slave for the wife and as a concubine for the husband.

[210]Reading *uwār* in *HSS* 5 67:22 (see *AASOR* 10, 1930, No. 2), following Speiser's alternative reading (E. A. Speiser, *Genesis*, p. 121), and following Postgate's collation of the Nimrud text ND 2307 in *OrNS* 44, 1975, p. 485.

[211]Laws of Hammurapi, para. 170; M. Schorr, *Urkunden* (*UZP*), No. 18.

[212]On this section as a whole, see above.

(9) A father's prohibition forbidding his prospective son-in-law to take a second wife in place of his daughter is found regularly in marriage contracts, as well as in Laban's covenant with his son-in-law Jacob (Gn. 31:50).[213]

(10) Since the function of Bethuel in the arrangement of his daughter's marriage is rather ambiguous (Gn. 24), one should note the several instances in the Old and Neo-Babylonian periods where a marriage was arranged by the bride's brother, either by himself or together with their mother.[214]

(11) The description of adultery as a 'great sin' by the Philistine king Abimelek (Gn. 20:9; cf. 26:10) is known also at Ugarit and in Egyptian marriage contracts of the first millennium B.C.[215]

(12) Certain oral statements were accompanied by recognized rituals and ceremonials which functioned as legal safeguards. These included the grasping or correct placing of the right hand, and actions of this kind may be seen as the legal background of Jacob's adoption and blessing of his grandsons (Gn. 48).[216]

(13) The use of the phrase *ʾākal kesep* in the complaint of Laban's daughters may be compared with the Akkadian equivalent (*kaspa akālu*), which is used five times in marriage contracts at Nuzi for the withholding of a dowry which was normally taken from the husband's marriage payment.[217]

Since the large majority of these examples show that the patriarchal customs can be compared without difficulty with a wide range of material from the ancient Near East, it may be concluded that the patriarchal narratives accurately reflect a social and historical setting which belongs to the second and first millennia B.C. More precise dates must of course be derived from other considerations, but neither van Seters' preference for first millennium material nor Thompson's assessment of the essentially nonhistorical character of the narratives can be supported by the evidence of the social customs. From the independent viewpoint of the historian, therefore, the social parallels make the historical existence of the patriarchs more likely.

[213]See above, p. 119.
[214]See above, pp. 119, 122.
[215]See above, p. 122.
[216]Cf. e.g. C. F. Pfeiffer and E. A. Speiser, *AASOR* 16, 1936, No. 56.
[217]See above, pp. 122-123.

But our conclusion also has hermeneutical and theological implications. Two examples must suffice. That Laban should conclude the details of Jacob's marriages twenty years after the marriages were agreed (Gn. 31:50), even though a marriage contract would normally have been drawn up at the beginning, is further evidence of his duplicity and of the difficulties with which Jacob had to contend. By contrast, Abraham's refusal to take a second wife or a concubine of his own in the face of Sarah's continuing infertility gives a new insight into his regard for Sarah's position as well as his faith in God's provision of the promised heir. A proper appreciation of the social and historical dimension of the patriarchal narratives thus leads to a more accurate understanding of Genesis' theological contribution, as in the specific application of Abraham's faith.

5
Abraham Reassessed
D. J. Wiseman

Discussion of the place of the patriarchs in history and tradition has recently tended to concentrate on a proposed first-millennium origin for the present text of Genesis and on the minimizing of comparisons hitherto made between extrabiblical evidence for the second-millennium period and the biblical narratives.[1] Thus, for example, van Seters has reviewed the common stance that the patriarchal 'stories present a portrayal of a nomadic way of life which can be documented from the textual remains of the second millennium B.C.' This has been the basis of many detailed studies which have mainly discussed the nature of the types of semi-nomadism reflected in the cuneiform texts from Mari.[2] Van Seters concludes that the picture presented in Genesis accords better with the late period, though several scholars have already challenged this.[3] The whole question is in turn influenced by the assumption, yet to be confirmed, that the environment and social and economic factors at Mari on the Euphrates are applicable to the experience of the patriarchs in S. Palestine whether they are to be placed in an early or late setting. The presupposition of these criticisms of the traditional view of a patriarchal period ante-dating the monarchy need to be re-examined.

1. WAS ABRAHAM A NOMAD?

The extant Genesis account describes the movement of Abraham and his family in clear terms. First, following a divine call and promise of a grant of land to his successors, Abram set out with

[1]T. L. Thompson, *The Historicity of the Patriarchal Narratives* (De Gruyter, Berlin & New York, 1974); J. van Seters, *Abraham in History and Tradition* (Yale UP, New Haven & London, 1975).

[2]On the latter see now V. H. Matthews, *Pastoral Nomadism in the Mari Kingdom ca. 1830-1760 B.C.* (American Schools of Oriental Research Dissertation Series, Cambridge, Mass., 1978).

[3]E.g. J. T. Luke, 'Abraham and the Iron Age: Reflections on the New Patriarchal Studies', *JSOT 4*, 1977, pp. 35-47.

his wife, father and nephew from 'Ur of the Chaldees' to go to 'the land of Canaan' (Gn. 11:31). After a break in the journey of undefined duration at Harran where the father Terah died, the divine call to Abram was repeated, but this time with the extension of a command to leave with his family group the territory they appear to have acquired there and go to a land which was yet to be shown him (12:1). The call was associated with a promise of extended influence over surrounding peoples. The text links the destination with the land of Canaan of the earlier call and, without any details of the journey, next shows them arriving in Canaan with all their possessions (Gn. 12:5).

It will be noted that no emphasis is placed on the long-distant phases of the journeyings, the route taken or the method or time of travel. There is no cogent reason for accepting Gordon's hypothetical equation of 'Ur of the Chaldeans' with one of the several towns named Ura^c in N. Syria, i.e. modern Urfa, c. 30 km NW of Harran, as the starting point of the journey.[4] Even were the designation 'of the Chaldeans' taken to be a post-ninth-century erroneous explanatory note, Saggs' counter-arguments supporting the traditional S. Babylonian location are strong. He stresses that the tradition is firmly one of movement from the east of the R. Euphrates (Jos. 24:2-3) and that, in addition to the philological weakness of equating Ur with Ura^c, it would be unlikely that a move eastwards, before retracing steps west toward Canaan, would need to be recorded.[5] In any event, this part of the long journey would have been through well-watered terrain. Thus far the narrative makes no statement which need be interpreted as supporting Abraham's movements as a nomad. Rather it points to a defined change of habitat from one city and its environs to another. No mention is made of any accompanying flocks until after the departure from Harran.

The ultimate destination was stated at the beginning of the narrative when 'Terah took his son Abram, his grandson Lot son of Haran, and his daughter-in-law Sarai, the wife of his son Abram, and together they set out from Ur of the Chaldeans to go to Canaan' (Gn. 11:31). After Terah's death at Harran Abram leaves his land, people and father's family-household for the new

[4]C. H. Gordon, 'Abraham and the Merchants of Ura', *JNES 17*, 1958, pp. 28-31.
[5]H. W. F. Saggs, 'Ur of the Chaldees', *Iraq 22*, 1960, pp. 200-209.

land which God will show him (12:1, usually taken as an early source and quoted by Stephen in Acts 7:2-4).

Genesis gives no detail after leaving Harran until Moreh near Shechem is reached (Gn. 12:6). Since the party is specifically said to have included their property (*rekūš* usually includes flocks and other animals) acquired in Harran (12:5) it may be assumed that the journey was a slow one. However, at whatever period it took place the route, whether via the Balih or Euphrates river banks, was marked by sizeable towns or settlements at c. 25 km intervals, with villages between. The caravan would never have been more than a day's march from well-inhabited and watered localities.[6]

At Moreh Abram built an altar to his God Yahweh after a theophany granted him the land where he then was (12:7). Here the first reference is made to the erection of a tent which may indicate that this refers not so much to his mode of living as the setting up of a tent-shrine to mark his acceptance of the divine land-grant, a form of token take-over of the promised land.[7] Similar action was taken at Bethel only a short journey to the south (12:8) to which he returned after the diversion to Egypt prompted through famine (13:4). Movements of peoples, not necessarily nomads, in search of food there, are known also from other times.[8] The duration of Abraham's stay there is uncertain.[9]

From a vantage point on high ground in the Judean hills Abram was called to look in every direction at the promised territory before walking through its length and breadth (Gn. 13:17; cf. Jos. 18:4-8). His onward movement was next to Mamre (13:18) where he stayed for a time near Hebron by agreement with local residents (18:1).[10] The southernmost point of his journeyings was Beersheba which Abram marked with the erection of an altar and a tent at what was then probably an uninhabited area near a

[6]B. J. Beitzel, 'From Harran to Imar Along the Old Babylonian Itinerary . . .' in G. A. Tuttle (ed.) *Biblical and Near Eastern Studies: Essays in Honor of William Sanford Lasor* (Eerdmans, Grand Rapids, 1978), pp. 209-219.

[7]D. J. Wiseman, 'They lived in Tents', in G. A. Tuttle (ed.), op. cit., pp. 195-200. For the 'tent-shrine' cf. B. Rothenberg, *Timna* (Thames & Hudson, London 1972), pp. 150-2; fig. 44, pl. XI.

[8]R. Giveon, *Les bedouins shosou des documents égyptiens* (Leiden, Brill, 1977), p. 132ff.

[9]B. Z. Wacholder, 'How long did Abraham stay in Egypt?', *HUCA 35*, 1964, p. 43, refers only to very late tradition.

[10]Cf. Gn. 14:13; cf. 13:18.

'sacred tree'. Later, Beersheba was symbolic of the southernmost point of the land, just as Dan (Tell el Qâdi), near the entry to Damascus to which area Abraham moved later in military action (14:14), was to become the north point—'from Dan to Beersheba'. To Beersheba Isaac was to return later (26:27, 25). For Abraham the only further travel mentioned is the temporary stay as a 'resident-alien' (gēr) between Kadesh and Shur in the territory of Gerar then ruled by Abimelek (20:1). This summary shows the comparatively restricted nature of Abraham's movements within Palestine. They were in fact less extensive than the journeys undertaken by Jesus Christ.

It is not argued here that Abraham did not live in tents on occasions. Town and village dwellers required these customary dwelling places in spring and summer, when there was limited transhumance for pasturage of sheep and cattle (cf. Gn. 4:20), religious festivals, and some agricultural field work (Gn. 9:21). In this way his grandson Jacob is said to have 'lived a settled life and stayed among the tents' (Gn. 25:27) which may indicate that 'tent' (ᵓohel) is already used of 'settlement, home' in contrast with Esau's life in the open countryside. Jacob is stated to have occupied a house near Paddan-Aram at Succoth (Gn. 33:17) though during his flight from Laban along the desert route taken by semi-nomads through Gilead and east of Jordan there is the rare mention of his tents and camels (Gn. 31:25, 33-34). After Rachel's death he 'pitched his tent' near Migdol, a fortified settlement (Gn. 35:31). Otherwise the only reference to Jacob's tent is when he (re)built the altar near Shechem now dedicated to ᵓEl—the God of Israel' (33:18).

The later traditional interpretation of Abraham's life was that 'by faith he made his home in the promised land like a stranger in a foreign country; he lived in tents, as did Isaac and Jacob, who were heirs with him of the same promise' (Heb. 11:9 NIV). The emphasis here is not so much on his life as a transient, he is described as resident-alien and exile (cf. 'stranger and passing traveller', NEB), but rather on his act of faith in settling into the divinely promised land. That is, his faith was demonstrated by claiming de facto what God had promised him de jure.

Van Seters has used the references to tents, or the absence of them, as an indication of the late origin of these narratives. 'It is a curious fact that tents are not mentioned in the Mari archives at all and only rarely in other second-millennium sources. This is in contrast to the encampments of the bedouin which are a most distinctive feature by the mid-first millennium B.C.[11] However, such a conclusion can only be reached by an *a priori* assumption that references to tents in Genesis must date from the first millennium B.C. In practice ancient near eastern texts from either millennium rarely mention the type of dwelling unless for legal reasons or as incidentally necessary to a narrative. Moreover extant references to tents in the first millennium are in fact fewer than the thirty so far attested for the preceeding thousand years. These include the '17 kings who lived in tents' of the Assyrian King List dating to the reign of Samsi-Adad I, c. 1750 B.C., the earlier Amorite 'tent-dwellers' of the Myth of Martu and administrative texts of the Ur-Isin-Larsa periods c. 2000-1800 B.C. as well as the Egyptian Tale of Sinuhe (c. 1960-1928 B.C.) and the reference by Ramesses III (1192-1161) to the pillaging of tents in Edom.[12] Van Seters gives insufficient weight to the references to the 'encampments' (*nawûm*) in the Mari texts themselves. There is no reason, on the ground of references to 'tents' alone, to argue against the descriptions of Genesis as a faithful representation of the practices of an early period. As with references to comparative customs, such rarely changing practices preclude the use of this type of criteria for dating purposes.

1.1 *Abraham the Hebrew*

Since long-range 'external nomadism' of the type known from central Asia or Arabia is not applicable to the patriarchal narratives, it has been customary to conclude that the closest affinity is found in the pastoral nomadism, herding of livestock and limited seasonal agriculture reflected in the Mari and other texts. This involved tribal communities who were never far from their urban settled brethren and the markets on which they depended.[13] They were part of a dimorphic society, where there was interaction between both nomad and sedentary and tribe and state.[14] Such

---

[11]J. van Seters, op. cit., p. 7.

[12]For details see D. J. Wiseman as n. 7, p. 198.

[13]M. B. Rowton, 'Autonomy and Nomadism in Western Asia', *Orientalia 42*, 1973, p. 252.

[14]V. H. Matthews, op. cit., p. 7.

'nomads' were far from renouncing obligations to society as has been proposed in the 'withdrawal' theories used to explain the latter Israelite occupation and settlement of the land by Mendenhall and Gottwald.[15]

Short-range semi-nomads engaged in pastoral nomadism with livestock and a few camels moved only slowly and never more than a day's journey from water supplies. Such groups were often designated by several names any of which might indicate the presence of the tribal group (e.g. Ubrabum, Yahrurum, Amnānum who formed part of the Benē-Yamina or 'Benjaminites' at Mari).[16] It has been suggested that Abraham's link with Aram (Nahur) reflects this link between nomads and sedentary members of a single tribe. Does the designation 'Abram the Hebrew' (Gn. 14:13, hāᶜibrî) applied to him by those outside his group mark him as a 'semi-nomad'? The meaning of the word is contested. The commonest opinion is to identify this with (H)apiru which, like the variants used at different periods and places—Amurru (Amorite), Aramu (Aramean) or later Arabu (Arab)—means 'semi-nomad' or the like. The Amorites ('Westerners') are first named (MAR.TU—Amurru) in texts from Fara (c. 2600 B.C.) and in a date formula of the reign of Šar-kalli-šarri (2250 B.C.) and last as an ethnic group in Babylonia in the time of Ammisaduqa (c. 1645 B.C.).[17] Their homeland is stated to be in Syria (Jebel Bišri) though their activities affected both the west and south-east (Babylonia) of the so-called 'Fertile Crescent'. The Hapiru are occasionally mentioned in early texts from Syria (Brak, Mari and Alalah) then increasingly so from the seventeenth century onwards. It is not certain whether these Hapiru (Egypt. ᶜprw) should be equated with the Hebrews (ᶜibrîm) either linguistically or functionally. The 'Hapiru' appears to be a sociological, and not an ethnic, designation, and for this reason the 'Hebrew' slaves of Genesis

[15]G. E. Mendenhall, 'Migration Theories vs Cultural Change as an Explanation for Early Israel', in G. McRae (ed.), *Society of Biblical Literature Seminar Papers, 1976*, pp. 135-143; N. K. Gottwald, 'Were the Early Israelites Pastoral Nomads?', *Rhetorical Criticism: Essays in Honor of James Muilenberg* (eds. J. Jackson and M. Kessler, Pickwick, Pittsburgh, 1974), p. 234; *JSOT* 7 (1978), p. 46.

[16]Cf. M. Anbar, *Biblica 49*, 1968, pp. 221-232.

[17]M. Liverani, 'The Amorites', in D. J. Wiseman (ed.), *Peoples of Old Testament Times (POTT)*, (1973), pp. 100-133.

(39:14, 17; Ex. 1:15-19, etc.) may refer to semi-nomads.[18] From early days there are occasional references to the term Aramean (Aramu) both as a place-name (Naram-Sin, c. 2350 B.C.) and personal name (Mari, Alalah, Egypt, Drehem). Van Seter's assumption that any reference to Aramean, including the reference to 'the ancestor who was a roving Aramean' (Gn. 26:5 possibly Jacob), must be a late interpolation may be questioned.[19] 'Aramean' is an increasingly common designation of the 'semi-nomads' from the twelfth century until displaced by the term 'Arab', used for the tribes ranging from the Damascus region down to N. Arabia from the ninth century B.C. onwards. However, the close-knit Assyrian provincial system almost certainly precludes this later period (Iron Age) as a realistic historical background for the Abrahamic episodes as proposed by Thompson.[20]

Among the many suggestions for the meaning of the term 'Hebrew' are a denominative from the ancestor Eber (Gn. 10:21);[21] or 'one who passes through, crosses territory' (*ebēru*). The latter is unlikely since the term to pass through territory used in Genesis is ᶜ*ātaq* (Gn. 12:8; 26:22, elsewhere commonly in Job, cf. Mari *etēqu*). It may however have been so interpreted by the LXX of Genesis 14:13 which describes Abraham as a wanderer or transient. Other interpretations of 'Hebrew' as 'dusty ones' (*epru*); providing or receiving supplies (*epēru*, ᶜ*pr*); 'transferred, without a stable habitat' (ᶜ*apr*); or 'lord' (Hurrian *ewri*), now receive little support. The solitary mention of Abraham as 'the Hebrew' cannot of itself determine either the date of the narrative or the activities he undertook. It may again be questioned whether the purpose of the Genesis narrative was, as is commonly supposed, to portray him as a semi-nomad.

1.2 *Abraham the prince*

It has long been considered that the purpose and emphasis of the narratives concerning Abraham is to describe the divine covenant

[18]J. Weingreen, 'Saul and Habiru', *Fourth World Congress of Jewish Studies I* (1967; World Union of Jewish Studies, Jerusalem), pp. 63-66.

[19]A. Malamat, 'The Arameans', *POTT*, pp. 134-135; M. Richardson in a paper read at Tyndale House, Cambridge, on 14 July 1979 argues for ᵓ*bd* as meaning 'lost' not 'roving' in Dt. 26:5.

[20]T. L. Thompson, op. cit., pp. 325-326.

[21]G. Pettinato, *BA 39*, 1975, p. 47.

made with him, which included the grant of land and promise of posterity to inherit it. If, as is here suggested, the primary concern is not with Abraham as a 'semi-nomad', it is more clearly with his status as a 'resident-alien' in the promised land (gēr, Gn. 17:8 etc.). He acknowledged this as his position (Gn. 23:4) when addressing others of this same status who lived in a mixed ethnic situation, possibly as a minority among the Canaanites who yet held land themselves in the Hebron area. These men called Abraham 'the Prince' (nāsīᵓ; Gn. 23:5 AV). Abraham had by this time lived in the area for sixty-five years (cf. Gn. 12:4; 17:17; 32:1) and was treated with respect by Ephron the Hethite,[22] from whom he sought to purchase the cave of Machpelah. 'You are a mighty prince among us' (Gn. 23:6 NIV), they said, and the title appears to have been used sincerely and in accordance with local custom. Whether the phrase is interpreted here as a superlative,[23] or as an acknowledgment of his appointment to the position by his God, it is in any case used by a man of another ethnic origin and religion and denotes a position of respect and leadership.[24] It is used of the chiefs of the men of Shechem (Gn. 34:2) who, with the chiefs of the Midianites (Jos. 13:21; Nu. 25:18) and Edom were concerned in the same promise as made to Abraham (Gn. 17:4-8). This same title of 'prince' (nāsīᵓ) was later applied to David and Solomon (1 Kgs. 11:34) but appears to have fallen into disuse after the adoption of the title 'king' (melek, 1 Sa. 8:5, cf. Ex. 22:28).

It is possible that the use of this title for Abraham implies some idea of an election procedure by the peoples of ten ethnic groups named as holding land adjacent to Abraham (Gn. 15:18-21).[25] Abram had earlier made an alliance with Mamre, Eshcol and Aner among other local 'Amorites' (Gn. 14;13, 21). Abraham was their acknowledged leader (14:24).

Abraham's rank and dignity were also acknowledged by the Egyptian king (Gn. 12:10-20) who would otherwise have dismissed an insignificant foreigner, especially if he were a suppliant for

[22]On the Hittites in the patriarchal narratives see H. A. Hoffner, *POTT*, pp. 213-214.

[23]D. W. Thomas, 'A consideration of Some Unusual Ways of Expressing the Superlative in Hebrew', *VT 3*, 1953, pp. 210-219.

[24]E. A. Speiser, 'Background and Function of the Biblical Nāsiᵓ', *CBQ 25*, 1963, pp. 111-119.

[25]Speiser, loc. cit., p. 115.

relief or a mere herdsman-nomad, whose action had affronted the court. Instead Abraham is given lavish gifts (12:16, 20) and made 'a very rich man' (13:2) though he was previously recognised as a person of substance (12:5; cf. 24:22). The pharaoh may have seen in his relationship with Sarah as 'sister' some covenant relationship which included an obligation to protect her beyond the extent normally due to a wife (12:14), much as Abraham did for Lot who, though his nephew (11:34) was described as his 'brother, ally' in 14:14 (cf. 13:8). Abraham and Sarah rejected any 'covenant-relationship', as commonly made between equals, which any marriage bond with Egypt would have implied (12:17).

Similarly, in his dealings with another foreign ruler, Abimelek, king of Gerar, Abraham is treated as a person of equal status to the extent that a covenant treaty between them included provisions of land tenure which were normally matters of royal prerogative (20:15). That this parity agreement was conceived of as 'inter-state' rather than 'inter-individual' can perhaps be adduced from the curses to be invoked in case of defection. When this occurred through the unwitting action by Abimelek over Sarah the curse was against the city-state and its ruler and to be paid off publicly (20:7, 9, 16).

Moreover the agreement made by Abimelek and his army commander bears all the hallmarks of an ancient parity treaty including provision for the parties to keep each other informed of any transgression of border or well rights (21:26-27). Another indication of the high status and power of Abraham is the clause requiring Abraham never to deal falsely with Abimelek, his children or descendents, and to show reciprocal good will (*ḥésed*). Abraham was thought powerful enough to be able to interfere with internal policy within Gerar or to maintain relations on a 'state-equivalent' basis. That Abraham countered with claims of his own (13:25) is an indication that he was not acting as a mere vassal. This treaty lasted at least until ratified by Isaac (26:28-29) and probably until the time of the judges in early Israel (Jdg. 13:1).

Objection has been taken to this narrative because of the supposed anachronisms in the references to 'Philistines' in this patriarchal narrative. Abimelek's territory is said to have included the 'land of the Philistines' (21:32, 34) and in the days of Isaac's dealing with the same Abimelek, or a succeeding king of that name or throne-name, was titled 'king of the Philistines' who were the main inhabitants of Gerar at the time (26:1, 8, 14-18). Van Seters finds this 'anachronism' to be evidence for the late and fictional origin of the narrative,[26] though most scholars take these notes to be an erroneous gloss by some later editor or a later editorial assumption that these areas, though originally Canaanite, were those subsequently occupied by Philistines. Most agree that the 'Philistines' were among the 'Sea-peoples' who fought against Ramesses III and in the late thirteenth century settled in SW Palestine in a pentapolis (of which Gerar was, however, not one such city) ruled by lords (serānîm). Certainly at the time of the exodus there were Philistines in the same area (Jos. 13:2-3; Jdg. 3:3; Ex. 13:17). These references are, therefore, not proven late anachronisms. It is noted that the inhabitants of the Gaza area appear to have been the Avim who were then replaced or joined by the Kaphtorim (Dt. 2:23). The mixed population of the area can be judged by the personal names; Abimelek and Ahuzzat (Semitic), and Phicol (Anatolian?), though they concluded treaties using formulae and procedures long attested throughout the ancient Near East.[27] The weight of evidence points to a more easterly location for Caphtor (Egypt. Keftiu) usually identified with Crete. The artistic evidence put forward by Wainwright and the recent archaeological studies by Strange, however, point afresh to Cyprus and the adjacent coastlands as the possible location of Caphtor at this early period. This would also coincide with the appearance of Cypriote wares in Palestine in Middle Bronze I-II.[28] If the 'Philistines' were the bearers or importers of this ware it would accord with their small numbers and limited location before the larger quantities of Cypriote 'bichrome' wares found in the early Late Bronze Age, the period (MB-LB) taken by Bimson's revised ceramic chronology as evidence for the late fifteenth-century conquest.[29]

This argument is perhaps the same as the earlier one that small groups of 'Philistines', as an offshoot of other Aegean peoples,

[26]J. van Seters, op. cit., p. 52.

[27]The framework of the treaties of the patriarchal period is the same as the so called 'Hittite' treaties of the second millennium. The latter are, however, 'Mesopotamian' in language and style.

[28]R. Amiran, *IEJ* 19, 1969, p. 225; cf. R. S. Merrillees, *Levant* 3, 1971, pp. 56-79.

[29]J. J. Bimson, *Redating the Exodus and Conquest*, JSOT supp. 5, 1978, pp. 168-172.

had come as immigrants into the Gaza area at an early period, just as Philistines from Kaphtor (cf. Am. 9:7; Je. 47:4) were already in the same area according to Deuteronomy 2:23. Aegean trade is attested in the Middle Minoan II period and the name 'Philistines' could have been used to denote such traders. If Bimson's proposed chronology for the patriarchal period is accepted with Middle Bronze I for Abraham and Middle Bronze II for Jacob (see his essay in this volume), then the mention of Philistines in the time of Jacob and a district of Philistines included in an earlier Abimelek's territory would be understandable.

What was Abraham's role as a 'prince'? As will be shown, this term may have 'dynastic' overtones. Meanwhile, an examination of the means whereby Abraham exercised his function as leader or prince ($n\bar{a}s\bar{\imath}$) shows that he carried out the function of the local or district governor. This office of 'governor' ($\check{S}\bar{a}pi\underline{t}um$) is well attested from the Mari documents c. 1800 B.C.,[30] but also appears to have been exercised in the city-state of Ebla earlier. Such governors acted within their region on behalf of the supreme ruler who had appointed them. Regional governors are attested in Palestine in the period of the so-called judges ($\check{s}\bar{o}p\bar{e}\underline{t}$; Jdg. 2:16-18, better translated 'governor'). Abraham acknowledged the Lord God who had called him, granted him the land and instructed him to 'walk about' (i.e. act as judge) through the length and breadth of the land (Gn. 13:17).[31] For him God was 'the supreme Governor of all the earth who does right' (Gn. 18:25; cf. Jdg. 11:27). To 'do the right' is the principal role of judge in the exercise of law and order.[32]

The maintenance of justice, law and order is the first requirement of the governor within his designated area. So Abraham

---

[30]A. Marzal, 'The Provincial Governor at Mari: His Title and Appointment', *JNES* 30, 1971, pp. 186-217.

[31]Heb. *Hithallek*, even without the preposition 'before (God)' is more frequently used figuratively than literally. Rather than just to 'live' it denotes action according to the divine law expressed in judicial processes. Cf. 1 Sa. 12:2; 25:15 and referring to land-tenure, Jos. 18:4, 8; Jdg. 21:24. Since this use of the hithpa^cel is more frequent than that of literally 'walking to and fro' (as 2 Sa. 11:2) it may be asked whether this significance does not apply to Gn. 13:17 and to Enoch (Gn. 5:22, 24) as to God's active presence among his people (Lv. 26:12; 2 Sa. 7:6-7; Dt. 23:15). (A fuller study of this term will follow.)

[32]D. J. Wiseman, Law and Order in Old Testament Times'. *Vox Evangelica* 7, 1973, pp. 5-21.

acted dominantly in settling disputes both within his own family (Gn. 13:17) and also over water rights (21:25). Abraham had to order his own family and set an example of 'keeping the way of the Lord' by the exercise of justice and law (18:19). In carrying out this responsibility the patriarchs were like a local chief (abbītim) working in the name of the king or deity. Provincial governors were usually granted lands in lieu of salary for their maintenance by the overlord, and Abraham's grant of land may have been for a similar purpose. Sometimes the governor was required to take military action in support of law and order. For this local forces were employed. As in a case at Mari, Abraham faced a problem of involuntary deportation, so using his trained retainers together with men supplied by his allies he recovered Lot (14:14, 24). Other juridical action includes his adjudication in land disputes (as 13:7). As a judge or governor he would sit in the court at the gate. For an inter-ethnic group case he sat with other local elders (23:10). The 'righteousness and judgment' which characterize God as the supreme and ideal ruler had to be reflected by all to whom he gave responsibility as sub-governor. They themselves would be judged by how far and in what manner they kept the 'way of the Lord'.[33]

Diplomacy, especially with neighbouring states, was also a concern of the governor on behalf of his overlord. This may perhaps be seen in Abraham's relations with the kings of Egypt and Gerar, in both of which Abraham intervenes and in which the giving and receiving of gifts are part of the process (12:16, 21; 21:23, 27). The 'misunderstandings' about Sarah might have been part of this process since the interchange of females or other persons was sometimes involved.[34]

Another responsibility was the collection of tribute, dues and taxes which a governor would forward to the authority or hold for his local use. This might include dues used in the support of a local cult-centre. The incident with Melchizedek may reflect this. Abraham 'gave him (Melchizedek) a tithe of everything' (14:20, according also to the traditional interpretation of Heb. 7:4, 10).

[33]Note the rare use of the singular here, cf. Jdg. 2:23; 2 Kgs. 21:22; Pr. 10:29; Is. 40:3; Ezk. 18:29.

[34]Often the interchange of daughters marked the ratification of parity-treaties, cf. Solomon's many such marriages (1 Kgs. 3:1; 9:16; 10:24-25). The acquisition of Hagar in Egypt may have been part of the royal gift (Gn. 12:16).

This act would not only acknowledge the identity of El-Elyon here with Yahweh, but would also support practice of a levy on war-spoils.[35] It is possible, though unlikely, that 'he gave him' could refer to a payment by Melchizedek to Abraham as the local representative of God.

A local governor was also often involved in commercial transactions both on behalf of his superior and on his own account. This has led some to classify Abraham as 'a merchant-prince',[36] but the evidence for this is not easily found. As a local governor he had to keep his overlord informed of all matters affecting both his own land and its principal citizens and also of affairs in neighbouring city-states. Abraham's intercession with Yahweh on the impending action against Sodom, which would be viewed as worthy of divine punishment for breaking the law, might come into this category.

A further duty fell upon a governor to provide accommodation, escort and hospitality to any dignitary who might pass through his territory, and especially for any messengers from the overlord. Thus Abraham treated the leader of the three men who came to Mamre with much respect, addressing him as a superior ('my lord'), and providing him with lavish hospitality and with information. Then when two of them departed he provided an escort, provisions and intelligence for the onward journey (Gn. 18:1-21).

This interpretation of the role of Abraham both in his movements within the promised land and his action within it has sought to act as a balance to the traditional view of him as a nomad chief. Over-emphasis on the latter has led to an ungrounded comparison with extra-biblical data which has to be constantly reappraised or redated in the light of new evidence. As a result, changes in interpretation have led some to believe that the biblical narratives themselves have been found at fault.

1.3 Abraham the father

One argument brought against the placing of the patriarchs a millennium or so before the time of the Hebrew monarchy is the supposed improbability of long oral and/or written tradition

---

[35]Cf. Nu. 31:28. $m\,^csr$ is not only used of sacred payments but is sometimes comparable with the mks-tax.

[36]See n. 4.

going back over several centuries. This implies that the genealogical consciousness of the Hebrews is a later fabrication. The
biblical tradition itself is unanimous in placing the patriarchs
before the exodus from Egypt, that is at least 300, and possibly
more than 500 years before David. The text is consistent in
making each successive generation refer back to 'Abraham our
father'. Thus Isaac uses this title throughout his life (Gn. 26:24)
and finally when passing on his blessing to Jacob (28:4). Jacob
also refers to Abraham in this way (28:13), stressing his ancestry
when making a covenant with his father-in-law Laban (hence
'The God of Abraham, the God of Nahor' 31:53; cf. 31:42), and in
his turn while blessing his son Joseph (48:15-18). This reference
to ancestors in the form 'the Lord God of your fathers, the God of
Abraham, the God of Isaac, the God of Jacob' was to become a
dominant note both in the call of Moses (Ex 3:6, 15-16; 4:5; 6:3)
and in the subsequent authentication of his mission in bringing
the descendents of these three named persons into the land said to
have been promised to Israel's forefathers.[37]

This concept is not surprisingly reiterated when Joshua took
possession of the land (Jos. 24:2-3) and later during the monarchy,
by Elijah in his opposition to those who would alienate the land
from being God's possession to his people and thus thwart their
implementation of their spiritual obligations to him (1 Kgs.
13:33). Such passing allusions would have been both unnecessary
and meaningless if written by a later scribe, unless the pre-
existence of Abraham was a fact.

David, in emphasizing the continuity of his family, dynasty and
covenant with his ancestors Abraham, Isaac and Jacob (1 Chr.
16:16; 29:18) finds echoes with each succeeding generation concerned with their title to the land, Jehoshaphat (2 Chr. 7),
Hezekiah (2 Chr. 30:6 cf. Is. 29:32; 41:8) and Jeremiah (33:26). Of
these ancestors Abraham, both as the first and as the reputed
original recipient of the promissary oath, was the most frequently
named.[38] This tradition continued through the exile (Ne. 9:7; Ezk.
33:24), through intertestamental times, and into the New Testament when it was customary in thinking of ethnic and religious
origins to 'look to Abraham the father' (Mt. 3:9; Lk. 3:8; cf. Is.

---

[37]Ex. 32:13; 33:1; Lv. 26:42; Nu. 32:11; Dt. 1:8; 6:10; 9:5, 27; 29:13; 30:20; 34:4.
[38]Is. 29:32; Ps. 47:1; 105:6, 9, 42.

51:2) and affirm that 'Abraham is our forefather' (Jn. 8:39; Rom. 4:1). Jesus Christ took the same standpoint (e.g. Lk. 20:37) and his claim that 'Before Abraham was I am' would have been meaningless to his hearers if it indicated, among other assertions, merely a chronological precedence somewhere between David and the exile rather than a claim to pre-existence as the authority prior to Abraham, the much respected first forefather of Israel.

This clear and unbroken sense of ancestry was for the Hebrews, as for other nations in the ancient Near East, linked with the title to their land. In land transactions reference is usually made back to the original donor, often a king as the one who acquired the territory whether through conquest or purchase. Land-tenure was dependent on the ability to make proper reference back to the original forefather who held the title authenticating the registration and from then on transmitted the deeds.[39] Had Israel and Judah not been able to refer to their origin in specific terms, which for them included the transmitted tradition of the Divine promise quite apart from any *de facto* possession gained through conquest, they would have been considered by others as untitled holders of it.

It is not without significance that the same applied to other nations. Early in the second millennium B.C., and usually associated with a western or Amorite tradition already of earlier origin, the idea of family descent associated with the legitimacy of the ruler, king or dynasty is already attested.[40] An Old Babylonian text dated c. 1700 B.C. already shows that the earliest names in a list of kings or 'patriarchs' were synonymous with those of individuals, tribes or places named after them.[41] Finkelstein argued that this genealogical list of the ancestors of the First Amorite (Hammurapi) Dynasty at Babylon follows the same traditional type as that used in the Assyrian King List which records the ancestors of Shamshi-Adad I, king of Assyria, itself dated about the same time.[42] Both texts were probably written to 'legitimize'

[39]This is also implied by the Assyrian and Babylonian King Lists and by kudurru inscriptions of the second millennium B.C.

[40]W. G. Lambert in P. Garelli (ed.), *Le Palais et la Royauté* (P. Geuthner, Paris, 1974), p. 634.

[41]J. Finkelstein, 'The Genealogy of the Hammurapi Dynasty', *JCS* 20, 1966, p. 97-99.

[42]A. K. Grayson, 'The Early Development of Assyrian Monarchy', *UF* 3, 1971, p. 317-319.

the dynasty and both represent a consciousness of tribal origins as of major chronological significance. Moreover, there existed prior to both compositions a separate document giving the earliest traditions of 'the kings who lived in tents'.[43] Though once dismissed by some scholars as 'fictitious' or 'mythical', fewer would now suggest this following reference in the Ebla texts which include a treaty made c. 2300 B.C. between Ebrum of that place with one Tudiya of Assyria, who is named as the first in the Assyrian list.[44] Malamat has compared these lists with the biblical genealogies.[45] He classes the first nine to eleven names as the 'genealogical stock' or common antecedent generation which may be compared with the list of Abraham's predecessors in Genesis 11:10-26. These are followed by a statement of the 'determinative line' of the generations which bridge from the common genealogical stock to the pedigree of the tribes giving rise to the immediate line in question. For Babylonia this was the Amnānum and Yahrurum, well known from the Mari texts, and for Assyria Abazu and Apishal. It is noteworthy that these, like the 'determinative' line of the Hebrew patriarchs Abraham, Isaac and Jacob all trace back to the same region of NE Syria. Following this the Old Testament traces its pre-Davidic ancestors through the tribal lines of Judah and Benjamin (cf. 1 Chr. 2:5, 9-15; Ru. 4:18-22). It could be that the designation of Abraham as 'the Hebrew' was to single him out as the founder of the 'determinative' line which led to David.[46]

Two further indications of the purpose and use of this early Babylonian genealogical list can be noted. First, the list was taken by the king in question (Ammiṣaduqa of Babylon, c. 1645 B.C.) as a true record of his lineage with respect to the 'throne'. When David instituted the liturgy in Jerusalem, his new capital (1 Chr. 16:16) and handed on the dynasty to his successor (1 Chr. 29:18) he made reference to Abraham as his forefather. Secondly, the Babylonian genealogy appears to be associated, or compiled for use, with mortuary offerings (kispus) made to the spirits of royal

[43]W. G. Lambert, JCS 22, 1968, p. 2.

[44]G. Pettinato, BA 39, 1976, p. 48. (Since writing this identification is seriously questioned.)

[45]A. Malamat, 'King Lists of the Old Babylonian Period and Biblical Genealogies', JAOS 22, 1968, pp. 163-173.

[46]Ibid., p. 167.

ancestors. David's association with Saul on a similar occasion (1 Sa. 20:5, 18) acknowledged Saul's rightful place in the royal lineage which should normally have taken precedence over David's personal annual remembrance of his own ancestral line (verses 6, 29). The importance of 'gathering to his fathers' a deceased member of the royal line has long been noted and this is already reflected in the patriarchal period for Abraham, Isaac and Jacob being so revered (Gn. 25:8; 49:29, 33).[47] This tradition also was linked with inheritance of the land (cf. Gn. 50:24-25; Ex. 13:19; Jos. 24:32). Possession of the land is specifically the subject of psalms in which the covenant with Abraham is mentioned (Ps. 47:9 cf. verse 4; 105:6, 9 cf. verses 11, 44).

It is suggested that all these varied references which show that a pre-Davidic consciousness of patriarchal ancestry, with extra-biblical examples of a similar realization of early origins, cannot all be assigned to some reworking of the text by a number of different later editors to whose work they are commonly attributed.

Another aspect of genealogical consciousness is the evidence of Mesopotamian historical texts which make reference to earlier persons and events. While some might argue that this could be explained by the individual nation's or family group's attempt to justify its place by positing early origins, this would be most unlikely over so wide a range of texts unless it could be shown to be a widespread literary phenomenon. This is unsupported by other forms of historical verification. For example, Assyrian kings from Shalmaneser I (1273-1244) to Esarhaddon (680-669 B.C.) make reference back to their ancestor Shamshi-Adad I c. 1820 B.C. naming intermediaries and events in precise terms from 60 to 580 years earlier in relation to temple building. Although in a minority of cases there is disagreement over chronology, there is none concerning the historical nature of the forefather.[48] The chronological note linking the beginning of Solomon's temple-building with Israel's coming out of Egypt (1 Kgs. 6:1), though variously interpreted chronographically[49] is a similar reference back in like circumstances within Israel's history.

[47]Gn. 25:8; 49:29, 33. Cf. M. Bayliss, 'The Cult of Dead Kin in Assyria and Babylonia', *Iraq* 35, 1973, pp. 115-125.

[48]H. Tadmor, 'The Chronology of the Ancient Near East in the Second Millennium B.C.', B. Mazar (ed.), *World History of the Jewish People* 2 (Massada Publishing Co., Tel Aviv), pp. 69-71.

[49]J. Bimson, op. cit., pp. 88-92.

References to ancestors are well attested in colophons to literary texts and records from the patriarchal period could similarly have been transmitted through the four centuries to the time of Moses and onwards.[50] Genealogies spanning a long period of time are known from both Mesopotamia and Egypt, usually giving the male line. Seven long Egyptian genealogies are known, each spanning several centuries. That of Ukhhotep who lived in the reign of Amenemhat II c. 1925 B.C. (a period often ascribed to Abraham) lists fifty-nine ancestors going back to the IXth Dynasty of Egypt c. 2500 B.C.[51] The genuineness and early transmission of these documents are beyond dispute, and they provide sufficient warrant for the feasibility of transmission of the knowledge of ancestors, both orally and in writing, by the close-knit Hebrew peoples. In this they were in step with other ancient near-eastern traditions and there is no need to fall back upon any theory of a fictional creation of 'founding fathers' at some late first-millennium date.

1.4 *The name of Abraham*

Thompson has rightly made two points. First, the contention that the name Abram fits 'only' or 'best' into the first half of the second millennium B.C. is false. Secondly, the occurrence of similar personal names in any given period is not, of itself, chronological evidence for the historicity of a patriarch bearing the same, or similar, name.[52] While at present it does appear that names like Ab(i)ram follow a form structure and language common in W. Semitic at all periods, there is wide divergence as to both its meaning ('Father is exalted', 'Exalted father', 'the Exalted (one) is (my) father' etc.) and the validity of the parallels drawn with extrabiblical texts.[53] It should be noted that of the few possible names cited by Thompson for the first millennium most are questionable: (1) the supposed Egyptian place name $sb3rm^c$ has to be taken as a personal name (Abirama); (2) the seventh-century

[50]P. J. Wiseman, *Clues to Creation in Genesis* (Marshall, Morgan & Scott, London, 1977), pp. 68-71.

[51]Cf. also for details K. A. Kitchen, *The Bible in its World* (Paternoster, Exeter, 1977), pp. 66-68.

[52]T. L. Thompson, op. cit., pp. 35, 22.

[53]T. L. Thompson, op. cit., pp. 25-36.

female name ˹AD-ra-mi⁵⁴ may be explained otherwise than Abi-
rami (cf. Alalah Idrimi). This means that, apart from the Abiram
of 1 Kings 16:24 (ᵓbyrm) there are very few attested similar names
for this late period. Even should the name-type Ab(i)ram be
proven to be common at all periods, that of the form Abraham
(ᵓbrhm) is not. Special emphasis is given to the fact that 'Abraham'
is a new and distinctive name (Gn. 17:5). Even if the name is to be
taken as a dialectical variant of Abram⁵⁵ the context clearly
provides a unique even if popular etymology as 'Father of multi-
tudes' which is closely linked with the covenant and promissary
oath.⁵⁶ It was a God-given name declaring that God would make
Abraham, then childless, ancestor of both his own people (12:2)
and of many different groups (17:5-6). It is thus a form of
'dynastic' ancestral name.⁵⁷ The change of name marks both a
new era and a new status and is consistently used in the subsequent narrative 'probably much the same as in a king's assumption
of a special throne-name'.⁵⁸ It is not necessary to view the interpretation of the name, be it a 'popular etymology' or 'word-play',
as a literary device to interpret a later theology of promise,⁵⁹ for it
would be more logical to expect that the belief in God's choice of
the patriarchs and his promises to them were present in Israel
from the very beginning.⁶⁰ Such a view is already present in what
is considered to be one of the earliest poems in the Bible (12:3 cf.
Nu. 24:17-19). Moreover, such 'popular etymologies' usually refer
back from the monarchy to an earlier pre-monarchic tradition,⁶¹
and from early historical periods a new line or dynasty was
marked by the introduction of a new name (e.g. Sargon, Shamshi-
Ad(d)u) and with a new or re-emphasized relationship with a

[54]K. Tallqvist, *Assyrian Personal Names* (Acta Societatis Scientarum Fennicae
XLIII/1, Helsingfors, 1914), p. 5; M. Noth, *ZDMG* 81, 1927, p. 31.

[55]T. L. Thompson, op. cit., p. 23; E. A. Speiser, *Genesis* (Doubleday, Garden
City, NY, 1964), p. 124, takes the median -*ha*- as a secondary extension in a
manner common in Aramaic.

[56]The assumption that Gn. 17:5 offers a word play on *abraham* for ᵃ*birham*,
'chief of a multitude' does not seem to allow for *ab hᵃmôn goyîm* being a
separate explanatory note on a rare (old?) use or *r-m* for *r-h-m*.

[57]So the specific reference to 'royal' succession in Gn. 17:6.

[58]E. A. Speiser, op. cit., p. 129.

[59]T. L. Thompson, op. cit., pp. 24-25.

[60]J. Bright, *Covenant and Promise* (SCM, London, 1977), p. 26.

[61]T. L. Thompson, op. cit., p. 24.

particular deity.[62] While the name 'Abraham' as compared with 'Abram' may not be of the same order of differentiation as other dynastic names, it is significant that, as with other such names, the name of Abraham is applied throughout the Old Testament to the patriarch alone.[63] Evidence of its application to other individuals is attested only after the sixth century A.D.[64]

It is suggested that the foregoing aspects of the person and function of Abraham are in keeping with his role as a 'great man' and worthy founding father of a nation, and need to be taken into account in any assessment of the historicity of the patriarchal narratives.

[62]E.g. the throne-name Nebuchadrezzar (I) was linked with a resurgence of the worship of Marduk; W. G. Lambert in W. S. McCullough (ed.), *The Seed of Wisdom: Essays in Honour of T. J. Meek* (Univ. of Toronto Press, 1964), pp. 3-13.

[63]M. Noth, *Die israelitischen Personnennamen . . . (1966)*, p. 60, attributes this to respect, but the matter needs further investigation in comparison with other 'throne/dynastic' names.

[64]None of the many hundreds of the names of rabbis in the Mishnah and Talmud bears the name of Abraham (or indeed of Moses, David or Solomon). Midrash Rabbah Gen. R. 49:1 states that a man should not give his son a name 'like Pharaoh, Sisera or Sennacherib but rather Abraham, Isaac . . . '. This does not appear to have taken effect quickly. The widespread use of Abraham as a personal name comes into common use in parallel with that of Ibrahim in the Islamic world after the seventh century B.C. (I owe this reference to Dr. M. Weizmann).

6
The Religion of the Patriarchs[1]
G. J. Wenham

1. INTRODUCTION

For well over a hundred years the religious ideas and practices of the patriarchs have attracted scholarly attention. In view of the place Abraham occupies in various religious traditions this is understandable. What is more surprising is that in the scholarly debate, no clear consensus about the content of his religion has emerged.[2]

At least four factors can be pinpointed which have contributed to this uncertainty. First, Genesis itself says relatively little about patriarchal religion. It tells us much about their religious experiences, but little about their beliefs or religious practices.

Secondly, the accounts of the patriarchs as we now have them are all post-Sinaitic, that is they presuppose the innovations in belief and practice that date from the time of Moses. Various texts allude to the differences between the religion of Moses and that of the patriarchs. For example Exodus 6:3 says: 'I appeared to Abraham, to Isaac, and to Jacob, as El Shaddai (God Almighty, RSV), but by my name the LORD I did not make myself known to them.' Joshua 24:14 states: 'Put away the gods your fathers served beyond the River, and in Egypt, and serve the LORD.' Both these texts appear to contrast the religious ideas and practices of the fathers with the post-Mosaic period. Yet Genesis itself gives very few hints that the patriarchs worshipped other gods. Indeed it usually describes the God who appears and speaks to the patriarchs as 'the LORD' (Yahweh), i.e. the God of Moses.

---

[1]This essay was written at the Hebrew University, Jerusalem, during sabbatical leave there supported by a grant from the British Academy. I should also like to thank Professor F. M. Cross and Mr. A. R. Millard for advice on several points.

[2]For a thorough survey of German Protestant views in the last 100 years see H. Weidmann, *Die Patriarchen und ihre Religion im Licht der Forschung seit Wellhausen* (Göttingen: Vandenhoeck and Ruprecht, 1968).

This prompts the question (thirdly): is this identification of the patriarchs' God with that of Moses a theological assertion by the writer of Genesis, who was sure the same God had spoken to Abraham as spoke to Moses? Or do the statements in Genesis implying that Yahweh revealed himself to the patriarchs correspond to the patriarchs' own conception of the God they worshipped? Answers to this most basic question are complicated by further considerations. It is generally held that Genesis is composed of several sources giving rather different accounts of the religion of the patriarchs.

And last but not least, the theological convictions of those who study Genesis affect their conclusions. Jews and Christians who regard Abraham as the father of the faithful are reluctant to accept that he was a polytheist who served strange gods. On the other hand, scholars who hold that religion is essentially a human creation are hardly likely to suppose that the patriarchs were pure monotheists.

These briefly are the main problems that confront a would-be historian of Old Testament religion in describing the beliefs and religious practices of the patriarchs. To arrive at the pure historical truth one needs to be able to shed one's own presuppostions, and distinguish between the interpretations of Genesis and the underlying facts. Such a programme is regrettably impossible. My aims are more modest. In this essay I shall first of all set out the statements of Genesis about patriarchal religion. These raw statements will enable us to grasp how the final editor of Genesis viewed patriarchal religion.

Since it is generally held that Genesis is made up of earlier sources J, E and P, the pictures of patriarchal religion found in them will be described next. Assumptions about the dates of these sources have played a large part in assessing the validity of these different pictures. But in an effort to distinguish the authentic early elements in the accounts from later interpretations more recent scholarship has emphasized the similarities between other early Semitic religions and the beliefs of the patriarchs. So a few of the most representative accounts of patriarchal religion will be surveyed next.

Finally an attempt will be made to evaluate the different suggestions. If one is not to fall back on dogmatic assumptions, there is only one way to do this: to ask which of the supposed reconstructions is most self-consistent and at the same time most true to the biblical data. In particular I shall focus on three questions. Did the patriarchs worship a God called Yahweh? Are the divine promises made to the patriarchs an early element in the tradition or were they added by later editors? Did patriarchal religion differ from later Israelite religion, or are the accounts in Genesis simply retrojections of later first-millennium beliefs and practices into the distant past?

2. THE RAW DATA

2.1 *The names of God*

According to Genesis God revealed himself to the patriarchs under various different names, and the patriarchs used a variety of divine epithets in their prayers. Abraham knew of Yahweh, Elohim, El Elyon, El Shaddai, El Roi, and El Olam. Isaac knew of Yahweh, Elohim and El Shaddai. Jacob knew of Yahweh, Elohim, El Bethel, Pahad Yishaq (Fear or relative of Isaac) and El Shaddai. However, since the use of some of these epithets may be ascribed to editorial identification of different deities, it is necessary to distinguish carefully between the various usages of the divine names, i.e. whether they occur in the framework of the story and therefore represent the editor's understanding of the situation or whether they form part of the dialogue in the story and therefore may represent the wording of the source, rather than an editor's understanding of his source. Sometimes more than one divine name is used in the same passage, and in such cases it is more possible that one of the items is an editorial addition identifying the two divine names. Such problematic cases will therefore be ignored in the following analysis. The results may be conveniently summarized in tabular form (see Table 1 on p. 164).

Full discussion of the data in this table will follow later, but three points are immediately clear. First, in all three cycles El Shaddai only occurs in the dialogue, never in the narrative framework of the stories. This suggests that at least this term is an early element in the tradition.

Secondly, in the Joseph cycle Yahweh is used only in the narrative framework, never in the speeches within the story. There, El Shaddai or Elohim is consistently used. This might be thought to be due to the setting of the stories, where the sons of

Table 1[3]

Distribution of Divine Names by Narrative Context

	Abraham		Jacob		Joseph	
	Framework (editor)	Dialogue (source?)	Framework	Dialogue	Framework	Dialogue
Yahweh	45	20 (2)	11	14 (0)	11	0 (0)
Elohim	24	11 (2)	14	28 (1)	2	30 (0)
El Shaddai	0	1 (1)	0	2 (1)	0	2 (0)
El (other names)	1	3 (0)	1	3 (2)	0	0 (0)
Adonai	0	6 (0)	0	0 (0)	0	0 (0)
Mixed	1	9 (0)	0	6 (1)	0	2 (1)

Jacob are constantly dealing with Egyptians and other foreigners. But in fact in many of the situations where God is mentioned, the brothers are talking to each other or with their father Jacob (e.g. 42:28; 45:5, 7, 8, 9; 50:25). This could suggest that the narrator identified the God of the patriarchs with Yahweh but that his sources did not refer to Yahweh, but only to Elohim or El Shaddai and that he faithfully preserved this feature in his dialogues. Whether this hypothesis can be sustained will be discussed further below.

Thirdly, and this apparently contradicts the second point, in the Abraham cycles Yahweh and Elohim are found both in the narrative framework and in the dialogue. In these stories then, both Yahweh and Elohim have equal claims to originality. If only one of the terms originally belonged to the traditions, later editors have not only reworded the narrative framework but also the dialogue. Another way of resolving this confusion is usually preferred, however, namely the postulation of different sources. It will be argued below that this solution is also fraught with difficulty.

[3]Notes on the table:
(1) The Abraham cycle consists of 12:1-25:18; Jacob 25:19-37:1; Joseph 37:2-50:26 (excluding the blessing of Jacob 49:22–27 which is poetry).
(2) The bracketed figures in the dialogue column refer to divine speech: the other figure covers human, angelic and divine speech.
(3) The references to household gods in 31:19, 30, 32, 34, 35 and 35:2, 4 are not included.

Discussions of patriarchal religion tend to concentrate on the names of God to the virtual exclusion of other aspects of their belief and practice, simply because the source material is so much more scanty in this respect. However, for a rounded picture it is necessary to mention the few details found in Genesis.[4] Altars are built, sacrifices, libations, and covenants are made; prayer, circumcision, tithes, vows, and ritual purification are other ingredients of their religion. Household gods were also highly valued. Apart from the last point the practice of the patriarchs apparently differed little from their successors. However, the texts are quite vague about the how and where of sacrifice. In general they worship in places that were well-known in later times for their sanctuaries. Yet the impression is conveyed that the patriarchs offered sacrifice outside the towns, presumably without the aid of the local priesthood. This would be somewhat irregular by later standards. It would of course have been even more surprising had the patriarchs regularly worshipped at Canaanite shrines staffed by Canaanite priests; though Genesis 14 does suggest that on one occasion at least this is what Abraham did.

If Genesis says little about the patriarchal mode of worship, it says much more about the divine promises made to them, and that for two reasons. First, their faith in these promises and their

[4]It may be asked why Genesis is so reticent about the religious practices of the patriarchs when the other books of the Pentateuch are replete with cultic details (cf. Ex. 19-40; Leviticus, Numbers, Dt. 12-18). There is a similar contrast between the books of Samuel and Kings on the one hand and the books of Chronicles on the other. The former tend only to mention religious practices in passing, while the latter describe the cult at great length. The reason for this discrepancy is clear. Samuel and Kings were edited in a period when the temple cult had become irrelevant. The bulk of the population was in Babylonian exile and unable to worship in the temple. The author of Kings regarded it as more important to explain the reasons for the exile than to recall nostalgically the elaborate temple rituals which it was no longer feasible to carry out. The author of Chronicles on the other hand was writing in a different situation, when many of the exiles had returned and the temple had been refounded. In order to encourage them to offer worship worthy of almighty God, he described at length the glories of the first temple in the hope that they would try to emulate the dedication of David, Solomon, Hezekiah and Josiah. It could be that a similar logic underlies the sparse details about worship in Genesis. Normal national worship is described in Exodus to Deuteronomy. The individualistic worship of the patriarchs without the aid of priests and prophets differed from later practice to such a degree that it is by and large passed over.

obedience to God's word served as a model to later generations of faithful Israelites. And secondly, the promises provided a justification for the settlement of the land. Three main themes recur, sometimes together and other times separately: they are the promise of numerous descendants who will form a great nation, the promise of the land and the promise of blessing on Abraham's descendants and through them to the whole world. These promises are spelt out very fully in many passages, and beside them the references to actual religious practices are relatively brief and fleeting.

How far is the picture of patriarchal religion modified by the classical source-critical analysis, which distributes the material among J, E, and P? A table will again be used to present the results.[5]

Table 2

Distribution of Divine Names by Sources

	Abraham		Jacob		Joseph	
	Framework	Dialogue	Framework	Dialogue	Framework	Dialogue
P Source						
Yahweh	2	-	-	-	-	-
Elohim	12	3	5	1	-	-
El Shaddai	-	1	-	2	-	1
JE Redaction						
Yahweh	1	-	-	-	-	-
E Source						
Yahweh	1	2	-	-	-	-
Elohim	12	8	9	19	1	27
El (Bethel)	-	-	-	3	-	-
El Shaddai	-	-	-	-	-	1
Adonai	-	1	-	-	-	-
Mixed	-	-	-	3	-	1
J Source						
Yahweh	41	18	11	14	11	-
Elohim	-	-	-	8	1	3
El Roi	-	1	-	-	-	-
Adonai	-	5	-	-	-	-
Mixed	1	8	-	3	-	1

[5]Notes on the table:
(1) Chapters 14 and 49 are omitted from this analysis.
(2) The source analysis is that of S. R. Driver, *An Introduction to the Literature of the Old Testament* (Edinburgh: Clark, [9]1913).

This table evaluating the use of the divine names on the basis of the source analysis gives a more nuanced picture than the simple analysis offered earlier, but the same three facts are clear. First, El Shaddai is found only in the dialogue, never in the framework. Secondly, in the Joseph cycle, Yahweh is used only in the framework of the story, never in the dialogues. There Elohim or El Shaddai is used. Thirdly, in the J, E and P versions of the Abraham cycle, Yahweh is used in the framework, and in the dialogue as well in J and E. Similarly, in the E and P versions of the Abraham and Jacob cycles, Elohim is found in both the framework and in the dialogues.

The source analysis by itself therefore does not give a clear answer to the question of the names under which the patriarchs worshipped God. The conclusions that can be drawn from these statistics depends on the assumptions made about the relationships between the sources. If the sources were completely independent and from the same period, their evidence should be given equal weight. On this basis it would be right to conclude that Elohim was certainly the earliest word for God. However, it is generally supposed that J is some hundred years older than E and nearly 500 years older than P, and that the later sources know the content of the earlier sources. On this assumption only J can be really relied on. This would suggest that Yahweh was the earliest name of God, and was later displaced by Elohim and El Shaddai. This is in flat contradiction to the usual understanding of Exodus 6:3 (generally assigned to P), which states that the patriarchs knew God as El Shaddai, not as Yahweh, which was a new name revealed to Moses. Though it has been argued that Exodus 6:3 does not really mean this, and that the usual tradition misconstrues it, advocates of the usual translation point out that the P passages in Genesis nearly always use Elohim or El Shaddai (Yahweh only occurs twice in P Genesis), which suggests that P indeed meant that the patriarchs did not know Yahweh as the name of deity. Yet this explanation side-steps a major problem: how could the author of P affirm that the patriarchs did not know the name of Yahweh when both the earlier sources J and E affirm that they did? If one supposed that the author of P was ignorant of all the material in J and E, which constitute five sixths of the patriarchal narratives,[6] this position would be defensible. But it

[6]In Genesis 12-50 about 630 verses are assigned to J, about 390 verses to E, and about 220 to P.

seems improbable, and some writers have gone further, affirming that P not only knew JE, but that these were the main sources of P.[7] It is evident that it is impossible to discover the content of patriarchal religion without making a number of judgments on the date and interrelationship of the pentateuchal sources.

2.2 *Religious institutions*

If the analysis of divine names is inconclusive, do the religious institutions mentioned in the different sources give any better clue to their relative dates and possible interdependence? Table 3 sets out the distribution of the references in the various sources.

Table 3
Religious Institutions in Genesis

	J	$\frac{1}{3}$J	E	$\frac{1}{2}$E	P
Divine Promises : descendants	6	2	2	1	3
: land	6	2	-	-	3
: blessing	5	1.7	2	1	2
Covenant : divine	1	.3	-	-	1
: human	1	.3	2	1	-
Altar building	4	1.3	3	1.5	-
Sacrifice	-	-	3	1.5	-
Pillar erection	2	.7	2	1	-
Libation	1	.3	1	.5	-
Tithe	-	-	1	.5	-
Vows	-	-	1	.5	-
Ritual purification	-	-	1	.5	-
Circumcision	-	-	1	.5	3
Household gods	-	-	2	1	-
Calling on the LORD	4	1.3	-	-	-
Intercessory prayer	4	1.3	3	1.5	-

In analysing this table two things must be borne in mind. First, the figures are not as precise as in the tables dealing with the divine names, because enumerating the number of references to

[7]E.g. L. Rost, 'Die Gottesverehrung der Patriarchen im Lichte der Pentateuch-quellen', *VT* Supp. 7, 1960, p. 350; S. E. McEvenue, *The Narrative Style of the Priestly Writer* (Rome: Biblical Institute Press, 1971); F. M. Cross, *Canaanite Myth and Hebrew Epic* (Cambridge, Mass.: Harvard UP, 1973), pp. 294-295.

such things as promises is rather subjective. What I have tried to do is to list the number of occasions an institution is referred to rather than the number of times a particular word appears. Thus because only one altar is meant in Genesis 35:1, 3, 7, it counts only once in the table though it is mentioned three times. Similarly the numerous references to circumcision in Genesis 17 count as one. Second, it must be remembered that E is twice as long as P, and J is three times as long. Thus to make the figures of J and E comparable with P, those of E must be halved and those of J divided by three. These results are found in the second and fourth columns.

When this is done, it beomes difficult to see any clear trend between the sources. E contains references to a wider span of institutions than any other source, and P to the narrowest range. P's failure to mention altar building and sacrifice might be thought to represent his reluctance to portray the patriarchs offering sacrifice without priestly intervention.[8] But this is unlikely, for P (Genesis) also omits reference to other institutions which did not require priests, e.g. tithing, vowing, ritual purification and prayer. Furthermore the regulations in Leviticus 1, 3 (also P) clearly envisage the layman slaying sacrificial animals. The priests simply have to sprinkle the blood and place the carcase on the altar. In view of the brevity of the references in Genesis to sacrifice, it seems unlikely that the potential usurpation of priestly prerogative by the patriarchs can be the reason for the omission of sacrifice from P. More likely it is statistical variation. The brevity of P makes it intrinsically less likely that it would give such a comprehensive coverage of the religious institutions as J or E.

Analysis of the distribution of religious institutions is thus of little use in determining the relationship between the sources or their relative age. Since everything mentioned in P is also found in J or E, P could be either earlier or later than the other sources. If, as is customary, it is assumed that J and E are earlier than P, it follows that no religious institution mentioned in the patriarchal narratives is later than the composition of these sources, for nothing is found in P which is not already found in J or E. These religious institutions could therefore date from patriarchal times.

[8]E.g. L. Rost, *VT* Supp. 7, 1960, p. 350.

This preliminary discussion of the question of the divine names and religious institutions has proved inconclusive, because the analysis of the material depends too much on *a priori* assumptions about the existence, extent, date and interrelationship of the sources. For this reason modern discussions of patriarchal religion have skirted round the source-critical problem and attempted to make comparisons between other near-eastern religions and the data of Genesis to arrive at a picture of patriarchal religion. But here again assumptions have to be made. With which type of religion should Genesis be compared? The point of comparison chosen and the individual scholar's evaluation of the reliability of the patriarchal tradition have largely determined his final picture of patriarchal religion.

3. THREE VIEWS OF PATRIARCHAL RELIGION

3.1 *A. Alt and 'The God of the Fathers'*

The extraordinary influence of Alt's essay 'The God of the Fathers'[9] is proved by its longevity. Though first published over fifty years ago, it was not translated into English until 1966 and it still is the point of departure for modern discussions of patriarchal religion. For this reason, our survey of critical theories about patriarchal religion begins with Alt.

Alt begins his essay by surveying the problem of recovering the content of patriarchal religion. The compiler of Genesis identified Yahweh with the God of Abraham, and the God of Isaac with the God of Abraham and so on. For him these were different names of the same God. But according to Alt the historical development of the religion was more complex, and often the compiler of Genesis has read his own ideas into the traditional material, thus distorting the picture of the patriarchal age.

In reality in the earliest phase of their religion the patriarchs worshipped the gods of the fathers. The oldest names for the patriarchal deities in Genesis are 'Fear of Isaac' and 'Mighty One of Jacob', alternatively described as 'the god of Isaac' or 'the god of Jacob'. A third deity is also mentioned, viz. 'the god of

---

[9]A. Alt, *Der Gott der Väter* (Stuttgart: Kohlhammer, 1929) reprinted in *KSI* (Munich: Beck, 1953), pp. 1-78, ET by R. A. Wilson in A. Alt, *Essays on OT History and Religion* (Oxford: Blackwell, 1966), pp. 3-77. Quotations are from this English edition.

Abraham'. According to Alt these were three different gods worshipped by different tribes or groups of tribes in their nomadic
period, i.e. the patriarchal age prior to the settlement of Israel in
Canaan. He tries to demonstrate the antiquity of these names by
comparing them with Nabataean and Palmyrene inscriptions in
Greek and Aramaic dating from the first century B.C. to the fourth
century A.D. These tribal peoples were also nomadic and they
worshipped 'the god of X', where X was the name of the founder
of the cult. Different tribes worshipped different deities. When a
god revealed himself to a person, that person established a cult for
him, and the god in question guaranteed the protection of the
worshipper's group or tribe.

Now according to Alt different tribal groups arrived in Canaan
at different times bringing with them different deities. The largest
group, the Jacob tribes, worshipped the god of Jacob and settled
in the east and north of the country. Another group, the Isaac
tribes, settled round Beersheba and worshipped the god of Isaac,
while the Abraham group settled round Mamre and worshipped
the god of Abraham. In course of time the El gods of the local
Canaanite shrines were identified with the gods of the fathers,
thus giving these tribal gods their own name. Instead of an
anonymous god of Jacob, names like 'El, the God of Israel' (33:20)
were invented. Furthermore, interactions between the tribes led to
a pooling of their history. To prove that the tribes were related to
each other, genealogies of the tribal founders were constructed.
Abraham became the grandfather, and Isaac the father of Jacob.
Simultaneously the gods whom the different patriarchs served
were identified with each other, so that Genesis can talk about the
God of Abraham and the God of Isaac meaning the same deity.
The final stage in the development of pre-monarchic religion was
the introduction of Yahweh as the national God of all Israel in
the Mosaic period. Exodus 3 and 6 make it clear that the God of
the Fathers was first called Yahweh by Moses. The worship of
Yahweh by the nation did not exclude the worship of the tribal
gods, such as the God of Abraham, at the tribal sanctuaries, but in
course of time Yahweh was identified with these local deities as
well.

Now all the pentateuchal sources were written some time after
this religious evolution was complete, and they reflect their
different authors' understanding of the situation and many of the

texts must be regarded as anachronistic. They reflect the later writers' concept of the patriarchal religion, rather than describing the true historical situation. Thus the references to 'the God of Abraham' in Genesis 26:24 and 'the God of Abraham and the God of Isaac' in 32:10 are just the invention of J.[10] Alt does not give a complete list of the passages he regards as authentic reflections of the patriarchal religion, but the following five would seem to be the few that pass his critical sieve: 31:5, 29, 53; 46:3; 49:25. They are all found in the Jacob material. Though this may seem a narrow base on which to build a theory of patriarchal religion, Alt argued that it was a firm one, because the patriarchal religion he described was so similar to that of the Nabataeans, who centuries later gave up a nomadic way of life to settle on the eastern and southern borders of Canaan.

3.1.1 *Evaluation of Alt*   The dominating influence of Alt's theory of patriarchal religion can be seen in the standard histories of Old Testament religion. In view of the relatively few texts on which his theory rests, its widespread acceptance is perhaps surprising. If with the hindsight of more recent scholarship, his ideas seem to have certain weaknesses, to his contemporaries they had obvious merits. First, they showed that a thoroughly critical methodology could still discover authentic traces of the patriarchal period in the Genesis narratives. They were not simply the retrojections of later writers' imagination into earlier times. Secondly, though only a few verses actually go back to ancient times, the picture of the gods of the fathers in the authentic verses is remarkably like the God of Genesis. The essence of the tradition in its most ancient and its most developed form is the same: God revealed himself to the patriarchs; he promised them descendants; he protected them in their wanderings; and, enjoying a special relationship to him, they worshipped him and established holy places in his honour. Only in one respect was there a substantial difference between the patriarchs' religious experience and Genesis' interpretation of it. Each patriarch worshipped the particular deity who had revealed himself to him, but contrary to the assumptions of Genesis and its earlier sources, these deities were different, not one and the same God Yahweh. Though the Genesis editors try to show that Abraham, Isaac, and Jacob all worshipped

[10]Ibid. pp. 16, 19.

the same God, and were therefore implicitly monotheistic, critical analysis of the tradition showed that the patriarchs worshipped different deities and the earliest form of religion was essentially polytheistic.

Later discussions of Alt's work have drawn attention to two main weaknesses in his synthesis. First, Lewy[11] questioned his view that the patriarchal gods were really anonymous, known only by their worshippers' names, not their own names. He pointed out that old Assyrian texts from nineteenth-century Cappadocia also spoke of 'god of your/our father' as a description of the high god of Assyria. He argued that the real name of the patriarchal god was El Shaddai, and that 'God of my father Abraham' and similar phrases defined 'the worshippers' relationship to the deity and were not a substitute for his name. Subsequent studies have shown that phrases like 'God of my father' are well known in the Near East to describe named deities.[12] The second weakness of Alt's approach is the remoteness of his comparative material. The Nabataean inscriptions that he cites are nearly 2,000 years younger than the patriarchal period. In the same year that Alt's article was published, the first discoveries were made at Ras Shamra, ancient Ugarit. These have revolutionized scholarly understanding of second-millennium Canaanite religion, and there have been various studies arguing that the Genesis narratives make better sense understood against this background rather than later Nabataean religion.[13]

3.2 F. M. Cross and 'Yahweh and the God of the Patriarchs'

Of all the recent attempts to understand the religion of the patriarchs against the background of second-millennium near-eastern religion, F. M. Cross's essay 'Yahweh and the God of the Patriarchs' is the most thorough. It was first published in 1962[14] and was republished in an expanded form in 1973.[15]

[11]J. Lewy, 'Les textes paléo-assyriens et l'A.T.', *Revue de l'histoire des religions* 110 (1934), pp. 29-65.

[12]Summarized by F. M. Cross, *Canaanite Myth and Hebrew Epic*, pp. 10-11.

[13]See especially the essays of O. Eissfeldt in the bibliography and the work of Cross to be discussed next.

[14]In *Harvard Theological Review* 55, 1962, pp. 225-259.

[15]In F. M. Cross, *Canaanite Myth and Hebrew Epic* (Cambridge, Mass.: Harvard UP, 1973), pp. 3-75.

Cross begins by summarizing Alt's essay we have just discussed. Though he agrees with Alt's general picture of patriarchal religion as a personal clan religion based on revelation to the patriarchs, he disagrees with Alt in seeing the patriarch's god as originally anonymous. Cross maintains that the patriarchs worshipped the high god of Canaan, namely El. In other words the passages which call the God of the patriarchs, El Shaddai, El Elyon, El Olam, etc., are not secondary later elements that were added to the tradition after the settlement in Canaan, as Alt held, but represent the original name of the God worshipped by the patriarchs. Phrases like 'the God of Abraham' are not used in Genesis because the God Abraham worshipped was anonymous, but to bring out the special relationship that existed between Abraham and his God, El Shaddai.

Cross, like Lewy, argues that since named Assyrian gods could be called 'god of your father', similar phrases in the patriarchal narrative could be taken the same way.[16] Furthermore there is evidence of similar usage in other regions and periods, particularly among early second-millennium Amorites.[17] He further questions whether Alt was correct in supposing that the Nabataean deity Du-Sara was originally anonymous. Since the name was unknown in Transjordan prior to Nabataean settlement, it is likely that the Nabataeans brought the name with them. But whether or not Alt's reconstruction of primitive Nabataean religion is correct, the analogy with the patriarchal period is remote and inappropriate. In Genesis the patriarchs are associated with both Mesopotamia and Egypt, unlike the desert origin of the Nabataeans, and must be presumed to have known the names of numerous deities.[18]

Though names like El Elyon and El Olam are found in Genesis, does it follow that these names refer to El, the high god of the Canaanites? Cross admits that names like El Olam could either be understood as 'El, the eternal one', or as 'the god Olam'. To show that the first possibility is the correct one, he says it must be shown that Olam, Elyon, and Shaddai are appropriate epithets of El, as his character is depicted in extrabiblical texts. However, two titles at least are unambiguous in their reference to El. These

[16]*HTR* 55, 1962, pp. 228f.
[17]*Canaanite Myth*, pp. 10f.
[18]*HTR* 55, 1962, p. 231.

are ᵓēl, ᵓĕlōhê yiśraᵓēl (Gn. 33:20) which must be translated 'El, the God of Israel' and ᵓēl,[19] ᵓĕlōhê ᵓābîkā (Gn. 46:3) which must mean 'El, the God of your father'. El Olam (Gn. 21:33) finds a parallel in a fifteenth-century Canaanite inscription which mentions ᵓl d ᶜlm 'El, the eternal one.' Numerous texts describe El as an old man, the patriarchal head of the pantheon. Cross therefore finds no difficulty in taking ᵓēl ᶜōlām in the same sense, i.e. El, the Eternal. The antiquity of this name in Hebrew tradition is supported by the old poem Deuteronomy 33:27 which Cross[20] translates: 'His refuge is the God of Old, under him are the arms of the Ancient One (ᶜôlām).

The second title used in Genesis that is suggestive of Canaanite El is 'God Most High (ᵓēl ᵓelyôn) creator of heaven and earth' (Gn. 14:19, 22; cf. verses 18, 20). The epithet 'creator of heaven and earth' admirably fits El, the principal creator God in the Canaanite pantheon, and the only god described as (qōnē ᵓarṣ) 'creator of earth'. However, the epithet ᵓelyôn is unusual. In other non-biblical texts Elyon appears as an independent god alongside El. Cross conjectures that ᵓēl ᵓelyôn of Genesis perhaps represents an early form[21] referring to a single deity which later split to form a pair of gods.

The commonest El title in Genesis, El Shaddai, is also the most problematic. Cross argues that though it occurs mainly in the P source, there is good reason to hold that it is an authentic second-millennium name. Shaddai occurs in the blessing of Jacob (Gn. 49:25), generally recognized as an archaic poem. It also forms part of the names in the lists of princes in Numbers 1:5-15; 2:3-29. Though these lists are usually assigned to the P source, the names 'actually reflect characteristic formations of the onomasticon of the second millennium'.[22]

Cross thinks that the best etymology of šadday connects it with tdw/y meaning 'mountain'. Šadday would then mean 'mountain one', and certainly El was connected with a great mountain in the

---

[19]Cross regards the definite article in Gn. 46:3 hāᵓēl as secondary, dating from a period after the spelling was modernized and the definite article introduced in about the tenth century B.C. HTR 55, 1962, p. 232 n. 27.

[20]HTR 55, 1962, p. 236.

[21]ᵓēl ᵓelyôn also occurs in Ps. 78:35, 'an early context'. Canaanite Myth, p. 52 n. 29.

[22]HTR 55, 1962, p. 244.

underworld, where the divine council met.[23] However, El is not the only god connected with a mountain, and no Canaanite text actually describes him as *šadday*. Cross suggests that *šadday* may be of Amorite origin and that the patriarchs brought this epithet with them from Mesopotamia.[24]

Finally Cross argues that the hypothesis that the patriarchs worshipped El helps to explain various features of later Yahwism. In particular the name of Yahweh may be explained as an abbreviation of some such form as *ʾēl ḏū yahwī*, 'El who causes to be', i.e. 'El the creator'. Such a continuity between El and Yahweh would explain why El, Elyon, Shaddai and Olam continued to be perfectly acceptable titles of Yahweh, particularly in poetry, whereas Baal and all his works were fiercely rejected. In Canaanite mythology Baal was a new upstart god, a rival to El. Secondly, postulating that all the Israelite tribes worshipped El before they adopted Yahwism would explain their sense of unity better than Alt's theory of a diversity of religious allegiances among the tribes. Thirdly, it explains why Aaron and Jeroboam could set up bulls as the symbol of Yahwism, for this was also the animal that was associated with El. Indeed the designation 'the mighty one of Jacob' (Gn. 49:24) could be translated 'Bull of Jacob'.[25]

3.2.1 *Evaluation of Cross* The attempt of Cross and others to interpret the traditions of Genesis in the light of Ugaritic and other near eastern sources has been widely accepted in Old Testament scholarship, and it is not hard to see why. First and foremost, he uses extrabiblical material that is relatively close in time and place to the generally received view of the patriarchs. Secondly, his synthesis presents fewer problems than Alt's to theological readers of the Old Testament. Whereas Alt held that each patriarch worshipped his own god, and these gods were not identical with each other, Cross suggests that there is a basic continuity between the God of the patriarchs (who all worshipped the same high God El) and Yahweh, the God of Moses. Thus, although the authors of Genesis have oversimplified things by

[23]*HTR* 55, 1962, p. 245; cf. M. H. Pope, *El in the Ugaritic Texts* (*VT* Supp. 2, Leiden: Brill, 1955), pp. 61f.

[24]*Canaanite Myth*, pp. 57ff., adopting with some modification the suggestions of L. R. Bailey; *JBL* 87, 1968, pp. 434-438; and J. Ouellette, *JBL* 88, 1969, pp. 470f.

[25]*Canaanite Myth*, p. 15.

claiming Yahweh appeared to Abraham, Isaac and Jacob, for they only knew God as El, theologically they are correct in identifying Yahweh with El, because historically Yahweh was an epithet of El. Cross's reconstruction thus reduces the gap between theology and history in the patriarchal narratives.

Notwithstanding broad agreement that the patriarchs worshipped El, three aspects of the Cross synthesis have been strongly challenged. First, is Elyon really an epithet of El or is he a separate deity? Those[26] who maintain the latter draw attention to the Sefire treaty which names El alongside Elyon, and to Philo Byblius who apparently regarded Elyon as El's grandfather.

Against this Lack persuasively argued that Elyon was once an epithet of El but it later became an epithet of Baalšamen, and this explains why Elyon is mentioned alongside El in the Sefire text. It is part of a long historical process whereby Baal gradually took over the position and epithets of El.[27]

More attention has been focused on the epithet Shaddai. Ouellette,[28] followed by de Vaux,[29] suggests that šadday derives from šadû, to be understood in the sense of 'steppe' rather than 'mountain'. That it therefore probably referred to the god Amurru who is described as god of the steppe. Cross[30] is prepared to accept that šadday may represent an Amorite name of El, but not to suppose that it is an alternative name for Sin the moon god, as Bailey[31] supposed. More recently Abel has pointed to other features in the patriarchal narratives that could indicate that El Shaddai was identical with the moon god. He points out that the patriarchs settled in Harran, an important cultic centre of the moon god, and that several of Abraham's relations had names associated with the moon.[32]

[26]E.g. M. H. Pope, *El in the Ugaritic Texts*, pp. 55-58; R. Rendtorff, 'El, Baal und Jahwe', *ZAW* 78, 1966, pp. 277-291; R. de Vaux, *Histoire ancienne d'Israel* (Paris: Lecoffre, 1971), p. 262.

[27]R. Lack, 'Les origines de *Elyon*, le trés-haut, dans la tradition cultuelle d'Israel', *CBQ* 24, 1962, pp. 44-64.

[28]J. Ouelette, 'More on ˀÊl Šadday and Bêl Šadê', *JBL* 88, 1969, pp. 470-471.

[29]*Histoire ancienne*, p. 264.

[30]*Canaanite Myth*, pp. 57-60 and 57 n. 52.

[31]L. R. Bailey, 'Israelite ˀÊl Šadday and Amorite Bêl Šadê,' *JBL* 87, 1968, pp. 434-438.

[32]E.g. Sarai, Milchah, and Terah: *sārāh*//*šarratu* (Sin's wife), *milkāh*//*malkatu* (Sin's daughter), *terah*//*Ter* (a name of Sin//*yārēah* (moon). E. L. Abel, 'The Nature of the Patriarchal God "Êl Šadday", *Numen* 20, 1973, pp. 48-59.

Koch,[33] on the other hand, believes that etymology does nothing to explain the meaning of *šadday*. Its use in Job indicates that it was originally a separate name for God, expressing his nearness and protectiveness. In Genesis *šadday* blesses and grants many descendants. The character of *šadday* is therefore quite like Alt's gods of the fathers, and Koch suggests that the two types of deity were identified in the pre-monarchy period. Later Shaddai was identified with El giving the double name El Shaddai.

That such diametrically opposed interpretations of El Shaddai are put forward emphasizes the limits of our knowledge. With Koch one must acknowledge that the etymology of Shaddai is uncertain. Only if and when it is found as an epithet of a god in some extrabiblical text will it be possible to be more confident about etymology. However, Koch's idea that El Shaddai is a late formation is implausible. Though more frequent in P than in other sources, it also occurs in J[34] (Gn. 43:14) and El is paired with Shaddai in early poems (Gn. 49:25, Nu. 24:4, 16).

The case for believing that El was known to the patriarchs before they reached Canaan is strong. Il = El is a well-known member of the third-millennium Mesopotamian pantheon.[35] Whether El was ever identified with the moon god is uncertain. To judge from the names of Abraham's relations and the cult of his home town, his ancestors at least were moon-god worshippers. Whether he continued to honour this god, identifying him with El, or converted to El, is unclear.[36]

For different reasons Haran[37] has insisted on distinguishing between Canaanite religion and the religion of the patriarchs. He

[33]K. Koch, 'Šaddaj', *VT* 26, 1976, pp. 299-332.

[34]Koch suggests this verse is a P-influenced insertion into a JE context, *VT* 26, 1976, p. 304 n. 7. Since he admits the antiquity of the poetic passages, this looks like special pleading. Some divine name is required in this verse.

[35]See J. J. M. Roberts, *The Earliest Semitic Pantheon* (Baltimore: Johns Hopkins UP, 1972), p. 34: 'The picture, then, that the Old Akkadian names give of Il is a portrait of a high, but gracious god, who is interested in man's welfare, and who is particularly active in the giving of children'. On Il at Ebla see G. Pettinato, *BA* 39, 1976, pp. 48-50.

[36]From a theological standpoint it may seem easier to regard Abraham as a worshipper of El, the high creator god of the Canaanite pantheon, than as a devotee of the moon god. However, El's character had a much seamier side: for example child sacrifice was frequently associated with his cult (Cross, *Canaanite Myth*), pp. 25ff; cf. Gn. 22).

[37]M. Haran, 'The Religion of the Patriarchs', *ASTI* 4, 1965, pp. 30-55.

points out that as a rule the patriarchs do not seem to have worshipped at the existing Canaanite shrines. When God appeared to them they built their own altars. This fits in with their semi-nomadic lifestyle: they generally camped outside existing towns but did not settle in them. Furthermore their worship of El Shaddai, in common with other sons of Eber (Gn. 10:21) suggests that their God was not simply borrowed from the Canaanites,[38] but common to a wider grouping of peoples. Haran's points are well made, but their validity of course depends on the antiquity and reliability of the patriarchal traditions.

A final point needs to be made about Cross's understanding of patriarchal religion in the light of his view of the pentateuchal sources. He holds that JE, the oldest epic source, has been supplemented by a later priestly writer, and that P never existed in isolation as a separate document. Now on any view of the documentary hypothesis, it is strange that the latest source should represent most accurately the religion of the patriarchs: El Shaddai occurs more frequently in P than in any other source. But Cross's particular version of the documentary theory[39] would appear to be contradicted by Exodus 6:3, which says that the patriarchs knew God as El Shaddai but not as Yahweh. Yet the J source, which P is supplementing according to Cross, often describes the patriarchal God as Yahweh. How then can P say that they only knew El Shaddai? The question will be explored more fully below.

3.3 Westermann's traditio-historical approach

Alt and Cross restrict their investigations to recovering the most primitive and authentic features of patriarchal religion. They are not interested in discovering how the traditions have grown in the subsequent retelling, except in so far as it is necessary to recognize such accretions for what they are, so that they may be disregarded in historical reconstruction. Alt and Cross have also paid very little attention to the promises of land, posterity and blessing that dominate the patriarchal stories. How far do these go back to the patriarchal age, or how far do they represent later *vaticinia ex eventu* in the light of Israel's success in the conquest and monarchy periods?

[38]Haran, p. 42, ascribes Baalam's use of the term El Shaddai and its frequency in Job to its currency outside Israel.
[39]See *Canaanite Myth*, pp. 294f.

C. Westermann in two important works *Arten der Erzählung in der Genesis* (1964) and *Die Verheissungen an die Väter* (1976) has discussed these problems in detail.[40]

As its title suggests, the first book is concerned with defining the different types of narrative that are found in Genesis. Westermann endeavours to show that Gunkel's definition of the Genesis stories as sagas (*Sagen*) is not quite apposite. A saga suggests that those involved are engaged in extraordinary feats of heroism designed to make a name for themselves. Westermann classes the Gilgamesh epic as saga. Whereas the patriarchal stories are essentially about down-to-earth family problems, moving house, childlessness, domestic quarrels and so on. Westermann therfore prefers to call them *Erzählungen*, i.e. 'tales', 'stories'.[41]

Westermann suggests that comparison with Icelandic folk tales helps to clarify the origins of the Genesis stories. Icelandic sagas have been classified into three types, family tales, kingly tales, and tales about olden days. The first group resemble the patriarchal traditions in Genesis, and the third group correspond to Genesis' primeval history. This comparison with Icelandic traditions allows Westermann to affirm with confidence the antiquity of the patriarchal stories, though he holds that most of the promises contained within them are secondary additions by editors and compilors.

Whereas earlier scholarship simply distinguished two main types of promise in Genesis, the promise of land and the promise of descendants, Westermann is much more precise. One must distinguish promises of (1) son, (2) descendants, (3) blessing and (4) land, and various combinations of these promises.[42]

According to Westermann promises can be regarded as authentic (i.e. part of the oldest part of a patriarchal tale) only on two conditions: first, that the promise contains only one possible element, not a combination of various elements (e.g. land or descendants, but not both); secondly, that the promise is intrinsic to the narrative in which it occurs and is not just an incidental extra. The promise must resolve a tension within the narrative. On these grounds only the promises of a son to childless women

[40]The later work includes a reprint of the former. My references to *Arten der Erzählung* are for convenience all taken from *Die Verheissungen*.

[41]*Verheissungen*, p. 39 n. 23.

[42]Ibid., pp. 18ff. The promises of numerous descendants and blessing are never found alone, always in combination with other promises.

in Genesis 16:11 and 18:1-15 are certainly genuine.[43] He regards it likely that an early promise of land lies behind the present form of 15:7-21 and 28:13-15.[44] The promises of numerous descendants developed out of blessing formulae and are not really intrinsic to the narratives.[45] Thus all the other promises found in the patriarchal narratives represent the theological reflections of later editors. They do not go back to the most primitive version of the stories. This is particularly obvious in the case of the Jacob stories: with the one exception of Genesis 28:13-15 Westermann believes that 'the promise texts are all to be characterized as insertions, additions or short notes'.[46]

His second work, *The Promises to the Patriarchs*, begins by surveying the history of the discussion since Alt's article. He restates and defends his own views in the light of more recent research. He is inclined to accept Maag's suggestion[47] that behind Genesis 12:1-3 there may lie a promise of fresh pasture lands for the nomadic patriarch, and that this was subsequently transformed into a promise of a land to live in. This illustrates a criterion enunciated by Westermann for distinguishing authentic ancient promises from later editorial additions. Ancient promises must not envisage a change of lifestyle for the patriarchs. If the promises clearly envisage a way of life that was achieved only after the conquest of Canaan (e.g. settlement in the land, or the establishment of the monarchy), then they must be late.[48] On the other hand, the promise of divine presence (*Mitsein*), an additional type of promise (e.g. 31:3), which Westermann distinguishes for the first time in *Verheissungen*, may be authentic, since it reflects nomadic conditions and their need for divine protection and guidance on their wanderings.

In a final chapter he compares the promise of a son to Abraham with similar promises made to kings in the Ugaritic epic. This he thinks shows the authenticity of the son promise in Genesis. Though the same epic texts also contain promises of blessing and

[43]Ibid., pp. 19f.
[44]Ibid., pp. 29f.
[45]Ibid., pp. 25f.
[46]Ibid., p. 74.
[47]V. Maag, 'Der Hirte Israels', *Schweizerische Theologische Umschau* 28, 1958, pp. 2-28; 'Malkût Jhwh', VT Supp. 7, 1960, pp. 129-153, esp. n. 137-142.
[48]*Verheissungen*, pp. 118f.

numerous descendants, Westermann argues that these are essentially wedding blessings and not analogous to the Genesis parallels,
where the promise comes from God, and therefore that they offer
no support for the originality of these patriarchal promises.

3.3.1 *Evaluation of Westermann*   The most positive assessment
of Westermann's method has come from R. Rendtorff. In his *Das
überlieferungsgeschichtliche Problem des Pentateuch* he accepts
Westermann's thesis that the patriarchal stories were originally
independent units usually lacking any promises. For Rendtorff
the addition of the promises to the earlier traditions serves to
unite and interpret them. He believes the promises served first to
link the stories about Abraham into a cycle, and the stories about
Jacob and Isaac into other independent cycles, and that at a later
stage more promises were added to combine all the patriarchal
stories into a large unit.

Negative reactions to Westermann have come from very different
directions. On the one hand van Seters[49] holds that Westermann's
claim that most of the patriarchal tales show signs of oral origin
is mistaken. Very few stories about Abraham show clear traces of
oral composition. Van Seters argues that these are early fragments
inserted into an essentially unified literary composition from
which it is often impossible to extract the promises without
spoiling the point of the story.

While van Seters holds that Genesis is a late literary composition, from which the promises can rarely be excised without
damaging the narrative, others, believing that the book does
indeed reflect the patriarchal age with some accuracy, have argued
for the authenticity of the promises on extrabiblical grounds.
Eissfeldt[50] pointed out that in the Ugaritic texts El promised land
and descendants to his adherents; while Cazelles[51] pointed out
that in inscriptions from the third to the first millennium B.C.
near-eastern deities repeatedly made such promises as we find in
Genesis. Westermann rejected these parallels on the ground that

[49]J. van Seters, *Abraham in History and Tradition* (New Haven: Yale UP,
1975).
[50]O. Eissfeldt, 'Der Kanaanäische El als Geber der den israelitischen Erzvätern
geltenden Nachkommenschaft- und Landbesitzverheissungen', *KS* 5, 1973,
pp. 50-62.
[51]H. Cazelles, *Dictionnaire de la Bible Supplément* 7 (Paris: Letouzey, 1966),
pp. 144-145.

the promises were made to kings.[52] But this seems inconsistent with his appeal to the Keret texts to prove the authenticity of the son promise, for Keret, the recipient of the promise, was a king. And the Ugaritic texts also contain more than one promise at once: for example blessing and numerous descendants. According to Westermann such combinations in Genesis are secondary.

This brief review of modern theories about patriarchal religion has highlighted some of the many problems that beset the researcher in this area. In this field, questions of pentateuchal criticism interact with questions of near-eastern religion in kaleidoscopic fashion. The data are like pieces of a jigsaw which each scholar puts together in the way that seems best in his own eyes. More recently still, claims have been made about the Ebla texts that could affect our interpretation of patriarchal religion. In the concluding section of this essay I shall try to peice together the currently available data guided by the following assumptions: first, that the patriarchs lived in the early second millennium B.C. when the worship of El was dominant in Canaan; secondly, that the present form of the patriarchal narratives reflects this period, though they of course interpret the patriarchs' religious experience from a post-Sinaitic perspective.

4. TOWARDS A NEW SYNTHESIS

4.1 *Introduction*

In evaluating the work of Westermann I have already referred to the studies of van Seters (1975) and Rendtorff (1977). Both works have in common a rejection of the documentary hypothesis, preferring instead supplementary hypotheses. Van Seters, who limits himself to the Abraham and Isaac traditions, believes it is possible to identify a few pre-Yahwistic oral traditions (e.g. Gn. 12:10-20), and a few short Elohistic developments (Gn. 20:1-17), but that most of Genesis 12-26 comes directly from the hand of the Yahwist (J). The priestly writer made a few later additions (e.g. chapters 17 and 23). In other words van Seters sees the present form of the Abraham cycle as an essentially literary creation mainly by the Yahwist.

Rendtorff is in certain respects more traditional than van Seters, and in others more radical. He is more traditional in following

---

[52]*Verheissungen*, p. 110.

Gunkel who supposed that most of the Abraham stories were originally independent and oral. However, he is more radical in rejecting the source-analysis terminology as well as its methodology. He considers that the Abraham stories were collected into an Abraham cycle, the Isaac stories into an Isaac cycle, and Jacob traditions were collected into a Jacob cycle, and that the Joseph stories are an independent literary work. While some of the promises to the patriarchs are integral to the independent stories, others were added when the cycles were collected to create a unity between the different traditions. The three independent cycles of Abraham, Isaac and Jacob were then at a later stage combined by the addition of other promises to form a large unit, on a par with the primeval history (Gn. 2-11), the exodus story (Ex. 1-15), or the Sinai pericope (Ex. 19-24). Thus whereas the traditional documentary hypothesis divides the pentateuch into independent vertical strands, beginning with creation and ending with the conquest, Rendtorff argues that we should think in terms of horizontal blocks of material each dealing with a particular topic (e.g. Abraham, or Joseph, or the exodus), and that these have been collected together by later editors. He thinks of a light P redaction, and possibly even lighter D redaction as the final stages in the edition of Genesis.

Graphically we may represent the difference between Rendtorff's understanding of the composition of the Pentateuch and the traditional documentary hypothesis as follows.

	Traditional Documentary	*Rendtorff*
Primeval History	P	Primeval History
Abraham	J	Abraham
Isaac		Isaac
Jacob	E	Jacob
Joseph		Joseph

Though at first sight van Seters and Rendtorff are proposing quite different analyses of the Abraham traditions, on one basic point they agree: that the cycle as it stands is a substantial unity whose present shape can be ascribed to one principal redactor. This redactor took over earlier material and integrated it into his own scheme. In a recent article[53] on the flood narrative I argued independently of Rendtorff that such a scheme fits Genesis 6-9 better than the usual critical supposition of two independent J and P flood stories. It is more congruent with the data to suppose that the flood story is an essential unity, to be attributed to the editor of Genesis who perhaps adopted a pre-Israelite story and reworked it to express his own theological understanding of the events. It seems to me very difficult to distinguish between the work of the redactor of Genesis and his source material, unless one supposes he borrowed directly from one of the extant Mesopotamian flood stories.

With the patriarchal narratives it is even more difficult to know where the source ends and the editor begins. Certainly the pervasiveness of the promise themes thoughout the patriarchal narratives focuses our attention on the editor's understanding of his material. And it may be that some of the promises do represent editorial additions to the earlier source material, but since these earlier sources no longer exist, dogmatism is impossible. It would seem wiser to begin with the explicit statements of the text about the editor's intentions and not rely merely on conjecture. As far as his treatment of the promises is concerned, the text is silent. But both Exodus 3 (generally assigned to E) and Exodus 6 (generally assigned to P) make explicit reference to the divine names used in Genesis. It therefore seems appropriate to begin our study with an exegesis of these passages.

4.2 The exegesis of Exodus 6:3

Exodus 3:13-15 is translated by the RSV as follows.

> Then Moses said to God, 'If I come to the people of Israel and say to them, "The God of your fathers has sent me to you", and they ask me, "What is his name?" what shall I say to them?' God said to Moses, 'I AM WHO I AM.' And he said, 'Say this to the people of Israel, "I AM has sent me to you."' God also said to Moses, 'Say this to the people of Israel, "The LORD, the God of your fathers, the God of Abraham, of Isaac and of Jacob, has sent me to you": this is my name for ever, and thus I am to be remembered throughout all generations.'

Moses' question in verse 13 appears to imply that the people did not know the name of the patriarchal God of Abraham. The

---

[53]G. J. Wenham, 'The Coherence of the Flood Narrative', *VT* 28, 1978, pp. 336-348.

divine answer in verse 14 then gives the personal name of the God of the fathers. However it is not quite clear whether this name is 'I AM WHO I AM' (Hebrew ʾ*Ehyeh* ʾ*ăšer* ʾ*ehyeh*, verse 14) or Yahweh (verse 15). The latter seems more likely.[54]

Exodus 6:3 clarifies the issue, if the usual translation is correct. 'I appeared to Abraham, to Isaac, and to Jacob, as God Almighty (El Shaddai), but by name the LORD I did not make myself known to them.' In other words the patriarchs knew God as El Shaddai, not as Yahweh. The latter name was revealed first to Moses.

For the student of patriarchal religion it is the second half of the verse that is problematic. The Hebrew reads *ûšmi yhwh lōʾ nôdaᶜtî lāhem*. The Greek and the Latin translate this clause literally: *kai to onoma mou Kyrious ouk edēlōsa autois, et nomen meum Adonai non indicavi eis*. The older targums render it equally literally: Onkelos *ûšmî yy lāʾ hôdaᶜît lahōn*, Neofiti *brm šmi tqipʾ yyy lʾ ʾodᶜit lhon*. It is apparent then that the early translators took this verse in its plain and obvious sense, and ignored the fact that several passages in Genesis imply that God did reveal his name Yahweh to the patriarchs.

The later targum,[55] pseudo-Jonathan, is aware of the problem though. Exodus 6:3 runs: *wʾtgliti lʾbrhm lyṣḥq wlyᶜqb bʾl šdy wšmi hʾ brm bʾpe škinti lʾ ʾtydᶜt lhon*. (I revealed myself to Abraham, Isaac and Jacob as El Shaddai and my name Yahweh but in the character of my Shekinah I did not make myself known to them.) In other words the patriarchs knew the word Yahweh, but did not experience the glory of the Shekinah usually associated with the name.

Similarly mediaeval Jewish commentators attempted to solve the problem by supposing that by his 'name' Exodus 6:3 means some aspect of his character. Thus though the patriarchs knew the word Yahweh, they did not understand the character that lay behind this name. This character was first revealed to Moses. For Rashi, the divine characteristic implied by Yahweh was the fulfilment of promises. The patriarchs received promises, but did not experience their fulfilment. For Rambam the difference between

[54]See R. de Vaux, 'The Revelation of the Divine Name YHWH' in J. I. Durham and J. R. Porter (eds.), *Proclamation and Presence: OT Essays in Honour of G. H. Davies* (London: SCM, 1970).

[55]The dating of the targums is very difficult. Pseudo-Jonathan contains both pre-Christian and post-Islamic traditions, so its final redaction must be late.

God as El Shaddai and God as Yahweh lay in the difference between the providential power of God and his miracle-working power. Thus the patriarchs simply experienced God controlling their circumstances and protecting them in ordinary natural ways, while Moses experienced supernatural miraculous divine interventions.[56] The same sort of explanation is offered by Cassuto.[57] He holds that El Shaddai refers to God in his character of giver of fertility, since where this term occurs in Genesis it is attached to promises of being fruitful and multiplying (e.g. Gn. 17:1-2; 35:11 etc.), whereas Yahweh means that 'He is the One who carries out His promises'. Some Christian commentators[58] have also held that *šēm* (name) really means character and this explains the remarks in Exodus 6:3. The patriarchs knew the word Yahweh, but did not experience the character implied by that name. That was first revealed to Moses.

A second method of eliminating the clash between Exodus 6:3 and Genesis is to suppose that the syntax of Exodus 6:3 has been misunderstood. W. J. Martin,[59] for example, suggests the clause should not be taken as a statement denying the name Yahweh was known to the patriarchs, but as a question implicitly affirming that they did know him as Yahweh. Verse 3 should then be translated 'I suffered myself to appear to Abraham, to Isaac and to Jacob, for did I not let myself be shown to them by my own name YHWH?' He points out that such an understanding of verse 3 is supported by the following verse which begins (*weḡam*) 'and also I established my covenant'. This implies that the immediately preceding clause ought to be positive, not negative as the usual translation implies. A slightly different interpretation of the syntax of Exodus 6:3ff. is offered by F. I. Andersen,[60] but he arrives at the same conclusion as Martin, namely that the verse is asserting that the patriarchs did know the name Yahweh.

[56]See N. Leibowitz, *Studies in Shemot I* (Jerusalem: World Zionist Organization, 1976), pp. 132-135.

[57]U. Cassuto, *A Commentary on the Book of Exodus* (Jerusalem: Magnes, 1967), p. 79.

[58]E.g. C. F. Keil, *Exodus (Biblical Commentary)*, ad loc. J. A. Motyer, *The Revelation of the Divine Name* (London: Tyndale, 1959).

[59]*Stylistic Criteria and the Analysis of the Pentateuch* (London: Tyndale, 1955), pp. 18f., followed by G. R. Driver, *Journal of the Ancient Near Eastern Society of Columbia University* 5, The Gaster Festschrift (1973), p. 109.

[60]*The Sentence in Biblical Hebrew* (The Hague: Mouton, 1974), p. 102.

The third method of dealing with the problem, adopted by the great majority of modern commentators, is to appeal to source criticism. They understand the passage in the same way as the ancient versions: that it is denying that the patriarchs knew the name of Yahweh. They claim that the author of this passage, P, could make this assertion because in the P-material in Genesis, God introduces himself to the patriarchs as El Shaddai not as Yahweh. The two P-Genesis passages, where Yahweh is mentioned occur in descriptive narrative description, not in divine speech (17:1; 21:1b).

A fourth possibility is put forward by Childs. He holds that the revelation to Moses involved both the new name and its meaning. In other words he combines the traditional Jewish understanding with the modern critical view. 'The revelation of the name of Yahweh is at the same time a revealing of his power and authority'.[61]

There are difficulties with each of the suggested solutions. The Jewish suggestion that the revelation of the name of God means the revelation of God's character, has problems in defining exactly what aspect of his character is expressed in the term Yahweh. Neither Rashi's explanation (that Moses experienced the fulfilment of the promises while the patriarchs did not), nor Ramban's suggestion (that the patriarchs knew only God's providence) exactly fits the data. The patriarchs did experience a partial fulfilment of the promises in the birth of children and the acquisition of burial grounds in Canaan, while Moses actually died outside the promised land. And while Moses' miracles were more spectacular, the birth of Isaac to an elderly couple seems more than the usual act of providence.

The syntactic solution is beautifully simple, but it is strange that the early translators are quite unaware of it. And the parallel passage in Exodus 3, which suggests that the name Yahweh was new to Moses, also tells against the syntactic solution.

The critical solution, which supposes that Exodus 6:3 is referring only to the priestly source, while solving one problem, creates another. How can the priestly writer who was writing after J have been ignorant of the fact that J uses Yahweh to refer to God and

---

[61]B. S. Childs, *The Book of Exodus* (Philadelphia: Westminster, 1974), p. 113.

occasionally allows God to introduce himself as Yahweh? The older documentary hypothesis, which held that P was the earliest source and that J was a later source avoided this problem. But by dating P after J, Graf and Wellhausen have created this strange anomaly. If it is held that this verse shows that P was totally ignorant and independent of J, one is still left with the problem of the redactor's understanding of the passage. How did he relate Exodus 6:3 to the statements in Genesis? Some sort of exegetical solution is required to complement the critical understanding of this verse as Childs has rightly seen. However, objections have already been raised to Rashi's exegetical solution, which Childs tries to hold in harness with the critical view.

4.3 Pre-Mosaic knowledge of Yahweh

It could lead to a more objective exegesis of Exodus 6:3 if it could be determined whether the name Yahweh was known before the time of Moses. To this we now turn. The evidence falls into two categories: indirect evidence about the use of Yahweh in pre-Mosaic times and the testimony of Genesis. The indirect evidence all suggests that El was a well-known god in early times, but Yahweh was not. Most of this material has already been discussed; here I shall just recapitulate and add a few extra observations.

The extrabiblical evidence shows clearly that El was the head of the west Semitic pantheon in the early second millennium B.C. This fits in with reference to El, El Elyon, El Shaddai and so on in Genesis. On the other hand there are no extrabiblical texts attesting the name of Yahweh before Moses. Recently Pettinato[62] has suggested that the texts of Ebla may include Yahwistic personal names, indicating that Yahweh was known in their pantheon. However, as Kitchen[63] points out, the *ya* element in Eblaite names may be just an abbreviation of other names. Archi has recently expressed a similar view.[64] F. M. Cross agrees with this, and, having seen a transcription of the term most confidently asserted to refer to Yahweh, holds that it is to be read quite differently.[65] Final judgment will have to await publication of the

[62]G. Pettinato, 'The Royal Archives of Tell Mardikh-Ebla', *BA* 39, 1976, p. 48.
[63]K. A. Kitchen, *The Bible in its World* (Exeter: Paternoster, 1977), p. 47.
[64]A. Archi, *Biblica* 60, 1979, pp. 556-560.
[65]In a personal conversation.

relevant texts, but at the moment there seems little evidence from outside the Bible that Yahweh is a pre-Mosaic name.[66]

Indirect biblical evidence also points in the same direction. Personal names among the patriarchs include several compounded with El, e.g. Ishmael and Israel, but none with Yahweh.[67] Similarly in the lists of tribal leaders in Numbers 1 and 2 there are several names compounded with El and Shaddai, but none with Yahweh.[68] It has sometimes been suggested that Jochebed, Moses' mother (Ex. 6:20) is a Yahwistic name, but this is far from certain.[69]

The testimony of Genesis has already been surveyed in the opening section. From this it was clear that the Joseph cycle by restricting Yahweh to the narrative framework and using Elohim or El Shaddai in the dialogue suggests that the editor of this section held that the patriarchs did not know the name Yahweh though he believed that he was their God.

In the Abraham and Jacob cycles the picture is not so clear-cut. While Yahweh is more frequent in the narrative framework than in the dialogue, the fact that Yahweh occurs in the dialogue suggests that the patriarchs were familiar with the name. Whether this is a necessary conclusion must now be examined. Passages where two names are used together, e.g. 'Yahweh El Elyon' (14:22) or 'Adonai Yahweh' (15:2) do not need to be discussed, since it seems quite possible that Yahweh has been added to show the identity of the older name with the new name. More problematic are those passages where Yahweh occurs alone.

The evidence for supposing that the editor sometimes introduced Yahweh instead of El or Elohim is quite clear. For example, Hagar is told to name her son 'Ishmael, because the LORD has given heed to your affliction . . . So she called the name of the

---

[66]Some discussions of the Ugaritic and Mari materials also suggested that Yahweh was mentioned in them, but this has now been generally rejected. See R. de Vaux, 'The Revelation of the Divine Name YHWH', in *Proclamation and Presence*, pp. 52-56.

[67]On Judah see A. R. Millard, 'The Meaning of the Name Judah', *ZAW* 86, 1974, pp. 216-218, who suggests it may be an abbreviation of $y^e h \hat{u} d y \bar{a} h$ or $y^e h \hat{u} d \bar{a}^{\circ} \bar{e} l$. In the light of the other evidence, I prefer the second possibility.

[68]Though these are attributed to P, the forms of the names are characteristically second-millennium. Cross, *Canaanite Myth*, p. 54.

[69]Most recently by M. Haran, *ASTI* 4, 1965, p. 51, n. 33. For a different view see M. Noth, *Die israelitischen Personennamen* (Stuttgart: Kohlhammer, 1928), p. 111, and R. de Vaux, *Proclamation and Presence*, p. 49.

LORD who spoke to her, "You are *El* Roi"' (16:11, 13). Similarly after his vision of the heavenly ladder Jacob awakes and remarks 'Surely *the* LORD is in this place', yet he goes on to call the place 'Beth*el*' (28:16, 19). In another encounter with God Jacob's name is changed to Israel and he calls the place Peniel (32:28, 30). In the last passage it seems probable that an original El has been changed into Elohim, whereas in the first two passages El has been changed into Yahweh. They show at any rate that the narrator felt free to use Yahweh instead of El, not only in his own narrative but when reporting the dialogue of human characters or the angel of the LORD.[70]

This is confirmed by an examination of the etymologies of the patriarchs in Genesis 29:31-30:24. Both Elohim and Yahweh are referred to, but the names given are quite unrelated to the title of deity. Within the narrative framework there is a clear tendency to mention Yahweh at the beginning and end of a scene e.g. 12:1, 17; 13:4, 18; 18:1, 33, etc. The same tendency is noticeable in passages where Elohim is used in the body of the scene, e.g. 17:1; 20:18; 21:1, 33. It may be that the same logic explains the frequent use of Yahweh in the opening and closing episodes of the Abraham cycle, i.e. chapters 12 and 24.

There are in fact only four passages in the patriarchal narratives where Yahweh speaks and uses this name on its own to describe himself. The first 'Is anything too hard for the LORD?' (18:14) is a proverbial statement cast in the form of a rhetorical question. Here the divine name is quite incidental to the thrust of the question, and therefore it would be unwise to read too much into this passage about the patriarchal knowledge of the name of Yahweh. Likewise though 18:19 mentions Yahweh twice, because it forms part of a divine soliloquy explaining God's motives, this verse does not imply that Abraham either heard these words or knew the divine name.

Much more germane to our discussion is the one other divine speech which employs Yahweh without any other epithet: 'I am the LORD who brought you (*hôṣîʾ*) from Ur of the Chaldaeans' (15:7). Other divine revelations mentioning one name of God refer to him either as El Shaddai (17:1; 35:11) or 'God of your father' (26:24). The uniqueness of 15:7 suggests there may be a special reason for the use of Yahweh here. Earlier commentators tended

---

[70]Cf. O. Eissfeldt, *KS* 5, pp. 52ff.

to see verse 7 as an editorial addition designed to link the two scenes that make up Genesis 15. More recent studies[71] tend to favour the integrity of verse 7 with what follows.

An examination of the usage of the formula 'The LORD who brought you out' in the rest of the Pentateuch suggests an explanation for the use of Yahweh here. 'The LORD, who brought you out' occurs twenty-two times in the Pentateuch. In every case except this one the reference is to God bringing Israel out of Egypt. It is clear that 'the LORD bringing you out of Egypt' is a stock phrase. It seems likely that the editor of Genesis was wanting to draw attention to the parallel between Abraham's departure from Ur and Israel's exodus from Egypt. He had to substitute Ur for Egypt in the standard formula. If he had also replaced Yahweh, the name for God usually used in the formula, the allusion to the exodus would have become inaudible. He therefore used Yahweh in Genesis 15:7 to make the typological point that the God who brought Abraham out of Ur was the same God who saved Israel from Egypt. So there is insufficient ground for supposing that here the editor was asserting that Abraham knew the name of Yahweh.

What seems more compatible with the evidence is that the Yahwistic editor of Genesis was so convinced of the identity of Yahweh and the God who revealed himself to the patriarchs,[72] that he not only used Yahweh in the narrative, but also more sparingly in reporting human and angelic speech. He showed even more restraint in modifying divine utterances. Often the old title of God was left unaltered. When the editor wanted to express the identity of the patriarchal God with Yahweh, he usually did it by adding Yahweh to an older epithet. Only in one case does

---

[71]E.g. G. von Rad, *Genesis: A Commentary* (Philadelphia: Westminster, 1961), p. 185; R. E. Clements, *Abraham and David* (London: SCM, 1967), p. 21; N. Lohfink, *Die Landverheissung als Eid* (Stuttgart: Katholisches Bibelwerk, 1967). C. Westermann, *Genesis 12-* (Biblischer Kommentar, Neukirchener Verlag, 1979), pp. 255-256.

[72]This could be the point made by Gn. 4:26, 'At that time men began to call on the name of the LORD,' which may be paraphrased, 'Then the worship of the true God began.' C. Westermann, *Genesis 1-11* (Biblischer Kommentar, Neukirchener Verlag, 1974) pp. 460-463, insists that this verse is tracing the origins of worship to the primeval period, and does not necesarily indicate that the divine name Yahweh was known then.

Yahweh replace an older epithet, for which (I have suggested) there is a particular theological reason.

If this is the correct understanding of the Genesis editor's method, it sheds fresh light on Exodus 3 and 6. Taken together these passages do suggest that a genuinely new name of God, Yahweh, was vouchsafed to Moses. And this is the way the ancient translators took it. However, this did not mean that there was a clash with the Genesis traditions, because they are not always verbatim reports of divine revelation. Where it suited his theological purpose the Genesis editor could add and even once substitute Yahweh in the divine speeches. However, the great reserve with which in practice he modified the wording of the speeches of God, as far as the use of the divine names is concerned, could well extend to the promises contained in these speeches. Westermann's hypothesis, which supposes that the promises were added to the tradition with great freedom, becomes somewhat implausible. If, where the editor's method can be checked, it can be shown that he was anxious to be faithful to early tradition, as is the case with the divine names, it is unreasonable to suppose that he acted without regard to the tradition in those areas, such as the promises, where we have no controls. When it is also remembered that it was not unusual for ancient Semitic deities to make such promises as Genesis contains, there is a good case for holding that the religious statements in the patriarchal tradition are just as old as any other part of the stories.

5. SUMMARY AND CONCLUSIONS

Though the sources that describe the patriarchs' religion are not as early or detailed as a religious historian would like, this study has tended to support the main conclusions of modern scholarship about the character of that religion. It involved the worship of the Semitic high god El, who revealed himself to the leaders of the clans. In so far as the patriarchs generally lived outside the main Canaanite towns, it seems more probable that they first started to worship El in Mesopotamia, not in Canaan. The God of the patriarchs was in a special relationship to their clans: Genesis 15 and 17 describe the relationship as a covenant, which involved promises of divine protection and supplying their needs of land and children. The writer of Genesis identifies the patriarchs' El with Yahweh and prefers to use the latter term when describing divine activity, yet in reporting the words of God to the patriarchs he uses Yahweh very sparingly suggesting that he wanted to transmit the traditional form of the promises, not create divine words *ex nihilo*.

The patriarchs' response to revelation took the form of the traditional acts of piety, sacrifice, vows, tithes, ritual cleansing, prayer and libations. They are portrayed as men of faith, who obeyed the divine commands and believed his promises. The story of the sacrifice of Isaac which exemplifies these themes may also represent a rejection of child sacrifice, which was a feature of some types of El worship.

The type of religion portrayed in Genesis has many points in common with later Israelite practice, but this is not to prove that the patriarchal stories are simply retrojections of first-millennium ideas into a fictional past. Revelation, prayer and sacrifice are features of most pre-Christian religions. But certain aspects of patriarchal religion are so different from later practice, that to suppose the traditions were invented in the first millennium seems unlikely.

There are at least four striking contrasts between the religion of the patriarchs and later Israelite practice. First, there is the use of the term El instead of Yahweh in divine revelation. From Mosaic times onward Yahweh was the characteristic self-designation of God. But in Genesis God usually reveals himself as El. This distinction between the El revelation of Genesis and the Yahweh revelation of later times is more than a verbal contrast. The exclusiveness, holiness, and strictness of the God of Exodus is absent from Genesis. Though the patriarchs are faithful followers of their God, they generally enjoy good relations with men of other faiths. There is an air of ecumenical bonhomie about the patriarchal religion which contrasts with the sectarian exclusiveness of the Mosaic age and later prophetic demands.[73]

Secondly, the complete absence of Baal from the patriarchal tradition points to its antiquity. In the second half of the second millennium B.C. Baal took over from El as the leading god in the west Semitic pantheon, yet he is never mentioned in Genesis. This is intelligible if the patriarchal tradition originated before about 1500 B.C., but not if it comes from later times.

[73]B. Gemser, 'God in Genesis', *OTS* 12, 1958, pp. 1-21.

A third feature distinguishing patriarchal religion is its un-mediatedness. God spoke to the patriarchs directly in visions and dreams, and not through prophets. In their turn they built altars and offered sacrifice themselves without priestly aid. Such religious immediacy fits in with the nomadic way of life of the patriarchs, but is quite different from the religion of the monarchy period where priests and prophets were the usual mediators between God and man.

The final striking difference between the patriarchal period and the first-millennium scene is the non-mention of Jerusalem. The patriarchs worshipped near other great sanctuaries, Shechem, Bethel, Hebron and Beersheba, but there is no unambiguous reference to Jerusalem. The town certainly existed in patriarchal times: it is mentioned at Ebla and in nineteenth-century Egyptian execration texts. Psalms 76 and 110 identify Salem (Gn. 14) with Jerusalem, while 2 Chronicles 3:1 identifies Moriah (Gn. 22:2) with Mount Zion. But in Genesis itself there is no hint of these identifications, and this is most easily explained if the patriarchal traditions not only originated, but were committed to writing, before Jerusalem became the principal cultic centre in the time of David.

These features of patriarchal religion are compatible with an early second-millennium date for the tradition, but they would be strange if it grew up in the later monarchy period.

7
Diversity and Unity in the Literary Structure of Genesis
D. W. Baker

Within the body of a text there are indications of internal divisions, especially on the higher discourse levels such as paragraph, story or episode. While these indications fall into a limited number of categories, individual examples are extremely numerous. These indications will be better understood in their context than presented in a list. This study will deal with the text as it appears at one period in time, namely the Hebrew/Masoretic text of the book of Genesis. This approach is a necessary preliminary to a study of the text, which some scholars believe is itself derived from sources. We must analyse that which is objectively determinable (the present Masoretic text) before we can study that which is subjectively proposed (the source documents). The existence of these documents is at times proposed on the grounds of the division markers in the text. To avoid a circular argument, we shall study the overt form and function of these markers before making a suggestion concerning their implications.

Scholars have already noted the importance of the study of the divisions of the text in Old Testament studies. Muilenburg, in his 1968 Society of Biblical Literature presidential address, took up Eissfeldt's call to study the inter-relationships between text sections rather than simply to multiply these sections by repeatedly dividing the text.[1] We must study the text as a literary unit to see where it is divided into smaller sections (which Kessler calls the 'macro-structure') as well as the devices used to mark the divisions and indicate the unity (which he calls the 'micro-structure').[2] Each passage must be seen in its objective *Sitz im Text* before it

[1] J. Muilenberg, 'Form Criticism and Beyond', *JBL* 88, 1969, pp. 1-18; cf. O. Eissfeldt, 'Die kleinste literarische Einheit in den Erzählungsbüchern des Alten Testaments', *Kleine Schriften* I (Tübingen: J. C. B. Mohr, 1962), p. 49.

[2] M. Kessler, 'A Methodological Setting for Rhetorical Criticism', *Semitics* 4, 1974, pp. 22-36.

can be studied in its often more vague and subjective *Sitz im Leben*.[3]

Muilenburg and others who espouse this approach do not deny that we should value the study of smaller literary sections in addition to a study of the larger units of which they are a part. One of the problems in this analysis of smaller sections of the text, however, and one which form critics also recognize, is how to determine where a literary unit begins and ends. To determine this, Muilenburg says, is the first concern in rhetorical criticism.[4]

Tucker noted that the study of the structure of literary units is valid not only in reference to ' "original" units of oral expression'.[5] A 'unit' can mean anything from the entire text down to a single word. These text units do not necessarily correspond to source-critical divisions and attributions, although the latter can enter into the study at a later stage, when they can be compared with the textual sections determined by form criticism.[6]

We can place indications of textual divisions in three general categories: (1) syntactical indications of a discontinuity in such areas as time, subject or venue, (2) structural indications of the framework of the text, including headings, subscripts and summaries as well as repeated literary patterns or formulae, (3) rhetorical devices which point to a self-contained unit distinct from its context.

1. INDICATIONS OF DISCONTINUITY

That the book of Genesis is a distinct unit is shown by the indications of discontinuity which occur at each end of the text. In the very first verse a temporal discontinuity is indicated by the adverb $b^e r \bar{e}^{\,} sh \hat{i} t$, 'in the beginning'. At the end of the book there is an implicit change of subject, since Joseph, the protagonist of the preceding chapters (Gn. 37-50), is dead.[7] These represent two

[3]Ibid.

[4]*JBL* 88, pp. 8-9; cf. also G. M. Tucker, 'Prophetic Speech', *Int* 32 (1978), pp. 32-33, and F. Schicklberger, 'Biblische Literarkritik und linguistische Text-theorie', *TZ* 34 (1978), pp. 65-81. The designation 'rhetorical criticism' is to be preferred to 'structural analysis', since the latter can lead to confusion with the entirely different study of 'structuralism'; see Kessler, *Semitics* 4, p. 32.

[5]Tucker, *Int* 32, pp. 32-33.

[6]Ibid.

[7]Gn. 50:26—'And Joseph died at one hundred and twenty years of age. They embalmed him and put him in a casket in Egypt.'

types of discontinuity which indicate divisions in the text: change of time and change of subject.

1.1 *Change of time*

Sometimes a narrative unit is specifically stated to begin or end. When Pharaoh was dreaming in Genesis 41, it is recorded after each of his dreams that 'he woke up' (verses 4, 7). Also, when the events foretold by his dreams were happening, the end of one textual unit is marked 'and the seven years of plenty were completed' (verse 53) while the next unit begins 'and the seven years of famine started' (verse 54).[8]

There are also a number of other textual divisions which are marked by an explicit time change. This is especially important when stress is laid on the progress of time; for example, in the flood narrative. The start of the flood is marked by a marginal time reference (that is, one on the periphery of the story unit) which gives Noah's age: 'and Noah was six hundred years old' (Gn. 7:6). Following the account of the entrance of the animals into the ark, the section is concluded with a wait of seven days (verse 10). Then, the exact date of the flood is given (verse 11), followed by other indications of time which serve to mark divisions in the narrative by marking gaps, or discontinuities, in time (verses 12, 17, 24; 8:4, 5, 6, 10, 13-14).

This same sort of division is seen in other literature of the annal type; for example, in the Babylonian Chronicles in which each section is headed by *mu* X ('the X year of'),[9] as well as in Kings and Chronicles.[10]

---

[8]These two verses, while indicating temporal discontinuity showing a boundary between sections, are united by their literary form (verb + seven years + subject clause) as well as by a word play on the verbs (*t^ehillênâ*/*tik^elênâ*) which are differentiated only by the distinction /h/-/k/ which is more graphic than phonetic. For other examples of an action being said to begin or end see Gn. 17:22 (P); 6:1; 9:20, 24; 20:8; 28:16, 18 (J); 22:3 (E); cf. Gn. 21:15 (E); 24:15, 22; 27:30 (J) in which a new section is headed by a note regarding the termination of something related to the previous section. For a discussion of the formula *wayyashkēm babōqer*, see D. Irvin, *Mytharion* (Neukirchen-Vluyn: Neukirchener Verlag, 1978), p. 25.

[9]A. K. Grayson, *Assyrian and Babylonian Chronicles* (Locust Valley: J. J. Augustin, 1975; cited as *Chronicles*), passim.

[10] E.g. 1 Kings 15:1, 9, 33; 16:8 and passim. This is not a statement concerning the relative dates of this type of division marker, but is saying only that it is common and does serve, when it occurs, to separate two text sections.

Andersen noted that ages are often indicated as time references marginal to a story either at the beginning or the end, or else between episodes within a story.[11] An example of this is the division between Genesis 16 and 17. In Genesis 16:16 Abram is said to be eighty-six when Hagar bore Ishmael. The next section, in which Abram is renamed and Yahweh institutes the covenant with him, starts out with a statement that Abram was ninety-nine years old (Gn. 17:1). The first of these marginal time references is of interest because it is a circumstantial clause with the inversion of the subject and the predicate 'Now Abram was eighty-six years old when Hagar bore Ishmael to Abram' (Gn. 16:16).[12] The second, 'Abram was ninety-nine years old', starts a new section concerning Yahweh's covenant with Abram. This is shown by the gap of thirteen years between it and the previous section which concerns the birth of Ishmael. Other such time references which start a new episode are Genesis 23:1; 26:34; 24:1[13] and 27:1 (referring to agedness, zāqēn, rather than a specific age);[14] 34:25; 37:2.[15]

This second marginal time reference is of interest because it is introduced by the verbal form $way^eh\hat{i}$, which Andersen and Gesenius-Kautsch noted as often marking the transition to a new texual unit.[16] This verb frequently signals a discontinuity in circumstances from the preceding section Most of these reflect a lapse in time, as did the example above in which there was a time gap between Ishmael's birth and the following events.[17] Thus, while 'the imperfect with wāw-consecutive serves to express actions, events, or states, which are to be regarded as temporal or logical sequence of actions, events, or states mentioned immediately before',[18] $way^eh\hat{i}$ in this form appears to stress the

---

[11]F. I. Andersen, *The Sentence in Biblical Hebrew* (The Hague/Paris: Mouton, 1974; cited as *Sentence*), p. 81; see also Irvin, *Mytharion*, p. 28.

[12]See section 1.2. For other marginal time references in the form of a circumstantial clause closing an episode, see Andersen, *Sentence*, p. 81.

[13]A circumstantial clause; see ibid., p. 80.

[14]A relative rather than an absolute reference to a discontinuity in time.

[15]Ibid., p. 87.

[16]Ibid., p. 63; GK, para. 111f; see also Schicklberger, *TZ* 34, p. 70.

[17]Andersen, *Sentence*, p. 63. See also G. S. Ogden, 'Time, and the Verb הִיה in OT Prose', *VT* 21 (1971), pp. 451-469, especially p. 462 where he notes that the wāw plus prefix conjugation of the verb indicate a 'break in thought between the two clauses in question' of a longer or shorter interval.

[18]GK, para. 111a.

discontinuity rather than the continuity between separated passages.[19] Again it is important to consider each case in its context, since the verb *hāyāh* can have other uses as well as that of indicating a temporal discontinuity.[20]

In addition to the absolute time indicators which separate text sections, there are also relative time markers which bind sections, as well as marking their boundary.[21] These include such phrases as 'after (this)' (*ʾaḥᵃr[ê kēn]*),[22] 'again' (*ʿôd*),[23] and 'also' (*gam*).[24]

Time changes also mark textual divisions in Akkadian texts, especially annals. For example, time is used as a division marker in Grayson, *Chronicles* 1, where each year's activities are separated from those of another year by a line.[25] The activities are arranged in the order of the months in which they occur.[26]

---

[19]G. Coats, *From Canaan to Egypt* (Washington: Catholic Biblical Association of America, 1976; cited as *Canaan*), p. 21 noted that *wayᵉhî* sometimes does not separate two completely new scenes but serves as a transition between (to use his terms) an exposition (background preparation) and a specific crisis in a new scene. In the previous section there is a sense of preparation for the one following, but there is still a discontinuity in time marked in both cases.

[20]Cf. e.g. GK, para. 116r and Ogden, *VT* 21, pp. 451-469.

[21]See I. L. Seeligmann, 'Hebräische Erzählung und biblische Geschichtsschreibung', *TZ* 18 (1962), pp. 310-311.

[22]E.g. Gn. 15:1; 22:1, 20; 25:26; 48:1. For other references see S. Mandelkern, *Concordance on the Bible* (New York: Schulsinger Brothers, ²1955), pp. 35 sub אחר, pp. 35-37; cf. Irvin, *Mytharion*, p. 27.

[23]E.g. Gn. 4:25 referring to verse 1; 8:12 to verse 12 to verse 6 and verse 12 to verse 11, 9:11, 15 to 7:21; 29:35 to verse 32; passim in chapter 30; 35:9 to verse 1.

[24]Gn. 3:22 (taking from the tree of life) referring to verse 6; 4:26 (son born to Seth) to verse 17ff.; 10:21 (son born to Shem) to verse 2(?); 27:31 (Esau makes tasty stew) to verse 14, 38 (another blessing for Esau) to verse 27, cf. verse 35; 32:20 (report of Jacob's arrival) to verse 18; 35:17 (another son born to Rachel) to 30:23.

[25]Cf. also Grayson, *Chronicles* 2-7, probably 8, 9-12, 15 and 16. 1:6-8 is a distinct section concerning an action continuing through several years. While it does not start with a specific year number as do the other sections, it does commence with a marginal time reference ('at the time of Nabû-nāṣir'). The line was omitted between iii 18-19 in BM 92502 but is included in BM 75976; see Grayson, *Chronicles*, p. 80.

[26]As noted by Grayson (*Chronicles*, p. 84, commentary on iv 19-22) the order of months in iv 19-22 seems to be confused, Shubria being sacked in Ṭebet (month 10), its booty taken to Uruk in Kislev (month 9) and the king's wife dying in Adar (month 12). This could possibly be due to the time at which Esarhaddon became king. He had been crown-prince from Nisan (month 1), 681 B.C. and his father, Sennacherib, was murdered in Ṭebet (month 10; cf. *RLA* I, p. 201), 681 B.C. Although he did not gain actual control of the throne until Adar (month

1.2 Change of subject

A change in subject matter can be an obvious indicator of a discontinuity in the text.[27] A passage giving the family tree of Noah's sons (Gn. 10) is clearly distinct from one concerned with the building of a town (Gn. 11:1-9). The same is true of passages in which different personnel are involved. On its most mundane level, this change of personnel marks sub-paragraphs such as those within a dialogue.[28] For example, in the discussion between Yahweh, the man and the woman concerning the couple's sin in Genesis 3:9-19, different text sections are shown by different grammatical subjects (verses 9, 10, 11, 12, 13 [two], 14) or indirect objects (verses 14, 16, 17), which comprise a speech formula such as 'X spoke/commanded/said to Y'.

Other larger sections can be marked by the introduction of a new character. Frequently this involves the use of a circumstantial clause, i.e. one which breaks the ordinary Hebrew narrative prose chain of $w\bar{a}w$-consecutive plus prefixed verb (or, more rarely, plus suffixed verb). Commonly this is done by inserting the subject, which generally follows the predicate in Hebrew prose, between the $w\bar{a}w$-consecutive and the verb.[29] Following the account of Yahweh's covenant with Abram in Genesis 15, a new person is introduced and a new section started by the circumstantial clause 'Now Sarai, Abram's wife, had not given birth for him' (16:1)[30] A circumstantial clause is not the only indication of subject change, however, since a new subject, or at least the resumption of a

---

12), 680 B.C., he could have counted his kingship from the month his father died, which would place Ṭebet before Kislev in the first full year of his reign. Cf. also Grayson, *Chronicles* 17 ii 12-14 and iii 10-11 and the notes on them for other dischronological accounts. The former might be explained as was the example just noted, but the latter specifically mentions year 19 before year 16.

[27]See W. Richter, *Exegese als Literaturwissenschaft* (Göttingen: Vandenhoeck & Ruprecht, 1971), p. 86; Schicklberger, *TZ* 34, p. 70.

[28]*Oxford English Dictionary* (Oxford: Clarendon Press, 1933), VII, p. 453 sub 'paragraph' 2, 'The words of a distinct speaker'.

[29]Andersen, *Sentence*, pp. 77-78; cf. also F. I Andersen, *The Hebrew Verbless Clause in the Pentateuch* (Nashville: Abingdon, 1970), p. 35 and S. R. Driver, *A Treatise on the Use of the Tenses in Hebrew* (Oxford: Clarendon Press, 1892), p. 201.

[30]See Andersen, *Sentence*, p. 87; also pp. 79-80 for further examples.

subject which has been already introduced, can follow a *wāw*-consecutive verb, according to the ordinary Hebrew narrative sentence structure of *wāw*-consecutive verb plus subject (e.g. Gn. 4:25; 11:1; 12:1, 4, etc.).

Andersen noted that circumstantial clauses can occur at the end of an episode, although it is at times difficult to determine whether the clause is at the beginning or the end.[31] Termination can be made clear by the introduction of a new subject in the following verse, thus starting a new section. For example, following a dialogue between Yahweh and Abraham in Genesis 18 it is stated that 'Yahweh went away when he had finished speaking to Abraham, and Abraham returned to his own place' (verse 33). The last clause is circumstantial in form and closes a section, since the following verse introduces new subjects, i.e. 'now two angels came to Sodom' (19:1).

Change of subject marks divisions elsewhere in the Old Testament as well as in other Semitic literatures. This is especially common in historiographic texts such as annals. Examples are abundant in the histories of the Israelite kings (eg. 1 Kgs. 1:1; 5:26; 10:1; 11:26 and *passim*) as they are in those of Mesopotamian kings; cf. A. Grayson, *Chronicles*, 14 (cf. p. 30), 18, 20-22 (cf. p. 56); L. W. King, *Annals of the Kings of Assyria* (1902; cited as *Annals*), p. 41:36; 47:89; 56:73; 57:88; 70:22 (Tiglath-pileser I: 1114-1076 B.C.) and other royal inscriptions. Some of these texts also include indications of a time change in conjunction with that of personnel.[32]

1.3 Change of time and subject: genealogical lists

Genealogical lists combine aspects of discontinuities in time and in subject. While they occur in Genesis (e.g. Gn. 5, 10 and *passim*), they are by no means restricted to that book. Recently Wilson published a detailed study of the form and function of genealogies in the Hebrew Bible.[33] He has compared these with

---

[31]Ibid., pp. 80-82 where examples are given.

[32]E.g. Grayson, *Chronicles* 23, 24. These two are both eclectic (see ibid. p. 60) and, although they start each section by a marginal time reference, could have only one per reign so that subject and time changes are the same.

[33]R. R. Wilson, *Genealogy and History in the Biblical World* (New Haven/London: Yale UP, 1977; cited as *Genealogy*). See pp. 207-215 for a detailed bibliography.

contemporary oral genealogical lists among African tribes, and with other ancient near-eastern genealogical material. His rather general conclusion is that 'genealogies seem to have been created and preserved for domestic, politico-jural, and religious purposes'.[34] However, the function of genealogies in the literary structure of the text in which they occur is mentioned only rarely, and requires further study.

An abbreviated form of genealogical data, 'A son of B (son of Y)', is commonly used in the Old Testament as a type of epithet. These were used to identify an individual more precisely. The 'epithet' form does not usually serve as a structural division marker within the Hebrew text, except incidentally when the person identified by it is encountered for the first time. A genealogy marking the end of a text section is sometimes used to relate the main figure of the preceding narrative to some other known personnage. For example the genealogy in Ruth 4:18-22 links Boaz to the proverbial Perez in the past (cf. 4:12; Gn. 38:29) and to David in the future. While representing a change of subject, a continuity with the past is also indicated. Thus the genealogy serves to emphasize both discontinuity and continuity.

Genealogies also link narratives concerning two different time periods. For example, Noah is introduced by a genealogical link to Adam through Seth in Genesis 5:3-32, while in Genesis 11:10-28 Noah and his sons are linked through Shem to Abram and Lot. This use of a genealogy unites two groups of traditions in which a relationship is not internally clear. The basis of these genealogies is not natural descent alone, since other criteria must be used to determine the line which was to be pursued. As Williamson noted concerning the early genealogies in Chronicles, which he acknowledged as being taken from Genesis, the line followed in these genealogies is that of the elect, that is, it leads to the founding of the people of Israel.[35]

Genealogies are not necessarily restricted to the main line of biblical history, and may concern secondary lines which are not pursued beyond the end of the genealogy. Adam's line through

---

[34]Ibid., p. 199.

[35]H. G. M. Williamson, *Israel in the Book of Chronicles* (London: Cambridge UP, 1977; cited as *Israel*), pp. 62-63; cf. also M. D. Johnson, *The Purpose of Biblical Genealogies* (London: Cambridge UP, 1969), p. 73.

Cain is given in detail in Genesis 4:1-24 and subsequently abandoned, while the line of Seth is simply introduced by a two
generation genealogy in this chapter (verses 25-26). It is then
taken up and continued for ten generations in 5:3-23, as noted
above. Also, Genesis 10 takes up the lines of Noah's sons, Japheth,
Ham and Shem. The order appears to be a result of listing the
most important line last, with the least important, and youngest,
first.[36] The lineage of Shem is then resumed, again for ten generations, in Genesis 11:10ff. Other secondary genealogies include
those of the lines of Ishmael (Gn. 25:12-18), Esau (Gn. 36:2-5, 9-14)
and Abraham's descendants through Keturah (Gn. 25:1-4).[37] All of
these are between major text sections, except the last, which
separates two episodes. In each case the genealogies mark divisions.

1.4 *Change of venue*

Another discontinuity which indicates a division between sections
in a narrative text is a change in the location or venue of the
events recorded.

Coats noted a formula which serves as a transition marker
between two units.[38] From the examples which he gives, this
could be called a 'settling formula', and it involves the subject
taking up residence (*yāshab*) at a given location. In some cases
this transitional formula has no clear relationship with either the
preceding or the following section. Following the genealogy of
Esau in Genesis 36, 'Jacob settled (*wayyēsheb*) in the land of the
residence of his fathers, that is, in the land of Canaan' (37:1). This
serves as a bridge between the preceding genealogy and the
following *tôlᵉdôt* formula and the Joseph story. Other occurrences
of this 'settling-formula' indicate either the beginning or the end
of a narrative unit.[39] There are also cases where synonyms of
settlement are used with the same function.[40]

---

[36]Cf. Williamson, *Israel*, p. 63; A. Guillaume, 'Paranomasia in the Old Testament', *JSS* 9 (1964), p. 283, n. 2.

[37]Cf. also Gn. 36:15-19, 20-28, 29-30, 40-44 for other examples; Wilson, *Genealogy*, p. 167.

[38]Coates, *Canaan*, p. 9, cites Gn. 4:16; 13:18; 19:30; 20:1; 21:20, 21; 22:19; 26:6,
17; 50:22.

[39]Other such transitions are Gn. 13:12; 24:62; 25:11b; 29:14 (with a time
reference); 47:27.

[40]*gar*—Gn. 21:34; *nāṭaᶜ*—21:33; cf. *shākan/nāpal*—25:18.

Some passages are bounded by a formula which contains a 'settling-formula' but is more complex. These have been named variously 'departure' or 'itinerary' formulae,[41] and involve a specific discontinuity in location as well as a settling down. These passages mention the departure from one place and the arrival at another. One of the more complex examples of this extended formula is Genesis 11:31 which makes a transition between the pre-history of Genesis 1-11 and the following patriarchal history when it records that 'Terah took Abram . . . and Lot . . . and they set out ($wayy\bar{e}s^{e^{\circ}}\hat{u}$) from the Chaldean Ur to go ($l\bar{a}leket$) to the land of Canaan. They came ($wayy\bar{a}b\bar{o}^{\circ}\hat{u}$) as far as Haran and they settled ($wayyesh^{e}bu$) there.' This is a complete itinerary from departure to settlement.[42] Other such formulae in Genesis are shorter,[43] and some of them use verbs other than $y\bar{a}shab$ to express the settlement aspect.[44] Some of these formulae do not contain the 'settlement' clause, containing only an indication of departure and arrival[45] or only one of these elements.[46] At times there is only a verb which indicates that travel is taking place.[47]

Venue change as mark of textual division in narrative texts is by no means limited to Genesis but is common in other Old Testament narrative texts as well.[48] A form of venue shift also indicates divisions in other literatures. For example, in the Sumerian King List the material is divided according to the different locations in

[41]Seeligmann, *TZ* 18, pp. 307-310; see J. Wilcoxen, 'Narrative', *Old Testament Form Criticism*, ed. J. H. Hayes (San Antonio: Trinity UP, 1974), p. 91, and G. M. Coats, *Rebellion in the Wilderness* (Nashville: Abingdon, 1968), pp. 47-48 and *passim*; cf. C. Westermann, *Genesis 12-50* (Darmstadt: Wissenschaftliche Buchgesellschaft 1977), pp. 49-51.

[42]See Westermann, *Genesis 12-50*, p. 159.

[43]E.g. 12:8; 36:8; 38:11; 50:7-10 ($n\bar{a}ta^{c}$ / $^{c}\bar{a}taq$).

[44]E.g. 31:25 ($taqa$ / $nasag$); 33:18 ($h\bar{a}n\bar{a}h$ / $b\bar{a}^{\circ}$); 35:21 ($n\bar{a}ta^{c}$ / $n\bar{a}sa^{c}$); 38:1 ($n\bar{a}ta^{c}$ / $y\bar{a}rad$).

[45]Gn. 8:11; 22:8-9 (see verses 3, 6); 28:10-11; 35:5-6; 43:15; 44:13-14; 45:24-25; 46:1, 5; 50:7-10; cf. 37:14; 46:28.

[46]Only departure—Gn. 8:18-19; 14:8, 17; 34:1, 6; 37:12; 41:45-46; 47:10; only arrival—Gn. 7:7, 13; 14:5, 13; 19:1, 23; 26:32; 27:30; 33:18; 34:20; 35:27; 37:23; 41:57; 42:5, 29; 44:14; 47:1.

[47]$n\bar{a}sa^{c}$—Gn. 12:9; 33:17; 35:16; $h\bar{a}lak$—Gn. 13:3; 14:11-12; 18:16; 21:14; 24:10, 61; 26:1, 31; 28:5, 7; 29:1; 31:55-32:1; 42:26; $y\bar{a}rad$—Gn. 11:5; 12:10; 39:1; $^{c}\bar{a}lah$—Gn. 13:1; 17:22; 26:23; 35:13; $sh\bar{a}b$—Gn. 33:16.

[48]See from different periods, for example Dt. 34:1 ($^{c}\bar{a}l\bar{a}h$); Ru. 1:1 ($h\bar{a}lak$); 2 Chr. 8:3 ($h\bar{a}lak$).

which kingship resided.[49] The same form of change of dynasty is also used in the neo-Assyrian Dynastic Chronicle, at least in some parts of the text.[50] In other cases, such as royal inscriptions concerning military campaigns, divisions (some of which are marked by extra-textual indicators) also have a change of venue to mark a discontinuity.[51]

2. INDICATIONS OF FRAMEWORK

At times the biblical text is divided into distinct sections by its formal literary structure. One method of this which is used in Genesis is panel-writing in which a structured set of component statements is repeated in the same form a number of times.[52] An example is found in Genesis 1 in which the pattern (1) speech clause ('and God said'), (2) command, (3) execution of command, (4) formula of divine approval, (5) ordering formula[53] is repeated eight times.[54] This panel writing is used to indicate sections in various lists such as genealogies (e.g. Gn. 5; 9:28-29; 11:10b-26). It can also be seen to unify narrative passages (eg. Gn. 9:12-17;[55] 15,[56] 17,[57]). Due to the fixed progression of elements within the panel, it is possible to determine the start and finish of each.

In addition to formulaic structure indicating the boundaries of a textual unit, there are also verbal formulae which can indicate the start or end of a section. One of these is the clause 'these are

[49]T. Jacobsen, *The Sumerian King List* (Chicago: University of Chicago Press, 1939).

[50]Grayson, *Chronicles*, p. 140: 4, 7, 10; cf. also col. v in which divisions were made according to the different locales from which the rulers came, i.e. 8-bala kur.a.ab.ba; 12-bala é-^{l}bazi; 15-bala [ela]m^{ki}; see p. 197.

[51]E.g. King, *Annals*, p. 49:7-8; 52:35-39; 59-60:7-9; 75:67 (Tiglath-pileser I) and passim in other royal inscriptions.

[52]See S. E. McEvenue, *The Narrative Style of the Priestly Writer* (Rome: Pontifical Biblical Institute, 1971), pp. 16, 17, 158-169.

[53]A marginal time reference indicating a discontinuity between one section and those before and after; cf. section 1.1. above.

[54]Cf. C. Westermann, *Genesis I-XI* (Neukirchen-Vluyn: Neukirchener Verlag, 1974) p. 117; B. W. Anderson, 'A Stylistic Study of the Priestly Creation Story', *Canon and Authority*, eds. G. W. Coats and B. O. Long (Philadelphia: Fortress Press, 1977), pp. 151-154; McEvenue, *Style*, p. 17.

[55]Ibid., pp. 77-78.

[56]Ibid., p. 155; cf. N. Lohfink, *Die Landverheissung als Eid* (Stuttgart: Katholisches Bibelwerk, 1967), p. 45.

[57]McEvenue, *Style*, pp. 158-159.

the *tôlᵉdôt* of X' which occurs eleven times in Genesis.[58] I have
argued elsewhere that the formula is neither strictly a heading,
starting a new section, nor only a colophon, closing a section. It
appears, however, to be ambiguous, at times opening at times
closing a portion of the text.[59] Whichever way the clause refers, it
divides the text at a juncture where the concern of the narrative is
focused down to a smaller group of people until finally it is
focused, in the Pentateuch, on Aaron and Moses,[60] or in Ruth, to
David. As well as this theological interpretation of the formula, it
should be noted that it always occurs in conjunction with other
division markers.[61]

There are also other formulae with the same demonstrative
pronouns (*ʾēlleh* 'these') which are commonly used as summary
statements in Genesis, and most commonly refer to the preceding
text section,[62] but at times refer to the following, as headings.[63]
Therefore, while these demonstrative formulae do mark a division
between text sections, it is the context which determines whether
they are anaphoric (summary subscripts) or cataphoric (summary
headings). It is also the context which indicates whether they
mark paragraphs or larger units such as episodes or complete
stories.

In addition to formulaic summaries which indicate textual
boundaries, there are other different clauses which serve this
function. In Genesis 50, Pharaoh gave Joseph permission to go
and bring his father to Egypt '(7) so Joseph went up to bring his
father. There went up with him all of Pharaoh's servants, the
elders of his house, and all of the elders of Egypt; (8) also all of
Jacob's house and his brothers and his fathers's house . . . (9) there

---

[58]Gn. 2:4; 5:1; 6:9; 10:1; 11:10, 27; 25:12, 19; 36:1, 9; 37:2.

[59]The arguments are presented in Appendix C of the author's Ph.D. thesis
'Some Scribal Techniques in Ancient Israel with Other Semitic Parallels' to be
submitted to the University of London.

[60]O. Eissfeldt, 'Biblos geneseos', *Kleine Schriften* III (Tübingen: J. C. B. Mohr,
1966), pp. 461-462. cf. J. Scharbert, 'Die Sinn der Toledot-Formel in Priester-
schrift', *Wort-Gebot-Glaube*, ed. H. J. Stoebe (Zürich: Zwingli Verlag, 1970),
p. 45, who notes that the formula occurs at different turning points in history.

[61]Time change: Gn. 2:4; 5:1; subject change: Gn. 6:9; 10:1; 11:10, 27; 25:19;
35:1; time and venue: Gn. 25:12; subject and venue: Gn. 36:9; subject, time and
venue: Gn. 37:2.

[62]Gn. 9:19²; 10:5, 20, 31²; 36:10 and passim.

[63]Gn. 36 passim. See Schicklberger, *TZ* 34, p. 70.

also went up with him chariotry and cavalry, it was a large group.' Here the final clause serves to summarize the list. This ends the text unit, because in the next verse a change of venue is marked, starting a new unit. Summaries are not restricted to lists, however, since the action of a whole passage can be summarized at the end. Thus, after an account of Abraham circumcising his whole household (17:23-25) we are told '(26) On that day Abraham and Ishmael his son were circumcised, (27) and all of his retainers, houseborn or purchased from others, were circumcised with him.'[64]

These division markers fall into two general categories. One set of markers is syntactical, indicating a discontinuity between two literary units. This can be a discontinuity of time (indicated by references to ages and dates, by the verb or by more specific statements of temporal discontinuity—'after that', etc.—as well as implicit time gaps), or a discontinuity of location, indicating a movement from one place to another (along with the related 'settling-formula' and its variants), or a discontinuity of subject (in which new personnel are introduced or stressed). All three of these discontinuities can be marked by syntactical discontinuities, that is, a circumstantial clause which breaks the ordinary narrative chain of consecutive verbs.

The second general category of division markers is formal, involving those summaries which can serve either as introductions to or as final sections of a literary unit. These can be either fomulaic or non-formulaic in character. Into this category can be grouped explicit statements of the commencement or termination of a section. Panel-writing also belongs to this category.

3. RHETORICAL DEVICES INDICATING DIVERSITY AND UNITY

In addition to these division indicators there are also marks of literary unity and discontinuity, grouped under the title of rhetorical devices, which can also delineate units of greater or lesser extent. One of these is the repetition of vocabulary or phraseology at the beginning and at the end of a textual unit. This is called an *inclusio*, and sets the unit apart from its context.[65] An example of an *inclusio* is Genesis 1:1-2:4a. In 2:4a, all of the non-formulaic

---

[64]Cf. also the summaries in Gn. 8:1b; 23:20; 30:43; 31:21.
[65]See J. Lundbom, *Jeremiah: A Study in Ancient Hebrew Rhetoric*(Missoula: Scholars Press, 1975), p. 16.

vocabulary, i.e., all except for the *tôledôt*-formula itself, is a repetition of that found in the first verse, 'created, heaven and earth'. The pair 'heaven and earth' also occur in the same order in both verses. While this order is that most frequently used in the Old Testament, it is deliberately used here (as can be demonstrated by the second half of 2:4, in which the order is reversed) to indicate a dichotomy between the two halves of the verse. This *inclusio* thus marks the seven day creation account as a unit separate from the following section.[66]

This rhetorical device delineates literary units a few verses (e.g. 5:1b-2) to several chapters long. Coats suggested that the 'settling'-formula in 37:1, opens the Joseph story ('And Jacob settled in the land where his fathers had resided, in the land of Canaan'), and that the same formula in 47:27a closes it ('And Israel settled in the land of Egypt, in the land of Goshen'). This parallel, or *inclusio*, he suggests, not only defines the boundaries of the story, but also 'suggests . . . a structural dialectic in the Joseph story itself'.[67]

Andersen noted that a similar rhetorical device—the recapitulation or 'echo' of some important point, sometimes through the use of a circumstantial clause—can be used to close an episode.[68] The example of this device which he gives is the story of Noah's nakedness in Genesis 9. After being told, in a series of *wāw*-consecutive verbs, that Shem and Japheth went in backwards to cover their father, the action is 'echoed' in verse 23b, 'their faces were towards the back so they did not see their father's nakedness', a circumstantial clause. The new section opening with a time discontinuity in the next verse ('when Noah awoke from his wine'), shows that this recapitulation does in fact close the previous section.

The criteria derived from discourse analysis indicating a textual division is harder to control than some previously mentioned since, as McEvenue has shown, recapitulatory 'echo' is also used to link two or more units which are separated by a division marker. An example which he cites is the time reference 'after the flood' which forms part of the *inclusio* in Genesis 10:1, 32, and is an echo of 9:28a and is again mentioned in 11:10. Other components of this *inclusio* are also echoes.[69]

---

[66]The *inclusio* is recognized by Muilenburg in *JBL* 88, p. 9.
[67]Coats, *Canaan*, p. 9.
[68]*Sentence*, p. 81; see also McEvenue, *Style*, p. 38, concerning the 'echo'.
[69]Ibid., p. 38.

Therefore, as well as showing divisions between two sections of a text, the rhetorical devices mentioned above also indicate a textual unity. The *inclusio* was by definition a repetition of vocabulary at the beginning and end of a text section, thus dividing the text by showing a textual unity, i.e. that portion enclosed by the *inclusio*. The echo can also serve as a uniting feature, since in it one passage resumes a theme or vocabulary introduced in a previous passage. The latter must either predate or be contemporaneous with the former.

Another rhetorical linking device is the chiasm or 'palistrophe'.[70] Not only can a chiasm indicate the unity of one section in contrast to others,[71] it can also serve to unite two passages that have been shown to be distinct units into a larger whole. For example, the chiasm 'heaven and earth—earth and heaven' in Genesis 2:4 indicates a conscious unification of the two passages Genesis 1:1-2:4a and 2:4bff.

A rhetorical device in Genesis related to the echo that also repeats vocabulary of one section in another, is prolepsis, or the anticipation of an event or action before it is actually recorded. This occurs in the form of a summary note. For example, Genesis 6:5-7 records Yahweh's dissatisfaction with man's wickedness and his vow to destroy man. Verse 8, which ends a section by a circumstantial clause (cf. section 1.2.) tells of Noah's uprightness. After a *tôlᵉdôt*-formula division marker (Gn. 6:9), another circumstantial clause reaffirms Noah's good character (verse 9b) and verses 10-7:24 detail the destruction of man. This not only exemplifies the use of summary anticipation followed by detailed fulfilment, but also utilizes the chiasm A—vow to destroy B—Noah's righteousness, B'—Noah's righteousness, A'—destruction, to unite two separated sections.[72] Another interesting example is found in Genesis 37:36 and 39:1, which record Joseph's descent to Egypt and his purchase by Potiphar. The two notes of this sequence of events in these two verses are separated by the Judah-Tamar incident in Genesis 38. Genesis 39:1 is then a recapitulation and resumption (*Wiederaufnahme*) of the narrative which had

[70]Also called variously 'concentric inclusion', 'concentric structure' or 'complex inclusion', the structure procedes through a series and then returns through the same series in the form ABCC′B′A′; cf. ibid., pp. 29, 157-158.

[71]See McEvenue's discussion of the chiasm of Gn. 17 in ibid.

[72]Cf. R. E. Longacre, 'The Discourse Structure of the Flood Narrative', *SBL 1976 Seminar Papers* (Missoula: Scholars Press, 1976), pp. 236, 241.

been temporarily interrupted by the intervening chapter. The resumption indicates the unity of the passage as it now stands, including chapter 38.[73]

4. OTHER UNIFYING LITERARY FEATURES

In addition to these structural or rhetorical indicators of textual unity there are also explicit references in the text which show the same thing. Sometimes one section is specifically referred to in another, as when reference is made to a previous occurrence of an event. This has been already noted above in the discussion of relative time references (section 1.1.). The adverb 'there' (*sham*) is also used to indicate a place designated earlier in the text, thus uniting the two references.[74] Another unifying feature involves questions, commands and promises. They look forward to the response in which there is an answer, obedience, or fulfilment;[75] or, at the fulfilment or answer, reference can be made back to the original question, etc.[76]

Richter also noted the unifying character of verbal and nominal pronouns. Not only do anaphoric pronouns tie a clause to the previous explicit designation of the referent; so too do the personal elements in Hebrew verbs. These, in addition to the verbal component, also contain person, number and gender within themselves, so that a subject could be explicitly given at the start of an episode and resumed only in the verb during the course of the narrative. For example, in Genesis 21:14 'Abraham awoke in the morning and took bread and a sack of water and gave it to Hagar . . . she went and she wandered in the desert . . . (15) and she threw the child under a bush . . . (16) and went and sat . . . and wept . . . (19). She saw a well of water, went and filled the water sack and gave the youth to drink.' The resumed third person feminine subject here unites the whole passage.[77] Related to this

[73]Cf. Seeligmann, *TZ* 18 (1962), p. 315.

[74]E.g. Gn. 20:1 referring to 18:1; 32:29 to verse 23. See Schicklberger, *TZ* 34, p. 79.

[75]E.g. Gn. 1:28 to verse 30; 15:2 to verse 4; 20:7 to verse 14; 22:2 to verse 9; 24:2 to verse 9; verse 3 to verses 15ff., verse 4 to verse 10; 26:4-5 to verse 22; 27:34 to verses 39ff., 28:2 to verse 7; 29:15 to verse 18; 31:24 to verse 29.

[76]E.g. Gn. 3:17 to verse 3; 7:9, 16 to verse 2; 12:4 to verse 1; 17:23 to verses 10-11; 27:19 to verses 3-4. See Richter, *Exegese*, pp. 85-88.

[77]Other examples are Gn. 24:16-25, 45-47 (Rebekkah); 32:10-23 (Jacob); 25-28 (Jacob's adversary). Cf. Richter, *Exegese*, pp. 85-88; Schicklberger, *TZ* 34 p. 78.

are those passages in which a noun is introduced in one grammatical function and then is resumed as a pronoun with another
function,[78] e.g. Genesis 30:25: Jacob (subject) speaks to Laban
(indirect object), verse 27 Laban (subject) speaks to Jacob (indirect
object), verses 28, 29 Jacob—(subject) speaks, verse 31 he (Laban—
subject) speaks.

Similar to these two indicators of textual unity are the enclitic
personal pronouns which also resume previously specified nouns.
There are numerous examples of these pronouns referring to
something mentioned immediately before but there are also
occasions in which the pronoun refers to something several verses
previously. For example in Genesis 14:9 Chedarlaomer and his
colleages are mentioned by name and then resumed in an enclitic
pronoun six verses later when 'he (Abram) split up against him
by night, he and his servants, and attacked them and chased them
as far as Hormah' (Gn. 14:15). This example is noteworthy
because it binds together two sections which were divided by a
circumstantial clause in verse 10.[79] Another similar example is the
resumption of Abraham who is named in Genesis 17:26 and
resumed in pronouns in verse 27 and 18:1-2. The division between
the chapters was noted by Speiser and von Rad.[80] The anaphoric
pronouns uniting these two passages are especially intriguing
since critical opinion attributes Genesis 17 to P and Genesis 18 to
J, the latest and earliest sources of the Pentateuch respectively.
According to the structure of these chapters as they now stand, a
source critic would have to conclude that someone could make
reference to a piece of literature which appears five or six centuries later, a hypothesis which does not seem likely.

One further syntactical feature which can serve to unify a text is
the quasi-anaphoric use of the definite article.[81] We have already

[78]Richter, *Exegese*, pp. 85-88.

[79]For a note of this division, see Andersen, *Sentence*, p. 80. Other examples
uniting different sections are Gn. 22:1 to chapter 21; 24:22 to verse 16; 26:26 to
verse 18; 29:9 to verse 3; 32:23 to verse 10; 33:3-4 to verse 1.

[80]E. A. Speiser, *Genesis* (Garden City: Doubleday, 1964), p. 122; G. von Rad,
Genesis (London: SCM, 1961), p. 202. Other examples uniting two sources are
Gn. 26:15 (S. R. Driver, *Genesis*, London: Methuen, 1926, p. 252) to verse 13 (J);
28:13 (J) to verse 12 (E); verse 19 (J) to verse 11 (E); 30:4 (J) to verse 2 (E); verse 20
(J); Speiser, *Genesis*, p. 229) to verse 19 (E); 32:9 (J; von Rad, *Genesis*, p. 313) to
verse 2 (E).

[81]Cf. GK, para. 126d; P. Jouon, *Grammaire de l'hebreu biblique* (Rome:
Institut Biblique Pontifical, 1947), para. 137, 3; Schicklberger, *TZ* 34, pp. 80-81.

noted the resumption of definite nouns by the use of anaphoric pronouns. The same also occurs when a noun is detailed at one point (e.g. 'behold three men were standing before him', Gn. 18:2) and resumed with only the definite article later on ('the men turned from there and went to Sodom', Gn. 18:22; 'the two angels', Gn. 19:1; 'the angels', verse 15; 'the men', verses 12, 16). These latter forms presuppose the explanation in 18:2. This feature is common within passages attributed to one source[82] and can also indicate unity between different sections, either as determined by the criteria mentioned above, or those proposed by adherents to the documentary hypothesis.[83]

5. IMPLICATIONS OF DIVERSITY AND UNITY

The Hebrew text of Genesis fits well into its contemporary literary milieu as far as its structure is concerned. Divisions between text sections in other documents, while at times employing overt, extra-textual indicators of separate units (e.g. rulings or spaces) which are not used in the Hebrew Old Testament, share many similarities with those divisions which are indicated in Genesis within the text itself. There is nothing out of the ordinary in the structure of the book which might indicate that it is a heterogeneous amalgam of originally separate sources which have been melded, at times leaving evidence of crude joins, as some have proposed. As far as the matters discussed in this paper are concerned, Genesis appears to be a well-structured literary document.

Concerning the absolute or even the relative dating of the final composition of this book we can determine nothing significant from this study of textual division indicators, since the criteria used to determine section boundaries are not peculiar to any

---

[82]Gn. 1:3 ('light') is resumed by 1:4, 5, 18 (GK, para. 126d); 22:2 ('one of the mountains') by 22:3, 4, 9 ('the place'); 28:1 ('stone') by 22:22.

[83]E.g. Gn. 1:26 ('man'; P) is presupposed by 1:27 (P), 2:7, 8, 15, 16, 19, 20, 21, 22 (J); 2:8 ('garden'; J) by 2:9, 10; 3:1, 8 (J), 2:22 ('woman'; J) by 3:1, 4, 6, 13 (J); 6:14 ('ark'; P) by 6:16, 18 (P); 7:1, 7, 9 (J), 13, 17 (P) and passim; 21:2 ('son'; J) by 2:8 ('child'; E); 24:2 ('servant') by 24:5, 10, 17, 22; 24:15 ('Rebekkah'; cf. verse 14: 'girl') by 24:28 ('the girl'); 25:24 ('twins'; P) by 25:27 ('the boys'; J); 12:10 ('famine') by 26:1; 29:1 ('land of the Easterners') by 29:22 ('the place'); 29:2 ('well') by 29:3, 10; 31:19 ('household gods') by 31:34; 33:2 ('women and children') by 33:5.

specific period. We can, however, deduce something from an observation of the unifying features studied here. This paper has shown that in some cases texts attributed to E or P refer to material attributed to J. While this is not remarkable, similar references in the 'early' J to the 'late' P must be explained. This calls for a thorough re-examination of the theory of source documents, or at least of the relative dates of those proposed by classical source analysis.

Bibliography

W. F. Albright	*The Archaeology of Palestine and the Bible* (London and New York: Revell, 1932)
	The Biblical Period (Pittsburgh: Biblical Colloquium, 1950; Oxford: Blackwell, 1952)
	The Biblical Period from Abraham to Ezra (New York: Harper and Row, 1963)
	Archaeology, Historical Analogy and Early Biblical Tradition (Baton Rouge: Louisiana State UP, 1966)
	Yahweh and the Gods of Canaan (London: Athlone Press; New York: Doubleday, 1968)
A. Alt	*Der Gott der Väter* (Stuttgart: Kohlhammer, 1929)
	Essays on Old Testament History and Religion (Oxford: Blackwell, 1966)
	Kleine Schriften (Ch. Beck'sche Verlagsbuchhandlung, 1953–4)
A. Altmann (ed.)	*Biblical and Other Studies* (Cambridge, Mass.: Harvard UP, 1963)
F. I. Andersen	*The Hebrew Verbless Clause in the Pentateuch* (Nashville: Abingdon, 1970)
	The Sentence in Biblical Hebrew (The Hague: Mouton, 1974)
M. Avi-Yonah (ed.)	*Encyclopedia of Archaeological Excavations in the Holy Land* (London: OUP; Englewood Cliffs, NJ: Prentice-Hall, 1975–8)
K. Barth	*Church Dogmatics* III/I (ET, Edinburgh: T & T Clark; New York: Scribner's, 1958)
	Church Dogmatics III/II (ET, Edinburgh: T & T Clark; New York: Scribner's, 1960)
R. D. Biggs	*Inscriptions from Tell Abu Salabikh* (Chicago: Chicago UP, 1974)
J. Bright	*A History of Israel* (London: SCM; Philadelphia: Westminster Press, 1972)
C. F. Burney	*Israel's Settlement in Canaan;* Schweich Lectures, 1917 (London: British Academy, 1918)
E. Cassin	*L'Adoption à Nuzi* (Paris: Maisonneuve, 1938)
U. Cassuto	*A Commentary on the Book of Exodus* (Jerusalem: Magnes, 1967)

B. S. Childs	*The Book of Exodus* (Philadelphia: Westminster; London: SCM, 1974)
R. E. Clements	*Abraham and David* (London: SCM, 1967)
	A Century of Old Testament Study (London: Lutterworth, 1976)
	Old Testament Theology: A Fresh Approach (London: Marshall; Atlanta: John Knox, 1978)
G. Coats	*Rebellion in the Wilderness* (Nashville: Abingdon, 1968)
	From Canaan to Egypt (Washington: Catholic Biblical Association of America, 1976)
F. M. Cross	*Canaanite Myth and Hebrew Epic* (Cambridge, Mass.: Harvard UP, 1973)
F. M. Cross et al. (eds.)	*Magnalia Dei: The Mighty Acts of God, Essays in Memory of G. E. Wright* (New York: Doubleday, 1976)
R. J. Coggins	*Chronicles* (Cambridge: CUP, 1976)
E. L. Curtis and A. A. Madsen	*The Books of Chronicles*; ICC (Edinburgh: T. & T. Clark, 1910)
I. M. Diakonoff (ed.)	*Ancient Mesopotamia* (Moscow: USSR Academy of Sciences, 1969)
M. Dietrich, O. Loretz and W. Mayer	*Nuzi-Bibliographie, AOAT* Sonder. II (Kevalaer: Butzon & Bercker, 1972)
H. Donner	*Die literarische Gestalt der alttestamentlichen Josephgeschichte* (Heidelberg: Winter, 1976)
J. D. Douglas (ed.)	*The New Bible Dictionary* (London and Downers Grove, Ill.: Inter-Varsity Press, 1962)
S. R. Driver	*A Treatise on the Use of Tenses in Hebrew* (Oxford: Clarendon, 1892)
	Genesis (London: Methuen, 1904; ^{8}1911)
	An Introduction to the Literature of the Old Testament (Edinburgh: T. & T. Clark, ^{9}1913)
J. I. Durham and J. R. Porter (eds.)	*Proclamation and Presence: Old Testament Essays in Honour of G. H. Davies* (London: SCM, 1970)
O. Eissfeldt	*The Old Testament: An Introduction* (ET, New York: Harper & Row; Oxford: Blackwell, 1965. German original 1934, ^{3}1964)
	Kleine Schriften 1 (Tübingen: J. C. B. Mohr, 1962)
	Kleine Schriften 3 (Tübingen: J. C. B. Mohr, 1966)
J. J. Finkelstein and M. Greenberg (eds.)	*Oriental and Biblical Studies* (Philadelphia: University of Pennsylvania, 1967)

H. J. Franken   *Excavations at Tell Dier ͨAlla* 1 (Leiden: Brill, 1969)

A. H. Gardiner   *Egypt of the Pharaohs* (London: OUP, 1961)

P. Garelli (ed.)   *Le Palais et la Royauté* (Paris: P. Geuthner, 1974)

R. Giveon   *Les bédouins shosou des documents égyptiens* (Leiden: Brill, 1977)

N. Glueck   *The Other Side of the Jorden* (New Haven, Conn.: ASOR, 1940)

Rivers in the Desert (New York: Norton, 1959)

W. Goldschmidt   *Comparative Functionalism* (Berkeley: California UP, 1966)

C. H. Gordon   *Ugaritic Literature* (Rome: Pontifical Biblical Institute, 1949)

Introduction to Old Testament Times (New Jersey: Ventnor, 1953)

A. K. Grayson   *Assyrian and Babylonian Chronicles* (Locust Valley: J. J. Augustin, 1975)

H. Gunkel   *Genesis* (Göttingen: Vandenhoeck & Ruprecht, ²1902; rp of 5th edition 1964)

The Legends of Genesis (New York: Schocken, rp 1964)

A. H. J. Gunneweg   *Understanding the Old Testament* (ET, Philadelphia: Westminster; London: SCM, 1978)

R. Harris   *Ancient Sippar* (Istanbul: Nederlands Historisch-Archaeologisch Instituut, 1975)

R. K. Harrison   *Introduction to the Old Testament* (Grand Rapids: Eerdmans, 1969; London: Tyndale, 1970)

J. H. Hayes (ed.)   *Old Testament Form Criticism* (San Antonio: Trinity UP, 1974)

J. H. Hayes and J. Maxwell Miller (eds.)   *Israelite and Judaean History* (London: SCM; Philadelphia: Westminster, 1977)

F. Hesse   *Abschied von der Heilsgeschichte* (Zurich: TVZ, 1971)

D. Irvin   *Mytharion, AOAT* 32 (Neukirchen-Vluyn: Neukirchener Verlag, 1978)

T. Jacobsen   *The Sumerian King List* (Chicago: University of Chicago Press, 1939)

Towards the Image of Tammuz (Cambridge, Mass.: Harvard UP, 1970)

J. Jackson and M. Kessler (eds.)   *Rhetorical Criticism: Essays in Honor of James Muilenberg* (Pittsburgh: Pickwick, 1974)

M. D. Johnson   *The Purpose of Biblical Genealogies* (London: CUP, 1969)

P. Joüon — *Grammaire de l'hébreu biblique* (Rome: Institut Biblique Pontifical, 1947)

C. F. Keil — *Biblical Commentary on the Old Testament* 1, 2 (Edinburgh: T. & T. Clark, 1864)

K. M. Kenyon — *Digging up Jerusalem* (London: Benn; New York: Norton, 1976)

L. W. King — *Annals of the Kings of Assyria* (London: British Museum, 1902)

K. A. Kitchen — *Ancient Orient and Old Testament* (London: Tyndale, 1966; Downers Grove, Ill: Inter-Varsity Press, 1967)

The Third Intermediate Period in Egypt (Warminster: Aris & Phillips, 1972)

The Bible in its World (Exeter: Paternoster, 1977; Downers Grove, Ill: Inter-Varsity Press, 1978)

J. Klíma — *Untersuchungen zum altbabylonischen Erbrecht* (Prague: Orientalisches Institut, 1940)

J. Köhler and F. E. Peiser — *Aus dem babylonischen Rechtsleben* 4 (Leipzig: Pfeiffer, 1898)

J. Köhler and A. F. Ungnad — *Hammurabis Gesetze* (Leipzig: Pfeiffer, 1904–23)

Assyrische Rechtsurkunden (Leipzig: Pfeiffer, 1913)

N. Leibowitz — *Studies in Shemot* 1 (Jerusalem: World Zionist Organization, 1976)

N. Lohfink — *Die Landverheissung als Eid* (Stuttgart: Katholisches Bibelwerk, 1967)

J. Lundbom — *Jeremiah: A Study in Ancient Hebrew Poetry* (Missoula: Scholars Press, 1975)

W. McKane — *Studies in the Patriarchal Narratives* (Edinburgh: Handsel Press, 1979)

S. Mandelkern — *Concordance on the Bible* (New York: Schulsinger Brothers, [2]1955)

W. J. Martin — *Stylistic Criteria and the Analysis of the Pentateuch* (London: Tyndale, 1955)

R. Martin-Achard — *Actualité d'Abraham* (Neuchâtel: Delachaux, 1969)

V. H. Matthews — *Pastoral Nomadism in the Mari Kingdom ca. 1830–1760 B.C.* (Cambridge, Mass.: American Schools of Oriental Research Dissertation Series, 1978)

B. Mazar (ed.) — *The World History of the Jewish People* 2 (Tel Aviv: Massada, 1970)

W. S. McCullough (ed.) — *The Seed of Wisdom: Essays in Honour of T. J. Meek* (Toronto: University of Toronto Press, 1964)

S. E. McEvenue — *The Narrative Style of the Priestly Writer* (Rome: Biblical Institute Press, 1971)

A. R. Millard — *The Bible BC* (Leicester: Inter-Varsity Press, 1977)

J. A. Motyer — *The Revelation of the Divine Name* (London: Tyndale, 1959)

M. Noth — *Die Israelitischen Personnennamen* (Stuttgart: Kohlhammer, 1928)

A History of Pentateuchal Traditions (Englewood Cliffs and London: Prentice-Hall, 1972) German original 1948

Die Ursprünge des alten Israel; Arbeitgemeinschaft für Forschung des Landes Nordrhein-Westfalen (Cologne: Westdeutscher Verlag, 1961)

J. S. Paradise — *Nuzi Inheritance Practices* (University of Philadelphia PhD dissertation, 1972)

S. Parpola — *Letters from Assyrian Scholars, AOAT* 5 (Kevalaer: Butzon & Bercker, 1970)

A. Parrot — *Abraham et son temps* (Neuchâtel: Delachaux, 1962)

Abraham and his Times (Philadelphia: Fortress, 1968)

M. H. Pope — *El in the Ugaritic Texts, VT* Supp. 2 (Leiden: Brill, 1955)

J. N. Postgate — *Fifty Neo-Assyrian Legal Documents* (Warminster: Aris & Phillips, 1976)

J. B. Pritchard (ed.) — *Ancient Near Eastern Texts Relating to the Old Testament* (Princeton: Princeton UP, [1]1950, [2]1955)

G. von Rad — *Genesis: A Commentary* (London: SCM; Philadelphia: Westminster, [1]1961, [2]1963, [3]1972. German original 1949)

Old Testament Theology 1 (ET, Edinburgh: Oliver & Boyd; New York: Harper, 1962)

Old Testament Theology 2 (ET, Edinburgh: Oliver & Boyd; New York: Harper, 1965)

R. Rendtorff — *Gesammelte Studien zum alten Testament* (Munich: Kaiser, 1975)

Das überlieferungsgeschichtliche Problem des Pentateuch, BZAW 147 (Berlin and New York: De Gruyter, 1977)

W. Richter — *Exegesis als Literaturwissenschaft* (Göttingen: Vandenhoeck & Ruprecht, 1971)

J. J. M. Roberts — *The Earliest Semitic Pantheon* (Baltimore: Johns Hopkins UP, 1972)

B. Rothenberg	*God's Wilderness: Explorations in Sinai* (London: Thames & Hudson, 1961)
H. H. Rowley	*From Joseph to Joshua* (London: OUP, 1950)
	The Servant of the Lord and Other Essays (Oxford: Blackwell, 1965)
J. A. Sanders (ed.)	*Near Eastern Archaeology in the Twentieth Century* (New York: Doubleday, 1970)
W. Schneemelcher (ed.)	*Festschrift für D. Dehn* (Neukirchen: Neukirchener Verlag, 1957)
M. Schorr	*Urkunden des altbabylonischen Zivil- und Prozessrechts* (Leipzig: Hinrichs, 1913)
E. A. Speiser	*Genesis* (Anchor Bible) (New York: Doubleday, 1964)
H. J. Stoebe (ed.)	*Wort-Gebot-Glaube* (Zurich: Zwingli Verlag, 1970)
E. R. Thiele	*The Mysterious Numbers of the Hebrew Kings* (Grand Rapids: Eerdmans; Exeter: Paternoster, [2]1965)
D. Winton Thomas (ed.)	*Archaeology and Old Testament Study* (Oxford: Clarendon, 1967)
T. L. Thompson	*The Historicity of the Patriarchal Narratives* (Berlin and New York: De Gruyter, 1974)
G. A. Tuttle (ed.)	*Biblical and Near Eastern Studies: Essays in Honour of William Sanford LaSor* (Grand Rapids: Eerdmans, 1978)
M. F. Unger	*Israel and the Aramaeans of Damascus* (London: J. Clarke, 1957)
A. van Selms	*Marriage and Family Life in Ugaritic Literature* (London: Luzac, 1954)
J. van Seters	*Abraham in History and Tradition* (New Haven and London: Yale UP, 1975)
W. von Soden	*Akkadisches Handwörterbuch* 1 (Wiesbaden: Harrassowitz, 1965)
R. de Vaux	*Bible et Orient* (Paris: Editions du Cerf, 1967)
	Histoire ancienne d'Israel (Paris: Gabalda, 1971)
	The Bible and the Ancient Near East (London: Darton, Longman & Todd, 1972)
	The Early History of Israel 1 (London: Darton, Longman & Todd; Philadelphia: Westminster, 1978)
J. Vergote	*Joseph en Égypte* (Louvain: Publications Universitaires, 1959)
H. Vorlander	*Mein Gott, AOAT* 23 (Kevalaer: Butzon & Bercker, 1975)

H. Weidmann	*Die Patriarchen und ihre Religion im Licht der Forschung seit Wellhausen* (Göttingen: Vandenhoeck & Ruprecht, 1968)
J. Wellhausen	*Prolegomena to the History of Ancient Israel* (ET, Edinburgh: A. & C. Black, 1885; reprinted Gloucester, MA: Peter Smith, 1973. German original 1878, [2]1883)
C. Westermann (ed.)	*Essays on Old Testament Interpretation* (ET, London: SCM, 1963) =
	Essays on Old Testament Hermeneutics (Richmond: John Knox, 1963)
C. Westermann	*Genesis 1–11* (Biblischer Kommentar) (Neukirchen-Vluyn: Neukirchener Verlag, 1974)
	Die Verheissungen an die Väter (Göttingen: Vandenhoeck & Ruprecht, 1976)
	Genesis 12–50 (Darmstadt: Wissenschaftliche Buchgesellschaft, 1975)
J. W. Wevers and D. B. Redford (eds.)	*Studies on the Ancient Palestinian World* (Toronto: Toronto UP, 1972)
H. G. M. Williamson	*Israel in the Book of Chronicles* (London: CUP, 1977)
R. R. Wilson	*Genealogy and History in the Biblical World* (New Haven and London: Yale UP, 1977)
D. J. Wiseman	*The Alalakh Tablets* (London: British Institute of Archaeology in Ankara, 1953)
D. J. Wiseman (ed.)	*Peoples of Old Testament Times* (Oxford: Clarendon, 1973)
P. J. Wiseman	*New Discoveries in Babylonia about Genesis* (London: Marshall, 1936, included in *Clues to Creation in Genesis*, London: Marshall, 1977)
G. E. Wright	*God Who Acts* (Chicago: Regnery; London: SCM, 1952)
	Biblical Archaeology (Philadelphia: Westminster; London: Duckworth, 1962)
	Shechem: The Biography of a Biblical City (New York: McGraw-Hill; London: Duckworth, 1965)
G. E. Wright (ed.)	*The Bible and the Ancient Near East* (New York: Doubleday: London: Routledge & Kegan Paul, 1961)
Y. Yadin	*Hazor: The Head of all Those Kingdoms* (London: OUP, 1972)
E. Yamauchi	*The Stones and the Scriptures* (Philadelphia: Lippincott; London: Inter-Varsity Press, 1973)
S. Yeivin	*The Israelite Conquest of Canaan* (Istanbul: Nederlands Historisch-Archaeologisch Instituut, 1971)

Index of Biblical References

Exodus

Leviticus

Numbers

Index of Authors

Index of Subjects